The Art of the
Interesting

The Art of the Interesting

What We Miss in Our Pursuit of the Good Life and How to Cultivate It

Lorraine Besser, PhD

balance

New York Boston

Balance
Hachette Book Group
1290 Avenue of the Americas
New York, NY 10104
GCP-Balance.com
@GCPBalance

First Edition: September 2024

Balance is an imprint of Grand Central Publishing. The Balance name and logo are registered trademarks of Hachette Book Group, Inc.

The publisher is not responsible for websites (or their content) that are not owned by the publisher.

The Hachette Speakers Bureau provides a wide range of authors for speaking events. To find out more, go to hachettespeakersbureau.com or email HachetteSpeakers@hbgusa.com.

Balance books may be purchased in bulk for business, educational, or promotional use. For information, please contact your local bookseller or the Hachette Book Group Special Markets Department at special.markets@hbgusa.com.

Library of Congress Cataloging-in-Publication Data
Names: Besser-Jones, Lorraine, 1973- author.
Title: The art of the interesting : what we miss in our pursuit of the good life and how to cultivate it / Lorraine Besser, PhD.
Description: First edition. | New York : Balance, 2024. | Includes index.
Identifiers: LCCN 2024006630 | ISBN 9781538743201 (hardcover) | ISBN 9781538743225 (ebook)
Subjects: LCSH: Quality of life—Philosophy, | Interest (Psychology) | Motivation (Psychology)
Classification: LCC HN25 .B47 2024 | DDC 306.01—dc23/eng/20240318
LC record available at https://lccn.loc.gov/2024006630

ISBNs: 9781538743201 (hardcover), 9781538743225 (ebook)

Printed in the United States of America

LSC-C

Printing 1, 2024

Contents

The Art of the
Interesting

Introduction

ON THE CUSP OF TURNING FORTY, I FOUND MYSELF AT THE top of my game professionally and at the bottom of my game personally. This part of my story is a little clichéd, but sometimes things are clichéd for a reason. I'm one of these people we hear about a lot: married early, threw herself into her career, juggled having babies and working full-time, pushing herself year after year...until it all came falling down and I found myself divorced and alone with two young boys to raise. Only when it all fell apart did I stop, did I pause, did I think: *Who am I? What do I want my life to look like?*

I found myself yearning for the spirit of my youth, who was all about travel and adventure. I took up sailing again after twenty years. I stopped caring about what others would think, or about how different my life looked than those of my siblings. Soon I fell in love with a man who saw *me*, probably even more clearly than I did. We bonded together over our shared passions, for skiing, for water, for conversation, for each other. We had *fun* together. I stopped working so hard and leaned into everyday life just a little more. With him by my side, I learned to notice the little things, to laugh at them, to let things go a little, and to relish the very chaos of life. Life started getting better. Life started to become way more interesting. In fact, life was good.

Poetically, I'd dedicated my career to thinking about the very same problem that plagued my personal life. Namely, what makes life "good"? I was drawn to philosophy in the first place largely because it offered a framework to understand what counts in life, and why. Philosophy offers a way of getting under the hood of what makes living worthwhile. Sure, we can look at the lives other people live and try to see what makes best sense for us—this is an important piece of the puzzle of living well. But philosophers seek something more fundamental: a universal understanding of what it looks like to live our best possible lives.

My first academic book, *Eudaimonic Ethics: The Philosophy and Psychology of Living Well*, explores how important being virtuous is to living well, a topic that has its roots in Aristotle and continues to be an important theme among philosophers and psychologists. I published this book the year I got divorced, the same year I also got tenure. I then started to think more broadly about living well. Surely, there's more to living our best possible lives than being good people. I'd argued that developing virtue was essential to our psychological well-being, but I knew there was more to life. I started to ask: What does a Good Life—our best possible life—really look like?

I began to think more about happiness, and I soon started writing a book on the philosophy and psychology of it.[1] The more I learned about happiness, though, the more I became sure of one surprising thing: Happiness really isn't *that* big of a deal. It's challenging to pursue and ultimately a feeling that comes and goes. It's important to our lives, no doubt, but its role is limited—*way* more limited than people seemed willing to admit. Surely, the Good Life couldn't be all about happiness, and my own personal experience had taught me it couldn't be all about purpose or meaning, either.

My personal and philosophical journeys started to come together in 2014, when I got an email from a psychologist, Dr. Shigehiro Oishi, who was beginning a new research project and was interested in having a philosopher join his research team. He'd reached out to a mutual contact who had recommended he get in touch with me.

Oishi suspected that there was more to the Good Life than happiness and meaning, and he was interested in testing his hypothesis that psychological richness was an important aspect of the Good Life. A psychologically rich life is one full of experiences that stimulate and engage the mind, that provoke a wide range of emotions, and that can change your perspective. Oishi thought that this was a form of the Good Life that—amazingly—had not yet been appreciated by philosophers or psychologists.

He'd already begun conducting focus groups, asking students to describe "interesting, rich" experiences, along with "happy" experiences and "personally meaningful" experiences. This preliminary work suggested that the interesting, rich experiences were different from the others, and were correlated with novelty, variety/complexity, and a change in perspective. These markers, we've gone on to show, are distinctive to psychologically rich experiences, but not to other kinds of experiences.

With this basis established, the next task was to flesh out the nature of psychological richness, both theoretically and empirically, and together we secured funding from the John Templeton Foundation to pursue this important research. As the philosopher on the team, my task was the theoretical one: How do we understand and locate psychological richness in relation to the dominant theories of the Good Life that philosophers have developed over centuries? While philosophers had discussed elements of psychological richness in other areas, such as aesthetics, there was no developed notion of psychological richness construed more broadly, nor had other philosophers explored the possibility that psychological richness is itself an important part of the Good Life, independent of whether people derive happiness, meaning, or purpose from their experiences.

While I set out to show that psychological richness was separate and different from other philosophical conceptions of the Good Life, Oishi continued to conduct studies showing it is empirically distinct. Our 2020 coauthored paper, "The Psychologically Rich Life," brings together both lines of research and established the framework for subsequent empirical and theoretical analysis. At this point, I began the independent, daunting philosophical task of showing that psychological richness was good in itself. This research led me to focus more heavily on the interesting—the qualitative feature uniting and underlying psychological richness. My 2023 paper, "The Interesting and the Pleasant," argues that the interesting is an intrinsic, prudential value.[2] It's the value of the interesting that makes psychological richness good in itself.

Throughout this process, an amazing thing happened. My research on the psychological richness and the interesting brought together my professional and personal journeys and showed me the clear path forward.

Maybe you've shared a similar personal journey. Maybe you've crashed and burned. Maybe the toils of the pandemic pushed you to confront the status of your life. Maybe you're not satisfied with happiness, or with meaning. Maybe you are simply ready to live a better life, right now. Maybe you know, deep in your gut, that there has to be more to life. Whatever your reason for picking up this book, seize the momentum now. Because I have good news: There *is* more to life.

PSYCHOLOGICAL RICHNESS AND THE INTERESTING: AN OVERVIEW

A *psychologically rich life* is composed of complex, novel, and challenging experiences that stimulate and engage the mind, that evoke different emotions, and that leave you with a different perspective than you started with. At the time Oishi reached out to me, his preliminary empirical research suggested that this kind of life is one that people value, even if they can't label it. And his research showed that this kind of life couldn't be explained within the dominant frameworks, which tended to think about the Good Life in terms of happiness and meaning. The experiences that comprise psychological richness just don't always contribute to happiness or meaning. Sometimes they do, but sometimes they don't. We still think they are good.

To start to wrap your head around this idea of psychological richness, you might begin by thinking about the kinds of experiences that challenge you, that force you to feel different emotions, that leave a dent in your mind. But—for now—don't get too caught up in *what* those experiences are. Focus on what it feels like to have them. Psychological richness is something that we can notice in the mind.

Its definition describes the features of experiences observed to deliver psychological richness, but fundamentally, psychological richness is a psychological state. Notice, though, that observing its existence— while super important—doesn't actually give us clues as to whether it's good/helpful/worthwhile. Even though its name suggests something positive, it's still just a psychological phenomenon we've recognized. Implicit bias and anxiety are also patterns psychologists can name, and we know that neither of those is inherently good.

These days, we are used to looking to psychology to explain how we are in this world. We think that if we can understand our minds, emotions, and thoughts, we can diagnose how to be better. And some-times this diagnosis is very clear. Learning about the sneaky ways in which implicit bias affects us can help us be proactive in safeguard-ing us from its influence. Learning about our mind's proneness to anxiety can help us to prevent its arousal. But notice this only works when we know that these are states we want to avoid. Does psychol-ogy tell us this? *Can* psychology tell us this? Well, no. As a science, psychology delivers information about our psychological states and the experiences they are correlated with. It tells us implicit bias is cor-related with use of stereotypes; it tells us anxiety is correlated with rapid heartbeats and obsessive thoughts. It doesn't tell us these are bad. It can't.

What makes something good or bad is a philosophical question. Phi-losophers probe beyond the correlations; where science ends, we ask why. And this is my contribution to the research team. The empiri-cal work shows people think psychological richness is good. The philo-sophical work is to show *why* people think it is good.

What caught my attention about psychological richness as a potential key to the Good Life was precisely that it wasn't about meaning, and it wasn't about happiness. I'd thought about meaning and happiness for years, without ever being tempted to think that they told the full story. Certainly, they didn't grip me, and no philosophical argument about their value had ever quite satisfied. Seeing the results of the empirical studies, which delineated psychological richness from happiness and meaning, struck a chord with me. I was immediately convinced that psychological richness added value to our lives, and always has. But how could philosophers have missed this? And what were we missing? What kind of value have we overlooked that seems so clearly present in psychological richness?

The philosopher in me took hold—over years of research and thought, it became clear to me that psychological richness can enhance our lives because it makes them more interesting. And being interesting alone makes something valuable. As I write this now, it seems so obvious. Yet often the hardest and most important philosophical work is to make sense of that which seems so intuitive.

WHAT IS THE INTERESTING?

We use the word "interesting" in all kinds of ways. Have you used it today? This week? We think it while scrolling our news feed. "Hmm, that's interesting." We get into the habit of saying "Interesting" when no other words seem to suffice. A coworker shows you the website her teenager built about *Minecraft*? "Interesting." We use it to set up our stories: "I had the most interesting thing happen to me today." We use it to praise: "She's so interesting!" "This is the most interesting book!" And sometimes we use it in lieu of praise, when we find ourselves unable to say anything else good about something: "How was the drive? It was...interesting." "Wow! Your outfit is so, er, interesting."

We need to move a little past our ordinary ways of using the word "interesting" to get to the sense of the interesting that adds value to our lives. But not too far. Notice that almost all the ways in which we use the word "interesting" highlight the ways in which interesting things stimulate our minds—even the teeniest bit, such as the first *Minecraft* fan site we've seen, or the first time we've seen someone wear a particularly hideous combination of colors and patterns. We don't often realize it, but "interesting" describes the way we respond to things. No thing is inherently interesting. What's interesting is all about how we experience the thing.

When we talk about interesting books, or an interesting class, we speak as if the book or class itself is interesting—to all who may read it or take it. Really, though, there's no one book we all find interesting, just as there's no one class we all find interesting. This is because experiences are interesting, not things. Reading a book can be interesting, and often is—outside of a classroom, we don't really find ourselves reading books that don't stimulate or engage us. The ones that do, though? They are the interesting ones to read, the ones we recommend to like-minded people who we think will find them interesting to read. The interesting isn't about any one thing, or even a collection of things. It's about our experiences of things that stimulate and engage us.

The interesting describes a quality of our experiences, and interesting experiences make up a psychologically rich life. That a psychologically rich life is full of interesting experiences explains why we value it. Complexity, novelty, and challenge stimulate our minds and spark engagement with the world around us. While we often shy away from things that push us in this way, we are learning more every day about how much value they offer to our lives. It may be easier not to engage our minds, but, please, trust me: Our lives go better when we do.

There is so much more life has to offer than meaning and happiness, and thank goodness. We're all feeling the disillusion. Whether it's a general sense of feeling stuck in life, or the anxiety and exhaustion that builds up day by day as we strive for more, all while we're confused about what we're aiming for and why it's not working, these feelings of disillusion hit all of us. We're yearning for more.

It's little wonder we are struggling. All we know is to try to cultivate happiness, or to seek meaning, and it's just not working. We meditate, volunteer, take CBD, change careers, change careers again, go to therapy, try to make friends, become a seeker—and yet none of it has yet delivered on the promise we've been chasing: that if we can just find enough pleasure, enough purpose, or maybe both, that we, too, can lead a Good Life.

It's time to start going for more. Opening this book is your first move.

In part 1, we'll look at why living a life of happiness and/or meaning just isn't going to cut it, and why including the interesting allows us to live our best possible lives. Then, in part 2, we'll take a deeper dive into ways that we can cultivate the interesting on a day-to-day basis. Because even though all of our minds hold the capacity for the interesting, there is an art to unlocking its potential.

There's important work involved here, clearly. What could be more important than learning about what makes our lives go well? But work shouldn't always feel like work, especially work on the interesting. Thinking about the interesting is interesting in itself, and one of my aims here is to deliver you one interesting experience while you learn the skills you need to enhance your life.

This points to one of the coolest and most distinctive aspects of learning the art of the interesting. To better your life, you don't have to set aside all the plans and projects that you've already got going on. You don't have to go on a wine-and-gelato-fueled mission to find your true bliss, nor do you have to give up what you already care about in some search for true purpose. You could do these things, and maybe you'll be inspired to make big changes in your life upon reading this. It's just as likely, though, that you'll find value in the little tweaks, which pay off in big ways. The art of the interesting delivers the tools you need to enhance your life without having to change or fix them.

Don't get me wrong: Change can be a good thing, even when it comes disguised as the worst. Change can resolve our problems, and a life with less problems is always a better one, no matter who tells us otherwise. Problems weigh us down. Living from paycheck to paycheck. Living with chronic illness. Tensions between family members. Long-distance commutes. Long-distance relationships. All these things bear down on us, sucking our energy to no end. Even the little annoying things—finding a parking spot, paying bills on time, calling the plumber, having to reschedule a hair appointment—can clump together and become lead, simply dragging us down every day. If we can fix our problems, we should. Even those that seem most impenetrable, the ones buried so deep we feel we may as well keep them there, are worth fixing, too—even if at the slowest pace, chipping away, block after block, making us lighter with every small step.

But you know what? Sorry to be the bearer of bad news, but life can suck in so many ways that are outside of our reach. Not every problem can be fixed, and sometimes change isn't possible. Even when change is possible, there's no guarantee it'll fix the problem. You can change your job, even your career, but you likely can't change the demanding grind of capitalism. You can shatter ceilings everywhere you go but still struggle against racism, patriarchy, homophobia. We should take charge of our own lives, and we most certainly should take charge of making our lives go better, but changing and fixing is hard. And some things are just out of our control. Here's the catch: Even when we can't change and fix, and even when life might be downright miserable on the outside, we can make it more interesting.

A LESSON TO REMEMBER

Few knew this better than Aaron Elster. Born to a Jewish family in Poland in 1933, from the age of six Aaron was running for his life, moving with his family into the hidden corners of his town's ghetto. When even those hidden corners became less safe, and the rest of the family had to flee, Aaron somehow made it to the Gurski family's door. In better times, the Gurskis had been regulars at his father's butcher shop. Mrs. Gurski reluctantly let Aaron in and quickly shuttled him up to their attic.

Aaron spent two years, from age ten to age twelve, hiding alone in the attic. Watching clips of Aaron speak of his time in the attic, it is hard to imagine this tan, bushy-haired man, with a smile so quick to turn to laughter, could be the same boy who lived through such conditions, no doubt ghostly pale from the lack of sunlight, starving for food but much more so for companionship. Mrs. Gurski would deliver him food once a day; any more contact would have jeopardized everyone's safety. Aaron grew so lonely he'd pull the wings off of flies, so that they couldn't fly away and would keep him company.[3]

I could not begin to imagine trying to live under these conditions, the strength of will it must have taken to get up, day after day. To have to fight to simply live. How did Aaron make it through the hunger, the fear, the absolute loneliness of his existence?

There is no question in Aaron's mind what got him through these times, what allowed him to survive, in the dark, on his own, at such a tender age. It was his mind:

> I had the ability to daydream. I used to write novels in my head. I was the hero all the time. And we have that ability, to either give in to our misery and our pain and die, or to absorb physical pain but keep your mentality, keep your soul, keep your mind.

Stuck, so alone, scared, and desperate in the attic, never to see his parents again, Aaron somehow made the choice to live. And he found a way to make his life better without changing a damn thing about it. *He daydreamed. He wrote novels in his head. He was the hero all the time.* Aaron's capacity to create the interesting saved him and it delivered the only good aspects of his life.

My hope is that this book shows how we can all cultivate this same skill. May none of us ever have to use it in such horrific circumstances as Aaron found himself in, but let's also not forget that the interesting is always within our reach, because the interesting depends on only one thing: our minds. As long as we're alive in any meaningful sense of the word, we've got the capacity to use our minds, so no matter what else is going on, and no matter how limited our lives may feel from the outside, we hold the power to make them good.

So keep reading. Learn the art of the interesting. Take advantage of the opportunity this offers: to forever change the way we live, to live better lives, maybe even better than we thought was possible. The Good Life really isn't all about happiness. And it isn't all about meaning, either. To live truly Good Lives, we need more of the interesting.

PART 1

GOOD LIVES

Chapter 1:

An Ancient Dichotomy

THE TV SERIES *SOMEBODY SOMEWHERE* FOCUSES ON A woman named Sam who finds herself back in her Kansas hometown, pushing middle age, recovering from her own life crisis. She's trying to find her place back in this town she'd run from as soon as she could but now finds herself stuck in.

Sam could be me. She could be any of us. That's the point. She's just a regular person, trying to live a Good Life, in a regular town, among regular people, including Joel, a guy she barely remembers from high school and who by any external measure is Sam's opposite in every way. Sam and Joel form a surprising and unique friendship. They come together, really, because they are both desperate for something. What it is, they have no idea.

In one episode, Sam convinces Joel to spend a Saturday tailing her brother-in-law, who she thinks is dealing drugs in the park. (Spoiler alert: He is not.)[1] As they wait in the car, they begin to lament what they are missing, what they would have otherwise been doing. Yet it's all a bit of a joke, revealing more the emptiness of what they would have been doing than any real missed opportunity.

"What are you going to be doing later today?" asks Joel, after hearing Sam tell her mom on the phone that she's too busy to get together.

"Saturdays are pretty big for me," Sam replies.

"Oh, you have like a Saturday ritual?" starts Joel.

"I do. I like to sit down and write out a list of goals for the week. And, of course, I write down a list of accomplishments from the previous week."

"You do? That's so amazing."

Sam laughs. "I don't do any of that. I like to lay around drinking wine in my underwear. It's pretty fucking great."

"Hmm…Just sounds a little lonely."

"Yeah, well, it works for me."

She can't hide how pathetic it is. They laugh.

She then turns to Joel. "And what do *you* do with your Saturdays?"

He lists off all the volunteer organizations, all the meaningful activities he's lined up to structure his Saturdays: church outreach, youth group mentoring, choir practice, volunteering at the pediatric clinic, clowning for the kids at the hospital.

They don't laugh at Joel's activities, yet the tone is clear. Joel feels just as empty as Sam does. And he knows it: "I just try to keep busy. Make sure the terror doesn't creep in."

It's clear that neither feels they are living a Good Life. What's even worse is that they don't know what to do about it. They pursue the things they think count—for Sam, it's something like happiness and pleasure; for Joel, it's something like meaning and fulfillment—yet none of these pursuits are doing it for them. And they know this. They know they are not living their best possible lives. But they can't figure out why. They can't figure out what their lives are missing.

I think this is how a lot of us approach the Good Life. We have instincts that kick in every so often, reminding us that life could be better. But we don't have the information we need to harness this instinct.

If I asked you right now to describe the Good Life, what would your answer be?

You might tell me about your aunt's friend Barb, who retired to

Colorado with her husband and her dogs, works part-time at the local brewery, and hikes in the Rockies every day of her life. Or maybe you think of your cat, who sleeps, eats, luxuriates, and seems blissfully unaware of "problems." Or maybe it's the life of a yacht-enthusiast, jet-setting millionaire who travels the world and has staff to take care of the little things.

It's easy to look from the outside and try to draw inspiration from people who seem to be living a Good Life. And it's not a bad strategy—especially if you find someone who shares your passions and values. But the ways in which we might ordinarily think about the Good Life have their limitations.

Two are obvious: First, it's hard to tell from the outside whether someone actually is living a Good Life. We all know that people's lives can look very different on the outside than they feel on the inside. Good old Barb might seem to have it all in place, until we look deeper and see the cracks. That part-time job at the brewery? Maybe it's more of a necessity than a passion; maybe Barb struggles to pay her medical expenses, and that brewery job, working alongside twenty-year-olds, is all she could find. Maybe it tortures her to have to show up and smile. When we look at how people are living from the outside, it's easy to overlook the struggles, the tensions, the gaps that can occur between how someone's life is structured and how they feel about their life.

Second, we're all unique. We've all got different passions and values that influence how different pursuits make us feel. Maybe Barb doesn't need the money from her part-time job at all; maybe she's one of those people who thrives on being around folks younger than her. Or maybe she's a beer enthusiast, and that drives her to the brewery. What we bring to our pursuits matters a lot, and this makes it tricky to find people whose lives we can use as a template for our own.

While there's nothing wrong with thinking about the Good Life in these ordinary ways, we can do better. Resting in these passive wishes—thinking occasionally about how we could be living better, looking around for examples to inspire us—feels too much like stumbling through life.*

Take a second to think about what happens when we stumble through anything, though. I've stumbled through my fair share of enterprises, going through the motions without seriously thinking about it or putting in a real effort. Freshman year of college. My early years of "running." Housekeeping. Oh, and the dinners: So many times have I stumbled through the task of cooking dinner for my family. So many scrambled eggs. So many boxes of mac and cheese. Way, way too many frozen pizzas. This is what you get when you stumble. Frozen pizza. Even with talent and luck, you end up, at best, with mediocrity.

There are thousands of dinners to cook. And it is just food, after all. Stumbling through cooking dinner with frozen pizza is one thing. But to stumble through your life? The one, limited life you have?

There's no sense in, nor reason for, settling into a mediocre life. All it takes, really, is to start paying attention to what lights you up. What sparks you? What catches your attention, or raises your intrigue? This lit-up feeling is the foundational siren of the interesting. Because the interesting arises within our minds, when we focus more on what's going on inside our minds and worry less about what's going on outside of them, we're on our way to unlocking the art of the interesting. Our minds will have the power to enhance any situation. This makes the interesting—not happiness, not meaning—our most consistent golden ticket to the Good Life.

Once you know that the interesting is out there, it can be hard not to want to dive straight in. (And who can blame you!) But in order to appreciate the interesting's role in our lives, we need to back up a bit and shed the baggage of what we've been taught to think about the Good Life—namely, we need to break through the ancient dichotomy of happiness and meaning, and start to see our Good Lives not as a teeter-totter but as a three-legged stool.

---

* Sam and Joel? I'm sure they would agree they are just stumbling through life.

OUR BEST POSSIBLE LIFE

When philosophers talk about "the Good Life," what we are talking about is our best possible life. Aristotle describes this as our highest or most supreme end. When we live a Good Life, nothing is lacking. Our lives are complete. We've reached the top of the scale—we've made it to the 10. There's an umbrella in our drink and no problems for the next thousand miles.

Easy, right? Not really. It is easy enough to understand the idea of "a Good Life" by filling it in with other words that carry the same meaning. Yet describing the Good Life as "the best possible life" or "the supreme end" or "the 10" really just adds more empty terms to the mix. It doesn't tell us what is in those lives that makes them good. Words like "the Good Life" occupy a place within our minds and so have some kind of conceptual status. Yet they turn out to be pretty useless for anything other than representing the highest thing we can shoot for. Certainly, they are quite useless in terms of helping us to understand and to pursue the Good Life. To pursue our best possible lives, we need to know what we're looking for. This is where a little philosophy can help. A lot.

AN ANCIENT DICHOTOMY

Aristotle lived and wrote in ancient Greek, circa 384 BCE, back in the days when public debate was literally a matter of shouting at one's friends across the town square, face-to-face. He was a student of Plato, and his writings became so influential that for a long while other philosophers referred to him simply as "the Philosopher" or "the First Teacher."*

The Philosopher had a lot to say about the Good Life. And the very way in which he framed his investigation set the tone for pretty much all subsequent work in philosophy and in psychology on the nature of

---

* Although the poet Dante might have come up with the best nickname: "The Master of those who know." If anyone ever feels tempted to put that on my gravestone, please just go ahead.

the Good Life. Yes, I'm dead serious. The dichotomies he sets up in his *Nicomachean Ethics* were written thousands of years ago, at a time when one's place of privilege determined one's moral status, when being wealthy gave men free rein to decide who else even counted and how so. Those born male and wealthy were taken not only to be the ones entitled to an education; even worse, they were taken to be the only people capable of being educated. Born a woman? Born from a farmer? You literally didn't even count among the audience for whom Aristotle wrote. It should not be surprising his dichotomies are not working out for you. It's shocking, really, that these dichotomies dominated how we thought about the Good Life up until 2019, when our first papers on psychological richness started coming out.[2]

Aristotle began thinking about the Good Life largely by looking around him and at the mistakes he saw others (in his circle, obvs) making. He saw his friends driven by an intense desire to make money. He saw so many politicians driven by desires for power and respect. And he saw a lot of people overly focused on indulgence, on satiating the body.*

Aristotle worried that none of these lives really reflected the nature of human beings, and thus couldn't be Good Lives. He thought the ordinary sense of "happiness" most people have, then and now, was deeply misguided. We tend to think of happiness in terms of feeling good, in terms of feeling pleasure, what the Greeks called *hedonia*; but Aristotle thought there was a deeper, more important sense of "happiness" we ought to aim for that better reflects the highest end for rational creatures. This is a state of human flourishing he called *eudaimonia*.

And so, a great debate wages. Is the Good Life a matter of feeling pleasure? Or is it something beyond pleasure, something that makes use of reason? *Hedonists* believe that the Good Life is a pleasant life. *Eudaimonists* believe that the Good Life involves using our rational capacities in the best possible way. Aristotle thought this meant developing virtue, but others draw on this framework to emphasize the importance of

---

* Sounds familiar, doesn't it? I wonder: Have times changed at all?

achievement and of meaning, things that require and reflect the use of our rational capacities.[3] And thus, the dichotomy is framed.

Until just recently, philosophers (and psychologists) have looked at the Good Life like Sam and Joel, in terms of happiness and meaning. Happy lives are full of pleasant experiences, the stuff that feels good. That's kind of like Sam drinking wine on Saturdays in her underwear, although, um, there are better ways to have pleasant experiences. Going to a movie with friends, watching your kids play soccer, having a picnic on a sunny day. These are pleasant experiences that make us happy. In contrast, meaningful lives are full of fulfilling experiences. This is what Joel aims at through his work with kids and with the church. Helping others is a fantastic way to find fulfillment in life, as is contributing to a cause, being active in your community, and pursuing an impactful career.

Happiness and meaning, experiencing pleasure and fulfillment, are important aspects of the Good Life. There's a reason we've all focused so much on them, and we now have a tremendous amount of information at our fingertips about how to pursue them...but, really, thinking about pleasure and fulfillment alone just doesn't cut it for most of us, maybe for all of us. It's clearly not working for Sam and Joel. How is it working for you? What we've been sold as the formula for Good Lives doesn't pan out. Maybe you've asked yourself "Isn't there more?" and come up empty. Ask again. I've got the answer.

A MODERN ADDITION

Emerging new research shows that there is more to the Good Life. It uncovers the missing piece that explains the emptiness Sam, Joel, and likely most of us sometimes feel, and it shows the way out. This research shows that there's a kind of Good Life, described as a psychologically rich life, that is distinct from a happy life and a meaningful life. And it is breaking right through the dichotomy of Good Lives that has guided both philosophical and psychological research for, well, a very long time.

For centuries, philosophers were the only ones thinking about the

Good Life, and for the most part we did so by focusing, developing, and building on Aristotle's dichotomy. It took until the late twentieth century for psychologists to get in on this project. Before then, psychologists saw themselves as in the business of studying and fixing pathologies of the human mind, but not at all in the business of telling people how they ought to live.* It took a group of psychologists who were frustrated with these limits to help the discipline see it could contribute to these conversations about the Good Life. This was how the positive psychology movement, which calls for the scientific study of human flourishing, began, spearheaded by Martin Seligman.[4]

When positive psychologists started researching the Good Life in the late 1990s, they turned to the Philosopher to help them understand what they were after. The dichotomy of Good Lives Aristotle set up became further entrenched, this time as a framework for psychological research on the Good Life.[5] The philosophical theories of well-being he developed and inspired serve to direct scientific research on the Good Life by giving the research its target. With a philosophical understanding of the Good Life in hand, we know what we're looking for and can identify the people who live Good Lives. We can then study them scientifically to understand the skills and traits they have that are conducive to living Good Lives.

Using this framework, psychologists have uncovered a tremendous amount of information about happiness and about eudaimonia, which, by this point, has evolved into a cluster of concepts best understood in terms of *meaning*. You've likely seen for yourself the explosion of books, blogs, podcasts, and discussion of its major findings: on gratitude, resilience, optimism, authenticity.

---

* Many psychologists still see this focus as their primary aim, and controversy over the call to extend their scope to the positive dimensions of human experience lingers.

FIXING THE TARGET

Psychology is an inherently descriptive science. It describes the human mind and identifies patterns that are correlated with features of the mind.

Philosophy is an inherently normative enterprise. It tells us what is good, why it is good, and how we ought to live in order to get what is good.

We get the best of both worlds when we draw on both fields. Here's a very oversimplified example of how it works!

WHAT IS GOOD	WHY? (philosophy)	CORRELATED WITH ... (psychology)	WHAT WE OUGHT TO DO (philosophy)
Happiness	It is pleasurable.	Optimism	Be optimistic.
Meaning	It is fulfilling.	Rational activity	Use our minds.
Psychological richness	It is interesting.	Novelty	Embrace novelty.

Once we know what is good and why, we can use psychological methods to learn all sorts of things it is correlated with. We then know what we ought to do to get what is good!

Even among these very important developments, research on the psychologically rich life stands out as groundbreaking. It is breaking the ancient dichotomy of Good Lives. Essentially, a psychologically rich life describes a life full of engaging experiences, which may not be pleasant, which may not deliver fulfillment, but are nonetheless among the most exciting, rewarding, and impactful experiences many of us have. They are the interesting ones.

Many of us seek out these kinds of experiences already. We travel. We read books about different times and places, and we watch documentaries exploring different cultures and ways of life. We push our boundaries through engaging in adventurous activities—be it through rock-climbing and cliff-jumping or by bringing molecular gastronomy and tripe into our kitchens. We talk with each other about stuff that has no importance whatsoever, but we simply find so engaging an hour can pass in the blink of an eye.

Of course, we're also familiar with boredom, that deadening place where our minds want nothing more than to be engaged but keep coming up short. We put down boring books. We pick up our phone at every spare moment, forestalling the possibility that—yikes—we might get bored while waiting in the line at the grocery store. We fall asleep in boring lectures. It is a lucky person who got through the years of pandemic-induced limitations and isolations without becoming all too familiar with the dent boredom leaves upon our lives.

While we may not always realize it, boredom expresses craving for the interesting. When we're bored, it is because we crave something to engage our minds, to stimulate our thoughts, and to make us feel something new. And you know what? Our minds naturally strive to engage. They need uptake. Not all the time—minds get worn out just like bodies do, but our minds are built to engage, to question, and to create. Interesting experiences deliver the goods our minds need to thrive. That's why we need them in our lives.

PAYING ATTENTION TO BOREDOM

Boredom claws at us. It demands our attention. But have we ever really reflected on why? You can take a second to do it now. Maybe, like many, your reaction to boredom is often just to find something to occupy your time, to distract you from feeling bored. These distractions may help you feel less bored, but do they add any value to your life? Just how was that quick dip into social media while you were waiting in line? Did it deliver? Feeling bored is a cry for more, more of what the mind needs. Next time you're bored, don't look for something to distract you. Seek out something interesting to engage in. The more you start to flip the switch of boredom by engaging, the firmer your footing becomes on the path to living your best possible life.

REMIXING THE DICHOTOMY

Recognizing the importance of psychological richness and the value of the interesting makes clear the limits of the traditional dichotomy of Good Lives and explains why so many of us struggle to live our best possible lives. We're struggling because we're stuck in this dichotomy that tells us we'll lead better lives by chasing more pleasure and more fulfillment. But that's just bad advice. As we'll see in chapters 2 and 3, pleasure doesn't work this way, and striving for fulfillment comes with serious costs. All this means the more we stick within the dichotomy, the fewer gains we'll make, and the more we'll miss out on the interesting.

Yet if you think I'm asserting that you can live on the interesting alone, you're wrong. The point is not that pleasure and meaning are not part of the Good Life, not at all. The point is that when we rely on them exclusively, we're not giving ourselves a fair shot at living our best possible lives. The Good Life is like a three-legged stool. It needs the support of pleasure, fulfillment, *and* the interesting. Just as pleasure and meaning alone deliver a shaky stool, the interesting can't hold up the stool on its own, either.

We are so used to defining the Good Life in terms of pleasure and fulfillment, we probably are used to a shaky stool. Maybe we've felt the shake and tried to beef up on pleasure and fulfillment. A tropical vacation, maybe? Some community service? We like to think we'll finally get to that good place if only we had more pleasure and meaning, but I think we know, deep down, that's not going to work. Pleasure and fulfillment have their limits. No matter how much effort we may put into one or both, it won't be enough in the absence of the interesting.

KEEPING IT INTERESTING

If you're finding yourself stuck, thinking there must be more, you are not alone. You're also right: Burgeoning research on psychological richness and on the value of the interesting shows there's more. By understanding how psychology and philosophy work together to deliver robust insights into the Good Life, you'll be ready to use this research to make your life better.

Chapter 2:

Happiness and the Limits of Pleasure

W HEN WE THINK ABOUT HAPPINESS, THE '90S SITCOM *SEIN-feld* is probably not the first thing that comes to mind. Full of characters who bond over their apathy toward others, relish in the suffering of their enemies, and make bad choices all around, *Seinfeld* rings funny but not exactly laden with insights about happiness. But I'm going on record right now: The *Seinfeld* gang shows remarkable prescience when it comes to happiness.

Happiness is nothing new. We've all felt its seeds and, maybe, the glory of those seeds growing and building. We know just by experiencing it that it enhances our life. It's what we want for ourselves and our families. Shoot, it's the heart of the American Dream: Give someone enough freedom, they'll earn enough resources, and they'll be happy. Life, Liberty, and the Pursuit of Happiness. That's what it is all about, right?

Actually, no. It turns out happiness is not like this, and embracing this perspective does not help us to become happy. Take a second to think about what this perspective on happiness brings us. It leads us to prioritize happiness in our lives, and to focus on its pursuit, which, within a materialistic society like the United States, sets us down a path of accumulation.

We want bigger houses, softer mattresses, and better iPhones. It is so easy to think these things will make us happy. And it feels pretty shitty when they turn out not to. So, we quickly start pursuing something else. We chase the dream.

While we chase the dream, we make sacrifices along the way: We work longer and longer hours, to afford the bigger house. We search out and embrace shortcuts that help us get to the dream faster: Life hacks, faster technology, whatever eases the burdens of pursuit, we go for. But, alas, we are no happier for it. This is the lesson of the "Easterlin Paradox": Research shows that happiness rises with income, but only to a certain point. Past that point, more income, more money makes little impact on people's happiness.[1]

Those of us schooled in the Cult of Happiness that exists in the self-help world know better than to rely on the material stuff to make us happy. The sheer volume of literature out there—from *The Happiness Project*, to *10% Happier*, to *The Happiness Advantage*—has helped many people to step off this path and instead focus on the things that do tend to count, such as developing deep connections and embracing an optimistic mindset. But despite the abundance of media, the books and podcasts, and the robust thought leadership, do we really even know what it means to be happy? Do we really know what kind of role happiness plays within our best possible lives?

This is where the *Seinfeld* gang shines. While none of them seem to think they are leading happy lives, they aren't sitting around thinking, *If only I had more [money, houses, comfort], then I'd be happy.* Happiness just isn't on their radar as something to pursue or to stress over. And none of them would even take seriously the thought that there is anything wrong with this approach.

So what is so noteworthy about how they approach happiness? It all starts with the happy dance, the squiggling and goofing they do to express their good moods.* The time Elaine comes back from vacation

---

* By this I do not mean Elaine's famous dance moves, which are just plain scary.

and the gang spends minutes hugging and jumping and shouting their welcomes. The time Jerry and George celebrate Kramer's release from the LA county jail, where they dance on the courtroom steps, hands waving, feet skipping, the three just taking the moment in. The *Seinfeld* gang isn't always happy, but they let it rip when they are *and* they don't freak out when they are not.

What's their secret? How can we get to this place, where we stop worrying so much about happiness, and instead just embrace it when it lands on our doorstep? I don't think they have a secret, actually. I think this is just how they are, which from our vantage point seems a little naïve, a little more sheltered than most of us are now. The Cult of Happiness is a great thing, but it makes it harder to be as cavalier about the role of happiness in our lives as the *Seinfeld* gang is. It is hard to be bombarded with all the research promoting happiness as a pinnacle of the Good Life without starting to take it too seriously.

Regardless, *Seinfeld* has internalized something that we might have to work a little harder to accept: Happiness is limited. No matter how much we try to be happy, there are physiological limits to how often we can be happy. This is why a "Take it when it comes and let it go when it goes" attitude makes sense. This is also what makes it impossible to pin our Good Life on happiness. Unlike the interesting, happiness is out of our hands.

TWO SENSES OF HAPPINESS

What is happiness? We use the word constantly, and we've all probably asked this question at one point or another, but I know I'm not alone in struggling to answer it. One problem we face off the bat when we try to talk about happiness is that people use the word to mean different things. You may say that "happiness" is some long-term satisfaction with life, but when I say "I'm happy!" I mean "Yay! I'm feeling so good today!" But then we both read an article that talks about "happiness" as if it were welfare, the kind of thing satisfied by housing and health care. We use words all the time without knowing fully what they mean. This is definitely the case with the word "happiness." We know it's a good thing and we know we want it. But what is it, really?

In philosophy, we distinguish between two different senses of happiness. Philosophers are all about this kind of move, and yes, people make fun of us for it, but there is a reason why we do it! If we aren't clear about what we're discussing, we can't say anything meaningful about it, and we can't make progress in our efforts to understand it, let alone obtain it. Imagine someone tells you your apartment is "dank." It could be a compliment (edgy, excellent) or an insult (unpleasant, damp). Unless you know which, you won't be able to react, much less be responsive to the feedback. Where words have different connotations—and lots do—unless we get clear on them, they leave us frozen. We should all be pushing for clarity!

There are two very different senses of happiness. Sometimes we use "happiness" to mean a Good Life, and sometimes we use "happiness" to describe the feeling of being happy (or the "mental state" of happiness). These are importantly different things.

In promising its citizens "life, liberty, and the pursuit of happiness," the U.S. Declaration of Independence takes happiness to be the *goal* of life, to be the Good Life. Many of us share in this view. This is the sense of happiness we evoke when we think along the lines of *I just want my kids to be happy.* But are happiness and the Good Life really the same thing?

There's a simple test philosophers use to try to figure out whether two words mean the same thing. It's called the Open Question Argument.[2] It's a straightforward test. When you are tempted to think two words mean the same thing (say, "water" and "H_2O"), put them into the form of a question: "This is water, but is it H_2O?" If the question simply makes no sense, like this one, then it isn't an open question whether the two words mean the same thing. Water *is* H_2O. End of story. But if the question makes sense—if it makes sense to ask whether the two things are the same—well, then it is an open question whether they are the same. It is a question worth asking and answering.

Let's see how this goes with "happiness" and "the Good Life." Is it an open question whether obtaining happiness is equivalent to living a Good Life? Yes. The question makes sense, as do lots of related forms: "I'm happy. But do I have a Good Life?" or "Sarah has a Good Life. But is she happy?" The fact that these questions make sense, in a way that doesn't make sense when you do it with water and H_2O, shows that happiness and the Good Life are not the same thing. It's an open question whether "happiness" and "the Good Life" mean the same thing. They might, but we can't assume they do. We need to look further into it. And to answer this open question, we've got to first figure out what it means to be happy.

THE MENTAL STATE OF HAPPINESS

If we know anything about happiness, we know that it feels good. Following this lead, most interdisciplinary research defines happiness as a mental state distinguished by feelings of pleasure. We aren't here just talking about the visceral, physical sense of feeling good—the massages and the orgasms. There are the pleasures of enjoying company, of laughing, of reading David Hume's philosophy, of taking in art.[*] But the physical stuff is certainly part of it, and reminding ourselves of these feelings is an easy place to start wrapping our heads around the mental state of happiness.

Recognizing that happiness consists in a mental state distinguished by pleasure sets us on a path toward experiencing more of it. As I'll remind you over and over again, knowledge of what we're after gives us insight into how to get it, and in this case knowing that happiness is just a pleasurable mental state shows us that the way to achieve more isn't through endless pursuit of more. Rather, the smart way to experience more pleasure is to check in with yourself and use your own experience of pleasurable states as both your North Star and your launchpad.

---

[*] This was John Stuart Mill's pivotal observation: that human beings can experience pleasures of the mind and of the body (*Utilitarianism*, 2nd ed., ed. George Sher [1861; Indianapolis: Hackett Publishing, 2001]).

Let's start with our happy places: those spaces and places where feelings of happiness flow freely. When we're in our happy places, we're not pushing or pursuing, we simply find ourselves feeling happy—we can't help but feel happy when we're in them.

My happy place? There are a few of them, but nowhere am I happier than when I'm on the water, ideally on a sailboat, cruising over the waves, water splashing in over the sides. Knowing this about myself—or rather, explicitly being aware of this fact about myself—turns out to be a game changer. No longer will I accept years on dry land. I'm not going to chase that bigger house or the new car. But save up for a Sunfish? Yes. Work toward being able to live around water full-time? Definitely. Moves like this increase your opportunities for moments of happiness.

TAKE A HARD LOOK AT YOUR HAPPY PLACE

When was the last time you felt pleasure? What were you doing? Try to imagine yourself in the moment and rehearse the feeling. Start by thinking about physical sources of pleasure: having sex with someone you feel completely comfortable with; the feeling in your gut when you laugh with friends at trivia night; drinking a crisp glass of ice water at exactly the moment you needed it; taking in the warmth of the sun with a cool, mellow breeze coming from behind your back. Get your moment. Close your eyes. Feel it. That's the sensation of being happy. Now open your eyes. Is the feeling gone? Probably. The second we move away from our happy places, the feeling drifts. Our happy places tend to reflect bounded, short moments. That's just reality.

But notice that no matter what we do, we're not likely to be able to make the sensation of happiness stick around for longer than those moments. It turns out nothing really can, and that's just how it goes with happiness and pleasure.* This doesn't make happiness less valu-

---

* There's a scientific explanation that I'll get to later, but for now, just observe.

able; the pleasure it brings is valuable. That happiness is pleasurable explains both why we are so vulnerable to its lure and why moments of happiness are all that we can truly attain. We're stuck in one of those boomerang loops: The draw of pleasure is strong, but the more we chase it, the quicker and harder it starts to snap back.

THE VALUE OF PLEASURE

The sixteenth-century philosopher Michel de Montaigne observes, "Scratching is one of life's sweetest gratifications and the closest at hand."* I'm sure anyone who has ever broken a limb and wound up with an arm or a leg in a fiberglass cast for months knows *exactly* what he is talking about.

I love Montaigne's quote because it captures the heart of pleasure and of moments of simply feeling good. There really is something pure and simple about pleasure. Just feeling it makes you want to do the happy dance. Think about some of the most clear-cut examples of pleasure: a catnap on the couch, a hug from your child, the sparks that fly during a good first date. Pleasure can get complicated, but its value shines in these little moments. We could push, and ask why pleasure is valuable, why feeling good is good for us, but I don't think we're really being honest when we do so. We know pleasure is valuable simply through our experience of it, in the moment.

The goodness of pleasure is tangible and obvious. But look around. How many people do you see pursuing a life full of pleasure? Not a lot, probably. That's a helpful sign that should go a long way toward putting the Cult of Happiness into perspective. Happiness is not the pinnacle of a Good Life. Happiness does not exhaust a Good Life.

Many of us know this, deep down. Happiness isn't the most important

---

Observe where you feel happiest and observe the limited duration of these moments of happiness and pleasure.

* Montaigne seems to have been prompted to make this observation after considering Plato's description of Socrates's urge to itch himself upon being released from handcuffs during his trial (Michel de Montaigne, "Of Experience," 1588).

thing in life. It's important because it delivers pleasure, but pleasure isn't all that important to many people. Even if we can't help but value it.

Look around again, maybe more broadly, as this is a hard one. How many people do you know who strive to live a happy life and have been successful in doing it? Maybe you've heard the stories. Maybe you've witnessed the story.

The documentary *Happy*, which does a fantastic job of presenting happiness research, highlights a handful of people who claim, or seem, to be happy. All the time. One of them always stands out to me. A Brazilian surfer, tanned and wild-haired, lives in a shack by the surf, chickens running around, nothing electric in sight. He devotes his life to surfing. He seems very happy. He says he's very happy. We're meant to see him as one who genuinely discovered how to live a happy life. But still, I look closely. I hear his words, and the way he talks about the waves and the water. He's got a spiritual connection to the water that informs his very way of being. His eyes are wide and welcoming, almost as if he sees something I don't—and maybe can't.

When you look closely, it becomes clear that something else, beyond happiness, is driving him. It's just not the words, nor the look, you get from a pleasure-seeker. It's the words, and the look, you hear from someone connecting with nature in a way that brings them awe. Awe is awesome. It's one of the emotions we feel when connected to a greater thing.[3] Awe is one step away from wonder, which begets the interesting. But awe is not pleasure. Whatever our Brazilian surfer has going on, it's more than happiness.

DOESN'T IT ALL "FEEL GOOD"?

One thing I'm encouraging you to do here, and throughout this book, is to become clearer on the different kinds of feelings and mental states we associate with the Good Life. I promise, this isn't just the philosopher in me demanding precision! There are a few reasons why it is important to move past the generic descriptors as you begin to think seriously about your best possible life.

First, if you are just going after things that "feel good," your efforts will be haphazard chases, running-with-the-wind-type stuff, rather than informed pursuits of the prudential values that enhance your life. Sure, pleasure feels good, as does the interesting, as does fulfillment—if they didn't, it'd be downright shocking to claim that they are part of the Good Life! Being able to differentiate the ways in which these values "feel good" is crucial to understanding their respective contributions to your best possible life, as well as to developing a more nuanced understanding of your needs in the moment. For example, pleasure is felt more passively than the interesting; in moments of exhaustion, we're better off seeking pleasure, while in moments of boredom, we're better off seeking the interesting.

Second, moving past the generic "feel-good" descriptor gives us a better handle on our target, and on what we can do to get there. Consider the difference between feeling awe and feeling pleasure. Awe arises when you feel you're in the presence of something greater, whereas pleasure arises from known physiological triggers. Whether or not you are after awe or pleasure is essential, practical information. When you're equipped with this information, you'll more easily be able to reach the states and feelings you desire.

Third, the only way to take advantage of empirical research is by understanding what it shows. Psychological research reveals correlations between actions and thought patterns and specific states and feelings. To know which actions and thought patterns you are better off embracing, you need to know what they are correlated with, and whether that's something you want or need. Optimism is a thought pattern highly correlated with happiness and feelings of pleasure. Challenge is an action tendency highly correlated with psychological richness and the interesting. Just as being optimistic isn't likely to help you experience the interesting, challenging yourself isn't likely to help you experience pleasure. Whether you should strive to be more optimistic depends a lot on how satisfied you are with the amount of pleasure you experience, and whether you should strive to challenge yourself more depends a lot on how satisfied you are with the amount of psychological richness your life currently delivers.

You've opened this book to help you stop stumbling through life, hoping you'll end up with a good one. The more you latch on to the very different ways in which things feel good, the better you'll be able to stop stumbling, and start living your best possible life.

We get a more accurate portrait of a life of pleasure from Alex Garland's 1996 novel *The Beach*, made into a movie of the same name. The premise is simple: A backpacker traveling through Thailand hears talk of a beach where other travelers live in camps. It's paradise. It's bliss. It's nothing but pleasure. The backpacker goes on an adventure to find the beach, nestled among a chain of islands. He finds the beach. It looks like paradise. But the people living there? Not so happy. More like tormented. They'd found paradise and they lived with one purpose: being happy. Yet even paradise wasn't enough to deliver, and a *Lord of the Rings*–type mayhem ensues. People die. The backpacker escapes, having learned a very valuable lesson: The more exclusively and exhaustively we pursue happiness, the less happy we'll be.

It's depressing, I know. But realistic, as anyone who has tried to live the life of pleasure knows clearly. The life of a pleasure-seeker disappoints. The sad reality is that as human beings, we have tendencies that make it all but impossible not to fuck up our experiences of pleasure, especially when we take it to be the bedrock of our best possible lives. This makes happiness unstable and unsustainable as a sole foundation for the Good Life.

HOW WE FUCK UP PLEASURE

Human beings have a long and complicated history with pleasure that goes far beyond what's shown in *The Beach*. Our earliest stories are all about our proclivity to mess with a good thing. (Hello, Adam and Eve!) We've been messing with pleasure for a long time. It's our elusive holy grail: always tempting, yet somehow always out of reach. We aren't getting any happier. What are we doing wrong? It boils down to three things. While, unfortunately, we can't really fix the ways we screw it up, we can understand them, and this will help loosen our commitment to the belief that "if only" we were happy, everything would be great.

We think more is better

Here's the thing: While lots of creatures experience pleasure, human beings are calculators and quantifiers. Pleasure feels good. Being happy feels good. So, we want it. But when we want pleasure, we don't just lie on our backs, looking cute and waiting for someone to rub our bellies, like my dog Ruby. (She is irresistible!) Nope, we get one taste of pleasure and we think, *The more the better.* This is natural. For many, it's inescapable. We may try to level our instincts for more with social norms. We may try to learn from past experiences.* But there's no denying the irresistible line of thought that tells us more is better.

There's a reason "too much of a good thing" is a cliché—more pleasure is not always better, and believing that it is leads us astray. Not from some "right path" or anything like that. Paradoxically, chasing pleasure takes us further away from pleasure itself. The nature of pleasure is such that the more we go after it, the less we'll experience it.

Our experiences of pleasure have a natural shelf life. Pleasure, after all, serves a particular evolutionary function, which is to motivate us to act in ways that keep us, and future generations, alive. Consider again the simplest sources of pleasure: food, sex, social engagement. It's not a coincidence that these are also the things necessary for our survival. From a functional perspective, our experiences of pleasure lead us to engage in things that are good for us.[4] But to play this role, the good feelings we experience need to subside. If we could eat once and feel the pleasure of that meal forever, we'd never eat again. If we could hold on to the feeling of a single orgasm forever, we wouldn't be motivated to connect sexually and/or reproduce. So, it's natural that pleasure comes *and* goes. It is limited in duration by nature.

When we take this kind of scientific look into the nature of pleasure, we see that pleasure serves an important but limited purpose. It isn't an end goal of human beings but is more of a tool, motivating us to act in ways conducive to our own survival. But it's also natural for human beings to want more. This sets up a somewhat perverse ripple effect.

---

* I'm forever grateful to my sister-in-law's open chocolate buffet. One holiday, it enabled my five-year-old son to indulge so much that the pain of his subsequent vomiting led him to swear off chocolate for most of his childhood, therein giving me one less thing to fight about.

Pleasure has a shelf life, so it always ends. But because it feels good, we always want more. A tempting cycle emerges. We'll always want what will never really be attainable: a life of more and more pleasure.

Nowhere clearer do we see this cycle than in cases of addiction. The tendency to want more is in all of us, yet in some of us it takes hold more strongly and becomes pathological. It leads us to seek more and more of the same source of pleasure, be it food, drugs, or sex. We overindulge, continually going after the pleasure. But our brains simply can't handle more and more of the same pleasure, so it plays a trick. It adapts.* The same sources of pleasure stop becoming pleasurable. It's a mean trick. But it's unavoidable. Our brain is just doing what it is supposed to do in response to change. It's not even a trick, although it can certainly feel like it. And the more we seek to escape the cycle of adaptation, the more embedded in it we become. We're stuck in a pursuit of more that leads us to experience less.

We start to value pleasure for its own sake

A tricky and more philosophical way that we fuck up pleasure is by coming to value it, which is nonetheless tempting and unavoidable for most of us. We are all more philosophical than you may think. The "wanting more" problem is largely a factor of our physical reactions and compulsions toward pleasure that stand in tension with the basic function of pleasure and affective states more generally. The "valuing pleasure" problem is largely a factor of how we naturally come to think of and to embrace the things in life that make us happy.

Valuing comes naturally to human beings. It's a sign of our mind's ability to transform and to go beyond our experiences: to think, *This*

---

* In cases of drug addiction, for example, the brain adapts to the influx of drugs by delivering less of the good stuff it ordinarily would make. Addictive drugs produce high levels of dopamine, which our brain makes naturally. But if dopamine starts to reliably come from the drugs, the brain stops making it. Even more problematic is that the brain may even start to function in ways to *reduce* the elevated levels of dopamine delivered from the drugs, such as by eliminating dopamine receptors.

is good. And in most cases, valuing things helps us to get those things. When we value our education, for example, we see it as more than just the thing we do or are expected to do. More than a task, our education becomes important for its own sake. We start to see learning as its own reward. Valuing our education helps us learn. It leads us to think about our education in ways that are conducive to success in it.

Things work differently when we start to value pleasure. As natural as it is to value something that we experience as good, valuing pleasure sets up a self-defeating cycle.[5] When we value pleasure for its own sake, we begin to *prioritize* it over other things in our lives. We judge pleasure to be more important than the experiences that give rise to it.

Say you've worked hard preparing a presentation for work. And it pays off—praise from your colleagues is through the roof. You walk away thinking, *That felt good. I should give more presentations so that I can keep this going.* The next time around, toiling in front of the computer, you think, *Is it really worth working so hard on this presentation? No one will be able to know the difference if I just ask ChatGPT to write it up. Win/win.* So you do it. And no one figures it out.* The praise flows. Do you feel as good as you did the first time? Probably not.

Getting into this kind of mode is natural, even if we may not realize we are doing it. The problem is that it leads us to treat pleasure as an end goal when it isn't. Pleasure is designed to be the reward. It's the bonus, not the aim or point. When we treat it as an end goal, we mess with the basic design. If we feel pleasure after working hard on our presentation, we won't feel anywhere near the same kind of pleasure when we skip the work and aim just for the reward.

Sometimes we can get away with treating pleasure as the end goal. Sometimes we just want to feel good and know ourselves well enough to know what will deliver. We go on a luxury vacation. We get massages.

---

* This is a hypothetical example. Maybe there will be a time when your use of ChatGPT goes unnoticed, but ChatGPT has got to get a whole lot better for that time to come.

We have sex and eat tasty meals. But what if we act like this all the time, and make *all* our decisions on these grounds?

Frankly, nothing good. Valuing things for the pleasure they bring screws with our experiences of all kinds of good things. Philosophers often describe this in terms of a kind of "schizophrenia."[6] It's a breakdown of the ordinary connections between things. It arises when we start to define something's value—be it a piece of chocolate, a career, or a person—by the pleasure it brings us rather than by the things that attracted us to it in the first place. When we do this, our experiences of these things deliver less pleasure.

Friendship offers a great example. Spending time with friends can be one of the most pleasurable activities we can take on. We laugh, we support each other, we go on adventures, and we have fun. But we get these things only if we care about the people we are hanging out with and view them as friends. Once we start to see our friends as sources of pleasure, our relationships turn transactional. It's as if we expect our friends to be gumball machines for pleasurable experiences, but humans aren't gumball machines.

Here's another example: There's all kinds of fascinating research showing that the benefits of relationships depend upon reciprocal or mutual feelings of love.[7] One-sided relationships, where one party is into it and the other is not, aren't satisfying to anyone, regardless of which end you are on—the one who receives the love or the one who gives the love. Anonymous sex delivers orgasms, but over time the physical pleasure is most often outweighed by the stifling and inescapable feelings of loneliness. We can try to game the system, but in the long term we'll probably fail.

What we see happening here is, again, basic human instincts and tendencies standing in tension with the physiological realities attached to our experiences of pleasure. We can't experience pleasure just because we value it, nor because we want it. To feel pleasure, most of the time, we've got to step back, value other things, and just let it happen. We are powerful and smart creatures, but sometimes we've got to recognize the limits of what we can do. We can't *control* if and when we feel good.

But wait? Can't we? This is a hard point for most of us to accept. Not all people think this. And this leads us to the third way in which humans fuck up pleasure.

We think we can outsmart pleasure

The more we learn, the more power we have and, yes, the more god-like we become. We can fight diseases, we can defy gravity; maybe, even, we can stop climate change. As early as 2022, Meta CEO and founder Mark Zuckerberg went on record claiming that it should be possible within this century to all but eradicate disease. He describes the long-term goal of the Chan Zuckerberg Initiative, a foundation he runs with his wife, Priscilla Chan, as creating "tools for the scientific community to enable them to either be able to cure, prevent or manage all diseases within this century. And I think that's possible," he emphasized.*

Time will tell if he's right. But let's be clear: If we think we've got the ability to eradicate disease, why should we throw up our hands when it comes to our ability to feel pleasure? It is an easy step to think we've also got the power to fight the limits of pleasure. And why shouldn't we? Why should we accept the fleeting and transitory nature of being happy when we can change and control so much?

It is telling that the human potential to take control over our experiences of pleasure, and to find a way to experience long-lasting states of happiness, is one that has worried a lot of people. We've heard the warnings as early as Aldous Huxley's *Brave New World*, published in 1932, well before happiness research was even on the radar. He predicted the invention of a pill, soma, that provides the purest and best kind of pleasure, unmixed with the dangers of today's street drugs. He predicted the invention of movies, feelies, that literally provide sensory stimulation, making it easy, almost unavoidable, to enjoy the movie. And

---

* In an interview with Joe Rogan (*The Joe Rogan Experience*, podcast, episode 1863, August 25, 2022). Zuckerberg and Chan have pledged to donate an astonishing 99 percent of their wealth to this fund.

he predicted these inventions would create a dystopia. Why? Because they provided pleasure in the form of escape from the raw emotions of human life and so, in the wrong hands, they could become a form of social control, reducing people to pleasure-seekers willing to do anything for more. The pleasure-producing technologies became a way of creating what reads as almost a different race of people. A race of people so interested in feeling good, they don't care about anything else.

We see the warnings again in David Foster Wallace's 1996 novel *Infinite Jest*. Wallace's worry was less about the threat of political control and more about the threat pleasure presents to the human species itself, especially given ever-increasing technological capacities. He envisions a world in which we've become so caught up in the pursuit of easy pleasures that it becomes standard to eat one's dinner from trays attached to one's neck, so that one doesn't have to look away from the TV for even the second it might take to bring a fork from a table to one's mouth. There exists a film, referred to as "the Entertainment," that is so engaging, so pleasurable, that people watch it continuously and lose interest in all other aspects of life, including eating and drinking.* It's a form of pleasure so good it will literally kill you. People who watch it are found dead in their recliners, in clothes soiled from bodily fluids and excrement, their dinner rotting on the trays still attached to their necks.

It's tempting to write off *Brave New World* and *Infinite Jest* as warnings to a world about things that would never happen. But the common theme they explore is worth taking seriously even if we reject the sci-fi aspects. What if there were a drug that could make us feel happy continuously without the cycles of addiction and adaptation kicking in? What if we could spend the rest of our lives in constant pleasure? If pleasure is really that good, these are the kinds of things we should be striving for. Yet again, these are dystopian novels. They tell the story of all that we'd miss in our pursuit of pleasure, even if we were able to outsmart its natural limits.

---

* The idea of "the Entertainment" is modeled after experiments on rats, in which rats allowed unlimited access to morphine took so much they neglected to eat, and soon died.

Of all people, John D. Rockefeller—who remains the inflation-adjusted richest man in U.S. history—is notorious for writing, "I can imagine nothing less pleasurable than a life full of pleasure." This isn't because pleasure isn't good; it's because pleasure is good for us and so is part of our Good Lives, only in limited degrees. We experience its value by respecting its limited nature.

This is true both of those who swear they'd never take a soma and those who feel the temptation strongly. We can recognize the importance of being happy, and of feeling pleasure, without structuring our lives by it. Given the nature of pleasure, it turns out that limiting its role in our lives is the most promising route to experiencing it. We could fight the limits, but we shouldn't. Instead, we're better off acting like the *Seinfeld* gang: Enjoy happiness when you've got it, but don't worry about it when you don't have it. And now we can see exactly what they get right, which turns out to be a lot more than the happy dance. In fact, the *Seinfeld* gang are uniquely tuned in to the nature of happiness.

The season 3 premiere slips in some of the most insightful dialogue about happiness we can find. Jerry and George have gotten their dentist friend in trouble for insurance fraud after he wrote the gang prescriptions for massages. In the aftermath, the dentist's receptionist looks at them with scorn: "I hope you're both happy," she says, clearly intending the opposite. Without missing a beat, Jerry jumps in, announcing with no regret or remorse: "I'm not happy." And then George: "Me neither. I've never been happy." They keep going:

JERRY: I mean I'm happy sometimes, but not now.
GEORGE: In college, maybe. Those were fun times.
JERRY: Yeah, college was fun.

It's a weird conversation, but their perspective on happiness is spot-on. We should recognize that happiness is the work of moments, not a lifetime. We should accept that it is OK not to be happy. And we should put elsewhere our efforts toward living a Good Life.

REPLACING PLEASURE WITH PASSION

When I look at the lives I admire, that I draw on for inspiration, it's always the lives of people who do what they are passionate about. I bet the same is true for you. We don't get inspired by pleasure-chasers unless it's clear that they are driven by passion. The Brazilian surfer dude inspires because he's so passionate about surfing, much like my old friend from high school, Matt, who managed to set up a life in Hawaii revolving around his passion for surfing. I remember reconnecting with him over social media decades after we graduated. Simply learning that he'd pulled it off, and built his life around a passion that had seemed so far-flung and out of reach from the wooded northwest corner of Connecticut where we'd grown up, brought a smile to my face. And despite the challenges and hardships of my own job in academia, I'm consistently grateful to be getting paid to do something that I love, that I am passionate about. Remembering this inspires me. Remembering this makes my life go better.

We don't get inspired by the person working a grueling job, hours on end, just to make ends meet. We might, and probably should, respect this person, and aspects of their dedication to provide may inspire, but really, this kind of life does not inspire.* Nope, the ones who inspire are the passionate ones.

Even if we can't all be so lucky to get paid for doing what we love, with just a little bit of effort, we can tap into and realize our passions, and let them fuel our pursuits. As we do this, it'll help to begin to reorient our attraction to pleasure and happiness. We're all driven by pleasure, yes, but not exclusively so. We have passions, instincts within us, that point to ranges of experiences we'll find rewarding even if they don't happen to be pleasant. Learning to listen to our passions and letting them start

---

* I am a sucker for the Venn diagram we often see that points us to careers in something we are good at, that we can get paid for, *and* that we are passionate about. It's good advice because it's true—this is how we'll succeed at living Good Lives. Having to work is an inevitable fact of life for most of us. We should strive to find something that delivers more to our lives than financial security alone.

to infiltrate the spaces that pleasure and happiness simply cannot fill in puts us on a trajectory toward a better life.

Think about it: When was the last time you experienced passion in your life? Has it been too long? There's a common thread I've found among a lot of my friends who have been through a divorce. It's the realization that they've lost sight of what they are passionate about and that their lives are worse for it. It's the realization that life is going by too quickly to not have fun. It's the realization that they need to make time for themselves and take control of their own Good Lives.

While you start to pay attention to what you are passionate about, pay attention to dread, too—that heavy, torturous place we land when we're doing or about to do something that squashes our passions. Both are barometers of resonance.

"Resonance" describes the feeling we get when we're doing something that clicks with us, that connects to and sparks our passions. It's the gut feeling that arises when something meshes with us on a deep level. When something resonates, it does so wholeheartedly, for there is nothing pulling us in a different direction. It's the feeling we get when we are so sucked into a novel we find ourselves unable to put it down. It's the feeling we get when we listen to our favorite song. It's what makes something our favorite song in the first place.

As is often the case, we can make a lot of progress in recognizing what resonates for us by thinking about what does not resonate for us. Yoga is something that has never resonated with me. No matter how many times I've tried to commit myself to a practice, no matter how much I know about its benefits, no matter how much I want to like it, I simply cannot get into it. And it is only recently that I would even admit this to myself, let alone to all who might be reading this book.

We've all been there, stuck doing something we think we should enjoy but that really doesn't resonate with us.* Maybe it was a new book by

---

* Confession: In between writing the first draft of this section and its revisions, I quickly forgot this about myself, tried to commit to yet another yoga practice, and failed again. I meant it when I said this takes work.

your favorite author that you were looking forward to but just couldn't get into. Maybe it was a trip to the Eiffel Tower, where you found yourself staring and staring, wondering why in the world people attach so much romance and intrigue to a massive A-frame of metal plopped in a largely residential neighborhood. Just me? Well, regardless, it did not resonate. But maybe it did for you. Maybe you saw, even felt, the mystique surrounding the Eiffel Tower. That's what we are looking for.

One of David Foster Wallace's best nonfiction articles describes the despair, almost horror, he felt upon taking a luxury cruise. The luxury cruise promises "indulgences become easy" and "relaxation becomes second nature," and the crew is dedicated to delivering on its promises.[8] Sounds like heaven to me right now. To Wallace? Not so much. He felt *despair*, which is surely a mark of doing something that does not resonate. He felt despair at being trapped on a ship designed for one and only one passion that he did not share, that he balked against.

We all probably have a sense of the kind of despair Wallace gets at here, although hopefully not often.* Your friend's new boyfriend is going on about crypto again, or Jaime's mom won't stop talking about his latest adventures in solid starts. You open your news feed to find one more article you do not need on how to be happy. You find yourself among colleagues who are driven by some kind of passion for the parts of your job you dread. The despair that comes from finding yourself doing something while completely devoid of passion is the kind of stuff that makes you want to gouge your eyes out or, if you're like Wallace, it'll make you want to jump overboard from a luxury cruise liner.[9]

Despair and dread more generally arise when we're in a place or doing an activity that doesn't resonate, even if it promises pleasure or other good things at the end. In contrast, feelings of ease and wholeness indicate that what you're doing resonates with your own passions. Maybe you get these feelings when on a luxury cruise. Maybe you get these feelings sitting in the pew of your church. Maybe you get these

---

* Tragically, David Foster Wallace took his own life in 2008.

feelings up onstage. Maybe you get these feelings from aspects of your job. Wherever they come, notice them. Embrace them. Let them drive you. Doing so will help loosen your grip on pleasure. It'll help you recognize the role happiness plays in your life, for, despite what we've all been taught, happiness really just is a by-product, a reward that only sometimes delivers value to your activities. It's not something we can or should chase. We're way better off replacing the chase with a stronger sense of what resonates for us and allowing our passions to point the way.

KEEPING IT INTERESTING

Happiness comes and goes. It's something we experience in moments. It makes us want to throw up our arms and jump up and down. It appears quickly and often without warning, and then fades away. Its mercurial nature makes it unstable ground on which to pour the foundation of our Good Life, but that doesn't mean we can't enjoy the pleasure it brings us. The key to letting it become part of our Good Lives is to follow the *Seinfeld* gang's lead: Let it flow when it happens but don't begrudge the times when it doesn't. Replace that pursuit of pleasure with attention to your passions, and let your passions determine the shape of your Good Life.

Chapter 3:

The Irony of Fulfillment

RECENTLY I MADE THE MISTAKE OF GOOGLING "HOW DO I find purpose?" Yikes. This opened a soul-sucking enterprise that left me feeling like there was something fundamentally wrong with me. My first mistake, apparently, was in how I asked the question. I shouldn't have been looking for "purpose"—that search delivered no insight whatsoever, for all I found were stories of how other people have found the One thing they were destined for. I guess I should have been asking, "What am *I* here for?" or "What *should* I be doing to make the most out of my life?" It's not that Google could have answered these questions, but the reveal was in how quickly we move from recognizing the basic importance of having purpose in our lives, to embracing the idea each of us needs to find our own Unique Purpose™ for our lives to be meaningful. Believing that to have a Good Life, we have to find the sole, discrete purpose we were destined for just isn't a good idea. Even if it (amazingly) turns out to be true for you, it's not a good recipe for living a Good Life.

Don't believe me?

It's not that there are not good stories of people who have found and embraced their purpose. There are plenty of those. A forty-eight-year-old man beats brain cancer and commits to helping others live their fullest lives, addressing their issues before they stare down their own mortality. He claims his near-death crisis forced him to confront his life and to find his purpose. A thirty-five-year-old woman realizes her life isn't going as she wants. She quits her job and travels around the world. She finds comfort in a culture's tradition of writing affirmation notes. She returns home and starts up a company dedicated to publishing affirmation notes. She reports that her travels helped her find her purpose. She's never looked back.

These stories aren't entirely unusual. We've all heard them. We know it *can* happen that people find their purpose. The problems arise when we think it's going to work out like this for each of us, and that there's something wrong with us or our lives when we haven't figured it out, which is exactly how I felt after my little googling experiment.

The reality is that trying to discover one's unique purpose is a crapshoot, a pursuit largely available only to those with privilege, and without dependents, who can get away with quitting their jobs on a whim, picking up, and moving to another country, or who can survive for years without a paycheck while they strive to discover their purpose. Here's what seems to me a more realistic account of what happens when we search for our purpose:

We google. We sit. We think. We second-guess. We reject. We feel bad. We keep thinking. We keep googling. We keep sitting. We keep thinking. We keep second-guessing. We keep rejecting. We keep feeling bad.

That's a bit tongue-in-cheek. The process of finding one's purpose can be long, and there is research to draw on to help each stage go a little better than it did for me. For a lot of us, though, this is the cycle, no matter how committed we are and how seriously we take the project. We set our standards high, fail to live up to them, and feel bad about it.

If you've found and embraced your unique purpose, good for you. You've beaten the odds. If you've also found that devoting your life to your unique purpose delivers you a Good Life, good for you. You've won the cosmic lottery. For the rest of us, it turns out that it's just as difficult to live a Good Life exclusively devoted to purpose as it is to find one's purpose in the first place.

PURPOSE, ACHIEVEMENT, VIRTUE

"Purpose" is one of a cluster of concepts that track the dimension of the Good Life involving the contributions one makes to the world. Unlike the experience of being happy, which is good just insofar as we experience it, this dimension of the Good Life tracks factors that go beyond one's sensory experiences. Purpose opens the door to count the things that we've achieved and obtained, including not just the tangible stuff like degrees and promotions and stock portfolios, but also the people whom we have helped, the volunteer groups we've organized, the ideas that we've produced, and the commitments we've made to living our lives in ways that reflect a concern for the greater good.

Sometimes psychologists refer to this kind of life in terms of eudaimonia, invoking reference to Aristotle's theory that human beings flourish insofar as they live a life of reason and virtue.* Yet Aristotle's focus on the importance of virtue to eudaimonia mostly drops out in psychological discussions of eudaimonia, which use the word more as an umbrella term to describe the forms of life we might conversationally describe in terms of meaning and achievement. We can make it easy on ourselves and just talk about this dimension of the Good Life in terms of meaning. Doing so allows us to pull together this cluster of concepts (purpose, achievement, virtue) without prioritizing any one of them.

Finding a purpose in life can give meaning to our lives. Achieving

---

* Interestingly, Aristotle famously maintains that each human being has a purpose by virtue of being a human being. He'd reject the popular notion that everyone has a *distinct* purpose, and he'd argue that the way to find "purpose" is to reflect on what is distinctive about human beings considered as a species, which, he'd argue, is reason and our capacity to use reason to direct and regulate our emotions. This is a far cry from today's tropes about the nature of purpose.

things can make our lives meaningful. Using reason and developing virtue can make our lives meaningful. In essence, a meaningful life is one in which we can understand our activities, or life overall, in a way that makes them count.

Now, from a bird's-eye perspective, there's a clear connection between having meaning in one's life and the amount of objectively good things one puts out into the world. There's no question that Greta Thunberg, the Swedish climate activist who made headlines for her well-articulated challenges and criticisms of global leaders three or four times her age, finds meaning in her chosen role that derives from the objective importance she (rightfully) attributes to her activism.

But we're not interested in the bird's-eye perspective. We're interested in how to live Good Lives for ourselves. In the context of thinking about living Good Lives, the perspective of the bird in no way trumps the perspective of the actual person living the life.

That's an indirect way of saying that we can consider the value of one's life from many different perspectives. The bird's-eye perspective tracks *objective value*, while only the personal perspective can track *prudential value*, which is subjectively experienced. Objective value can add prudential value, as we would hope is true for Greta. Her contributions to the world, we'd hope, make her life go better. But it might not go like this. That someone's life has objective value does not necessarily mean their experience of their own life is enhanced. It's an unfortunate but true fact that the two can come apart.

Let me give you another example: Ernest Hemingway wrote books that were well received in his day, earning him both a Nobel Prize and a Pulitzer, and that went on to become American classics. The merit of his literary contributions is beyond challenge, and what's more, he succeeded in living the life that he wanted: being a writer. Despite achieving his ambitions, and making significant contributions to the world, Hemingway clearly did not live a Good Life. He married four times, suffered from depression and paranoia, and was a lifelong alcoholic. He took to hobbies like fishing and hunting because their violent nature satisfied his urges to harm himself: "I spend a hell of a lot of time killing animals and fish, so I won't kill myself," he once said.[1]

Hemingway did end up killing himself at the age of sixty-one. Afterward, a friend wondered how this could happen to someone so successful, "whom many critics call the greatest writer of his century, a man who had a zest for life and adventure as big as his genius, a solid marriage...good friends everywhere...[how could he] put a shotgun to his head and [kill] himself?"[2]

We get where his friend is coming from. It's hard to look at the trophies of such a successful life, at all that someone has and has accomplished, and imagine that it might not be a Good Life. Doing so would shake the bedrock of what so many of us have been taught to strive for since infancy.

It's heartbreaking to see so many examples of successful people who don't or didn't lead Good Lives. They've checked all the boxes, found success by any objective measure, contributed to the world, yet they don't feel the fulfillment that they were promised. Maybe this sounds familiar to you—maybe it's even the reason you picked up this book. What we've been told will bring us the Good Life isn't delivering.

It helps to name this, if only to change the scripts we tell ourselves. In an excellent article on the limits of achievement, *New York Times* bestselling author Ryan Holiday asks and answers the question for himself so, so well: "So how does it feel to have everything you wanted in life? And to have it earlier than you ever could have realistically expected? I can tell you: It feels like nothing."[3]

Even worse, there's solid research affirming the dent that searching for meaning makes in one's overall life satisfaction and well-being. Especially in the later years of life, the more folks have searched or find themselves searching for meaning, the less of a Good Life they seem to be living.[4]

It's not at all uncommon to feel empty in the face of our accomplishments, even and especially the most important ones. It's not at all uncommon to find ourselves caught up in a job or lifestyle that adds so much to the world, only to question, in the quiet moments, whether we're living the lives we really want. While meaningful lives might add objective value to the world, we shouldn't mistake that kind of value for the kind that necessarily contributes to our Good Lives.

The upside of this is that we can lead Good Lives that lack objective value. I, for one, am reassured by the fact that I can still have had a Good Life even if no one is reading my work in one thousand years, none of my students have gone on to change the world, and I haven't received any kind of Pulitzer Prize.* It means my Good Life isn't contingent upon being "successful," upon being fortunate enough to make a dent in the world. It means the Good Life isn't reserved just for the special, talented ones. It means there's hope for all of us, even if we are stuck in conditions that limit us. Whether we are limited by our resources, our talents, our locations, or our tastes, we can still live Good Lives. Whether we live Good Lives doesn't inherently depend on the amount of value we put out into the world.

At this point, you might be thinking, *But, Lorraine?! What about my volunteer work? What about my degree in research science? What about the books you have written? Doesn't any of that matter? I feel like it does...*And you'd be absolutely right. Just because meaning doesn't inherently give us a Good Life doesn't mean that it can't help.

Just like with happiness, though, we shouldn't go all in on meaning as a safe bet for a Good Life. We're not wrong to think that meaning is a part of a Good Life. It is. There's a ton of research and compelling arguments about the prudential value of living a meaningful life. But we need to focus less on the bird's-eye perspective and more on our own. We need to stop thinking so much about whether what we are doing is valuable and focus more on whether what we are doing is making for a Good Life. We need to ask ourselves: *What are these pursuits doing for me? How are they making my life better?* Putting the focus on the prudential value of meaningful lives helps us to better understand the role meaning can play in our Good Lives.

---

* Not that any prize like this exists for philosophers.

WHAT ARE THESE DIFFERENT TYPES OF VALUES?

Type of value:	Objective value	Prudential value (A form of subjective value)
Commonly known as:	This is "valuable."	This is "valuable for me."
Why valuable?	This is a very difficult question to answer.	Because it benefits *you*.
Gauge the value from:	An impersonal point of view (the bird's-eye view)	The personal point of view (your interests, desires, needs)
Examples:	Great works of art Human life Knowledge	Your projects Your relationships Your Good Life

FINDING FULFILLMENT IN OUR LIVES

The problem with devoting ourselves exclusively to living a life of meaning isn't just a practical matter of finding our purpose, or the difficulties involved in achieving something of objective value. There's also the very difficult step of finding fulfillment within our lives—that is what we're really talking about when we're talking about the prudential value of meaningful lives. For what we are doing to contribute to our Good Life, we've got to find prudential value in it. We have to find fulfillment. This turns out to be harder than we'd expect it to be.

Even if we set our hearts on achieving something, and achieve it, whether we will be fulfilled as a result depends upon a lot of factors, not all of which we can control or predict. We've all had the experience of feeling the initial seeds of fulfillment sprout after achieving something we've worked hard for, be it a college degree, a promotion, whatever. Sadly, I'm guessing we've all had the experience of feeling those seeds shrivel up just as quickly as they sprouted.

Why does it work this way? It can feel like a cruel twist of fate. This thing you've worked so hard for, that you've finally gotten, turns out to leave you feeling flat and empty. These stories are a dime a dozen. One man works for years producing a meaningful, important documentary. He finishes it, he's proud of it, and he's got a deal with Netflix. Yet three days later he finds himself crying in his truck in a Walmart parking lot.[5] A sixteen-year-old wins the championship at a national dance competition and feels joy...for an hour, until she finds herself alone in bed, feeling empty, anxious, and alone. She binges on food in the middle of the night to fill the emptiness.[6] Even post-tenure depression, afflicting those of us academics lucky enough to succeed in the most tangible possible way—a lifelong position—is a real thing.

There's nothing wrong with any of these folks, nor the choices they made. They all accomplished something important, both to them and to the bird. But they don't feel fulfillment, at least in any lasting sense of the word.

Psychologists describe this common phenomenon in terms of the arrival fallacy.[7] It's the mistake we make when thinking that *when we get X, we'll be satisfied.* It's a mistake because it presupposes there's a strong connection between achievement and fulfillment, when it's a pretty flimsy one. For one thing, achievements often depend on external validation. We need others to pat us on the back to feel like we've achieved. Anything that depends on others is sketchy at best. We can achieve things that go unnoticed. Even in those moments when we do get the pat on the back, well, it's a pat on the back! It happens and disappears in the blink of an eye. It is no wonder so many successful people feel so unfulfilled.

Another reason is that to benefit from the "If only I get this, I'll be fulfilled" mentality, it's got to be true that the thing you're aiming at will fulfill you. Otherwise, we just get the thing and not the fulfillment. For the strategy to pay off, we've got to be good at predicting how we'll feel when we get something we want. And, hands down, research shows we are really bad at making these predictions.

Dan Gilbert's fascinating work on affective forecasting shows, time and time again, how wrong we are about the things that we think will impact us the most: our choice of college roommate, for example. It is so tempting to think that who we live with is going to have a huge impact on our college lives. To think that if I have a good roommate, I'll enjoy college. Why wouldn't it have this impact? But whoever your roommate turns out to be will have very little impact on your life more generally. Same with getting tenure. In fact, Gilbert's research even suggests that we are more unsatisfied when we've chosen something—like a painting, for example—than when we're given something without getting to make any choice about it. We put so much weight on these things, which can put so much stress on us, and they turn out not to matter.

Again, this research is depressing yet liberating. Knowing these facts about ourselves gives us the golden ticket to stop stressing quite so much about the decisions we must make, or about what will happen if we fail. And comprehending the weak links that exist between achievement and fulfillment can help us to better understand (a) the role of meaning in our Good Lives and (b) the huge mistake we make when we assume meaning constitutes the entirety of our Good Lives. The value it promises—fulfillment—is elusive, and much less connected to achievements than we tend to think. This alone suggests we ought to limit the role a search for meaning, purpose, and achievement plays within our lives.

There's a further, perhaps more penetrating reason why we ought to limit the role of meaning in our lives. Living a life dominated by achievement, purpose, and meaning is hard. It's exhausting work that asks a lot of us. One big ask is that we prioritize our rational mind, and the plans and purposes it strives to form, over pretty much all other things. Is this the best approach to living a Good Life? Do the remarkable powers of our rationality consistently warrant priority? It's likely you were raised to think something along these lines. It's time to start thinking for yourself, both about what a life of prioritizing rationality entails, and about why we tend to think rationality is so important.

A (VERY SAD) LIFE OF REASON

Born in London in 1806, John Stuart Mill had the misfortune of being raised by a philosopher in the days in which philosophers were all like his dad, James: male, white, and elitist.* John was a child prodigy, the stuff of legends. By age three (!), he had learned Greek and mathematics. By age eight, he was not just reading Plato, but critiquing him. By age seventeen, he'd accomplished academically what typically takes others (okay, me) almost twice as long. By age twenty, he had suffered a life-changing mental crisis.

It is hard to find a better example of the downsides of being a child prodigy. In his autobiography, Mill laments being trained "to know rather than to do" and begrudges the fact that his father made no effort to make up for the practical skills Mill lost out on developing by virtue of being homeschooled. What comes to the forefront as most problematic is that, amid his extensive schooling in Greek and Latin, he hadn't learned to pay attention to feelings.

Well before his mental crisis, Mill had found his purpose. He'd been working with a group that included his father and Jeremy Bentham, whose legal reform project was gaining traction. Mill was committed to defending the utilitarian position and the merits of creating laws that promoted the greatest happiness. But, despite his commitment to this movement, he increasingly began to recognize something was missing.[8] While Mill was able to wrap his rational mind around the importance of happiness, he couldn't *feel* the pleasures of sympathy. He couldn't rejoice in the happiness he promoted.

This realization stopped him in his tracks. He'd built his life so that all his serious and permanent personal satisfaction rested on an end that "had ceased to charm." There was nothing to push him forward. As he put it so poetically, he found himself "stranded at the commencement of my voyage, with a well-equipped ship and a rudder, but no sail."[9] His

---

* We are getting better. Slowly.

rational pursuits gave his life structure, but structure is useless without something pushing forward.

Mill wasn't sure how he'd go on. He realized how off-track his life was. He'd focused all along on changing people's minds through argument. It hadn't occurred to him to worry at all about the cultivation of feelings, in himself or others. And, at the time of his crisis, Mill worried that there was no hope of feeling: "All feeling was dead." He reportedly spent a year in this state of crisis, absent emotions, before he found himself moved to tears by a book.

He was transformed by this moment of feeling. He realized he wasn't made of stone, after all, and that he had the capacity to find enjoyment in ordinary life. He returned to his philosophical mission, only this time, he sought to infuse utilitarianism with feeling. He returned with passion. John Stuart Mill went on to become a more influential philosopher than his father, and his defense of utilitarianism was, and is often still taken to be, the definitive one.

Here's the real problem with fulfillment, a problem that arises even if we find it, and especially if we focus too much on finding it. We see it clearly when we hold little John in our mind, learning Greek as a toddler. His father was so focused on ensuring that his son fulfilled his potential, living up to the (admittedly outstanding) intellectual promise he saw within him, that he cut him off from all the other parts of life. By making John live a life of reason alone, he even cut John off from parts of himself.

That's the irony of fulfillment. We focus so much on fulfilling one part of ourselves, that one little part wrapped up in purpose, achievement, and meaning, that we forget about the rest. There's a little bit of this in most of us, and sometimes a lot. It's the very misguided thought that if someone has "potential,"* they've got to structure their lives around making sure they reach the fullest extent of it.

---

* At this point, I really don't even know what "potential" means. Do you? We declare "potential" when we see an ability in someone that is advanced for their age and/or training. Yet why this means anything is really a mystery to me. Could

Why should being born with a capacity entail that our best possible lives will and ought to revolve around it? This seems a grave mistake. A rampant one we all fall victim to, but a mistake nonetheless.

We do figure this out with some things. "Don't let them know you're good at it!" is a well-known saying among professors with respect to the administrative stuff. Most of us are passionate about our research and teaching, and most of us are good at it. But there's administrative work to be done, too, such as chairing, and we are not all good at this. Sometimes the people who are good at it enjoy it, but more often, we don't. And it becomes a curse to be good at it, for the more you've got to do the chairing, the less you're able to do the stuff you're passionate about. And that's just unfortunate.

Being good at something shouldn't be a curse or a rail ticket to a single track. It's important only when you're good at things you are passionate about. Absent a foundation in passion, potential has no connection to the Good Life. In little John's case, devoting himself to his potential meant being cut off from fun and play, and all the emotions that come with them. This didn't just stifle his pursuit of a Good Life; it literally drove him to a mental breakdown.

Just because we have potential, even the distinctive promise for greatness that John showed, doesn't mean we should double down on it, taking the development of our potential to be the most important aspect of our lives. Too often, we feel that we must fulfill our talents, or we've failed as human beings. That purpose is figuring out what we're best at and going all in to maximize that vocation. The trouble is that even if we do happen to see our potential (or have someone see it in us), when we hyperfocus on it, our lives start to shrink. They may look good (from that bird's-eye perspective), but they don't feel good.

Whatever shape fulfillment takes for you—be it through developing potential, finding that unique purpose, or through achievement—it's

---

my sons have learned Latin and Greek before kindergarten? Maybe, if I were willing to do what it takes. But why would I want to torture them? Or myself?

worth rethinking its role in your life. It's no secret that great success in any of these areas requires sacrifice. But it's a myth that such sacrifice is always, even often, worth it. And it's time to put an end to that myth, and to look very clearly at what we end up sacrificing and why.

We sacrifice our Good Lives. We may squeeze in time for moments of pleasure during our missions to achieve, but we're much less likely to save space for the interesting in our lives. That's, first, because we probably aren't thinking about it, and second, because the interesting also arises in the mind and often involves challenges. Experiencing pleasure is a passive, easy thing. Experiencing the interesting can be easy, but it'll always enrich our lives in a way that rejuvenates and leaves our minds charged. The more we focus on fulfillment, the more liable we are to cut ourselves off from that magic of the interesting. That's a big mistake.

Why do we make it? Why do we think fulfillment warrants sacrificing the other good things life has to offer? We do it because we just can't shake the standards set for us eons ago by the ancient Greek philosophers, who held up rationality as the most important part of us, never to be sacrificed in the name of passion.

SHAKING THE BIAS OF THE ANCIENT GREEK PHILOSOPHERS

It's not surprising to hear that for centuries, philosophers have prioritized the development of reason over anything else. They did this for all the obvious reasons: Our cognitive capacities do make humans special, and using reason does open to us an all-things-considered-valuable way of operating in the world.* These are true things about us, but it's an altogether different claim to say we ought to be living lives devoted exclusively to the use of reason. It's a proposal that made sense to the philosophers advocating it, because it worked for them, given their circumstances. It doesn't work out so well for us.

---

* This is the exact line of argument Aristotle employs in his *Nicomachean Ethics* (chapter 1) to advocate for the inseparability of using reason from the Good Life.

The thing is, in ancient society, where the bias toward reason first arose, things were structured in a way that made it easy for the philosophers—obviously, all of whom were men—to privilege reason. It fit in with both their lifestyles and their theories.

Plato, Aristotle's teacher, warrants much of the credit and blame for this move. Plato advocated for a specialization of labor.[10] Rather than all of us doing everything, Plato recognized, we'll be more effective if we split it up, focus on what we're good at, and let others focus on what they are good at. While great in theory, we know exactly how this worked out for Plato and his friends. They were good at the most important stuff, using their reason. They shouldn't, needn't, and didn't do the other stuff, like use their bodies, or raise kids. Philosophers, he literally argued, ought to be kings.

Back in ancient Greece, philosophers could be kings, living lives focused only on the mind. It was a convention that worked for them, given the circumstances of their society. Children were raised by women, who were relegated to the household. When male children got to be of school age, they were sent away for their education. What could women teach them at this point, after all? It wasn't even clear to ancient Greek philosophers that women had reason, much less could use it the way the kings did.

And you know what? This may sound radical, but truthfully the women of ancient Greece were not capable of using reason the way the kings did. Why? Because they had no education and were taking care of the fucking kids at home. In ancient Greece, because of how society was structured, the elite males could focus on developing reason, living the virtuous life, and achieving.* They made sacrifices to do so, missing out on fatherhood, partnership, and all the exhilaration that comes from embracing one's emotions. But their philosophy justified their sacrifices (even denied that these were sacrifices), and their

---

* Interestingly, the ancient philosophers were elite yet not always rich—Socrates, for example, took a vow of poverty. The philosophers were elite in their associations with and their influence upon the ruling class.

society supported them in institutionalizing the separations that made their status as kings possible. The glory of reason reigned.

I'll admit, for a long time, I wished I lived in times where the philosophers were kings, where we could occupy ourselves solely by running around town, arguing, developing views. (Okay. It stills sounds fun.) Yet then I started to think about how one-sided that kind of life really would be, about how I'd have to sacrifice all that I do value. Why is this one part of life so important that we should surrender anything that might lure us away from it?

Even if there were a world where it would be possible to live as a philosopher-king, I wouldn't want it. And the reality is that there is not a world where philosophers can live as kings. We can't just cut ourselves off from the rest of the stuff like they did. We have to do the juggle almost everyone in life shares. And, because of some damn thing Plato said two thousand years ago, we make sure when we do that juggle never to drop the ball of reason. Anything else—friends, family, fun? We're told it's OK to drop those things, that their sacrifice is always warranted in pursuit of achievement, especially of our potential. And then we beat ourselves up when we understandably fail and feel overwhelmed by having to always prioritize just this one part of ourselves.

My saddest entry in the pandemic diaries is of lecturing to a computer, in my favorite orange room now suddenly exposed to the world, while my eleven-year-old son lay, hidden from the camera, on the black-and-white rug layered in dog hair, bored, depressed, and overwhelmed by remote classes that I did not have time to help him with.

We've all been there. Trying to juggle is hard enough. It's worse when we're still left with the baggage of philosopher-kings, and think one ball is the most important, never to be dropped. I will forever regret not dropping that damn ball and just helping my child.

Society has changed a lot since ancient Greece, and many philosophers have critiqued the heck out of their arguments privileging reason,[*]

---

[*] Hume is the best, simply claiming: "'Tis not contrary to reason to prefer the

yet overall, we still seem to have trouble shaking the bias toward reason. This is a problem. It is a problem to embrace Plato's lead and to devote yourself to reason, because it will fulfill at best only one small part of you, while requiring that you sacrifice the rest. Even the rich white males, John Stuart Mill included, couldn't escape the harms that arise when we try to devote ourselves exclusively to living a life of meaning. Don't condemn yourself to the same fate.

CONVENTIONS, SCHMENTIONS

Tempting as it may be to blame the individuals in our lives who pressure us toward a life driven by purpose, meaning, and achievement, we're all plagued by this same problem, reinforced over centuries, which is thinking that our true value lies in what we can obtain by reason. Some of us shake it—that awestruck Brazilian surfer comes to mind, as do rock stars, nomads, Deadheads, drifters. And notice what we call those who shake it: "unconventional." But can we please notice from where our conventions derive and ask ourselves whether it makes sense to embrace them as the conventions for our lives?

The very word "convention" implies a created standard that has come to be accepted by society. It's a convention that Americans drive on the right side of the road and British on the left. It's a U.S. convention that voting day is the first Tuesday in November. And it is a convention that women do the housework and take care of the kids.

Here's the thing: Conventions arise to coordinate behavior in ways that are helpful to a society. They are never set in stone, but at best present standards that function well under specific circumstances. If it's a convention, it can change. And it should, especially if the convention is no longer working out. Our Western convention of greeting another through a firm handshake? It went right out the window

---

destruction of the world to the scratching of my finger." His point is that morality has its roots in our emotional responses, rather than reason, and that reason can't influence our emotional responses. David Hume, *A Treatise of Human Nature*, ed. David Fate Norton and Mary J. Norton (Oxford: Clarendon Press, 2000), 2.3.3.6.

during the pandemic. A convention of touching strangers' hands, laden with germs, made no sense during a pandemic. And as we realized that, many of us came up with various fist-bump maneuvers and other substitutions—new conventions, designed to suit the new circumstances of our lives.

LABELING CONVENTIONS

Can you pick out the conventions that dominate your society or your microcosm? All of our lives are informed by conventions, whether we realize it or not. It's good to start realizing the conventions at play in our lives. Labeling them as conventions helps to loosen their grip, giving you space to ask: Does this standard that someone else has created work for me? Sometimes, the answer is an easy yes: No harm to me to drive on the right side of the road in the United States! But if the answer is not obvious, it's time to ask: What is the point of this convention? Might there be another way to go about this that works better for me? (I'll give you a hint: If you're asking the question, the answer is YES!)

Sometimes it's easy to recognize when new circumstances demand new conventions. But often those conventions are so deeply rooted, their hold lingers even after they've lost their purpose. There may have been a time when circumstances required a convention that women be responsible for the home stuff. Those circumstances are now long gone. But we haven't shaken the damn convention yet. It's well established that women who work outside of the house face a double burden by having to also be the ones in charge at home, which impairs their quality of life. Recognizing that women are equal players in the workforce should have meant getting rid of a convention created at a time when women were not seen to be equal. But look around. How ingrained is this convention, still, in your community?

Once we realize that our focus on the meaningful life and the belief that sacrifices made for it will always be worth it are mere conventions, we'll reach a place where we can loosen its grip. For in this case, it is very clear that the people who created these conventions did so because it worked for them. There is no reason to think this same standard could even possibly work for us. We need to stop pigeonholing ourselves and holding ourselves to these standards.

SAINTS AND HUMAN BEINGS

We learn from the philosopher-kings the dangers of devoting oneself to a life of reason alone. In contemporary society, though, the dangers take a different cloak. There're not many philosopher-kings around, struggling because they've prioritized reason at the cost of everything else. These days we hear a lot more about the do-gooders than the philosopher-kings. The philosopher-kings focused on fully realizing their potential (i.e., the potential they valued) as a means of fulfillment. The do-gooders focus on giving themselves away, on finding fulfillment through becoming selfless. But both make the same mistake. When we structure our lives exclusively around a life of meaning, we miss out on what makes it good.

Many of us know this, deep down. We watch our idols pursuing meaning and goals, from afar. We're glad they're doing it, but we don't necessarily wish we were the ones doing it, because we know the sacrifices this entails. The author Larissa MacFarquhar hits the nail on the head in her book *Strangers Drowning*. She explores the lengths to which some people go to do good: devoting one's life to prevent animal suffering, becoming completely selfless, or moving one's family to live in squalor so that they can help those already there. She observes the awe *and* the dread we view such "do-gooders" with, which she compares to the way we view a mountain or a rough sea. "Confronting it, you see its formidable nobility, and at the same time you sense uncomfortably that you would not survive in it for long."[11]

Reading through MacFarquhar's depictions of real-life do-gooders, it becomes clear just how amazing it is they survive as long as they do. She describes the struggles those who commit themselves in these ways face. A woman becomes so selfless and devoted to others, and so unwilling to compromise her moral principles, that she recognizes how "hellish" it would be to be married to her. She eventually finds someone who shares her moral values, yet their combined devotion to others stakes too big a hold on them. The decision of whether to have a child gets laid out on a spreadsheet. Their struggle is not about the morality of bringing a person into an overpopulated world. Their dilemma is whether it'd be morally acceptable for them to love the child with the preference it demands. After all, if all people are equally worthy, on what moral grounds can one prefer one's child?

If you find that question nuts, good. It should give us pause when we consider a moral demand so large it leads us to question the validity of the love between a parent and a child. Deep down, we might be able to see the argument. We might be able to see the reasons why it makes sense to view all people as equally worthy of our attention. But even if we see why, a lot of us could not even entertain the idea that it would be wrong to have a child because it would demand preferential treatment. We can't entertain it because we see how much sacrifice this commitment requires. It doesn't just require the sacrifice of petty things, like luxury vacations. It requires sacrificing much of the things that make us human beings.

In her influential paper "Moral Saints," philosopher Susan Wolf famously and refreshingly announced, "I don't know any moral saints, and I'm glad I don't."[12] Becoming a moral saint involves renouncing much of the stuff that makes us human, from our diverse range of interests and capabilities to our personalities. A moral saint doesn't have room for cooking projects, and certainly doesn't have room for sarcasm. She can't prioritize any of these things, or anything at all, except for her moral commitments.

It isn't just a commitment to morality that throws one off-track. A saintlike commitment to any source of fulfillment is problematic, be it a commitment to a religious life, a life of achievement, or a life of meaning. Why?

Mahatma Mohandas Gandhi sacrificed constantly during the decades he fought for India's independence from Britain's rule. His hunger strikes are legendary, as is his steadfast commitment to nonviolence. He renounced physical pleasures, remaining celibate until his death.* Gandhi accomplished great things in his pursuits. The bird would certainly approve of the value he contributed to the world. But what about Gandhi himself?

When George Orwell read Gandhi's memoir, he walked away not at all inspired, and instead with very mixed feelings about the shape of Gandhi's life. He argues that in his quest for sainthood, Gandhi gave up being a human being. And he worries about our practice of putting up lives like Gandhi's as ideal ones, as lives we should and would aspire to, if only they weren't so damn hard to pull off. Orwell thinks this takes us on the wrong track, for it leads us to think of ourselves, and of average human beings, as "failed" saints, when the reality is quite different: To succeed at being saints, we've got to give up on being human beings. Desiring to be a saint conflicts with desiring to be a human being.[13]

We act like saints whenever we sacrifice parts of ourselves for something beyond us. Sainthood requires giving up on many of the things that make us human beings. Take martyrdom. Its very premise is that commitment to a faith or belief requires sacrifice, and that we reach our true potentials only through sacrifice. Also consider the concept of marianismo, embedded in Latin cultures, which props up a life of painful sacrifice to one's family as the highest potential for women.[14]

Even in the absence of beliefs about true potentials, many of us act like saints through the guise of people-pleasing. Like saints, people-pleasers

---

* According to one biography, Gandhi took pride in celibacy, reportedly testing his own willpower in his late seventies by sleeping naked with his teenage grand-niece. Ramachandra Guha, *Gandhi: The Years That Changed the World, 1914–1948* (New York: Vintage, 2018).

sacrifice their own needs and replace them with something they gauge as more worthy. People-pleasers embody many virtues. They are agreeable, willing, and accommodating. Yet they, too, fall into an elusive search for fulfillment. And the elusiveness of their target is perhaps the worst: People-pleasers depend upon external validation, upon pleasing others, for their very self-worth. But this dependency creates an untenable situation, for in becoming so dependent, people-pleasers lose their very sense of self. Their actions are always aimed at some good beyond themselves, which takes priority over all other things. But how can we ever find meaning and feel fulfillment when we've rejected the very self that craves it?

We can't give up being human beings. But we can stop holding up as ideals aspirations that stand in tension with our lives as human beings. We can start to honor all parts of ourselves, and live lives that give all parts of us a chance to flourish. We can find moments of pleasure that enhance our lives. We can become comfortable using our minds to find the interesting, rather than using them only to achieve. And without question, if we are interested in living our best possible lives, this is what we should be doing. We need to live our best possible lives, not someone else's, especially those of the martyrs and philosopher-kings.

A MORE INTERESTING WAY TO USE OUR MINDS

Lest you think a philosopher is about to advocate jettisoning reason, it's worth pausing for a minute to consider how many other ways there are to use our wonderful minds beyond the service of fulfillment. Crossword puzzlers and Wordlers know something about the joys of using reason without getting caught up in plans and purposes.* If that isn't your thing, think about daydreams, banter among friends, immersion in novels, and especially those times when you simply find

---

* Tempted to try this out? Jump to the Wordle case study on page 88 for a taste of the interesting.

yourself thinking, *Why?* We are used to dismissing these tendencies of our minds as the unimportant ones, the distractions, even, but ummm, why?

One of the things we'll learn about the art of the interesting is the value to be had by using your mind in open-ended and unstructured ways. Often this begins just with noticing, something more easily said than done, especially for those of us adept at filtering out the distractions so that we can keep our eyes on some prize, that elusive promise of fulfillment. But look around—yes, right now. What do you notice?

Maybe you are, like me, sitting in a coffee shop. I'm sitting at a long table in a wonderful spot filled with a shocking number of very healthy plants, given the absence of natural light. I'm sitting across from two young women, plugging away at their laptops. They look like college students working hard on term papers, even though it's mid-July. One student has a FREE TIBET sticker on her laptop. Wow, that takes me back to the sticker I had on the old car I had in college, one that my anthropology professor joked about on a field trip to a Vietnamese community outside New Orleans, that I think was surrounded by rice paddies, although that now seems somewhat unbelievable. And I'm still not sure why my professor was joking about that FREE TIBET sticker.

The seeds of the interesting are contained within our minds. Our minds don't just strive for fulfillment, a trajectory structured by aims. Our minds strive simply to engage, to wander in thoughts without structure or aim. We find and create the interesting through giving our minds the freedom to wander. The ride is yours. You just gotta make space for it.

KEEPING IT INTERESTING

Your best possible life is yours. It should reflect ideals that reflect you. Maybe it made sense to hold up "sacrifices" as ideals when times were different, but not much good comes from sacrificing yourself in the name of the Good Life. Making difficult choices may be an inevitable part of life, but we're better off seeing these choices as a clash of priorities, for which there is not an immediate answer. The convention that tells us there is—that we should always prioritize meaning, purpose, or achievement—is just a convention, designed for another time, for other people. Embracing it now leads to an impoverished life. There's no reason it must be the most important ball in your juggle of life.

Chapter 4:

The Unique Promise
of the Interesting

G ROWING UP IN DENVER IN THE 1930S, A YOUNG BOY NAMED
Neal Cassady saw corners of the city most kids did not. In his
earliest years, his dad ran a barbershop in their home. One can imagine
the conversations Neal overheard throughout the day: story after story
of fast times and lots of just shooting the shit. By all accounts Neal's
dad, Neal Sr., was a drunk—a "wino," as they called them then. When
the barbershop failed and his parents split up, Neal moved with his dad
farther into the slums, where winos reigned and all kinds of characters
floated in and out of the tenement they stayed in, complete with a legless roommate called Shorty. Sometimes Shorty wouldn't come home
and the two Neals would search the streets for him, then carry him
home safely to the cubicle they all shared on the top floor.

Things like stability, comfort, and safety weren't part of Neal's life.
His hardships made it all but impossible to live a happy life. The structure of his life was that there was no structure. Someone else in these
conditions might have jumped right onto that hamster wheel, searching,
striving for meaning, imposing a structure onto their life. But not Neal.
Whether by force or by nature, Neal simply embraced the challenges
his life presented. He didn't fight them, and he didn't try to impose

meaning on them or find meaning within them. He just dove in, relishing each experience as it hit him.

The city became Neal's playground. He scoured the corners of the city, observing and taking in all the darkness that lies at the fringes. He hunted the dumpsters, "junking" to collect pocket money. His dad took him traveling but, no, not to visit his grandma's house in Florida. Neal Sr. taught him the art of "tramping." They hopped trains, hitchhiked, and stayed in hobo encampments, splitting cans of beans and pork with their fellow travelers—most of them, like Neal Sr., drunks living on the edge, working when they needed to and moving on when they had to. They adventured among the same kind of people with whom they lived, and all the while young Neal just took it in. He heard their stories, over and over again. He was indoctrinated by these stories, the "collective intelligence of America's Bums," he called it.

It is easy to imagine Neal's life staying and ending there, in the slums of Denver, following the path of his dad and the other winos. But Neal was also both smart and irresistibly charming. He attended school and caught the attention of one of his teachers, Justin Brierly, with whom he started corresponding.* He took delight in writing letters to Mr. Brierly and, soon, to a group of friends he met through him. His letters described, at a legendarily fast pace, all that he took in and all the mischief he created, from stealing cars to the tête-à-têtes with the drunks, to all the young women he claimed to have enticed, their defenses having apparently evaporated in his presence.

These letters showed much more of Neal's personality and zest for life than his grammatical skills. But the tone of the letters matches the craziness of their content. They describe a life on the fringes, absent any of the traditional markers of success—degrees, jobs, relaxing vacations—characterized instead only by Neal's insatiable appetite for *experience* and his ability to make every experience an interesting one.

---

* And, if we believe the rumors, with whom he also started having sex. Remember, he was both smart *and* irresistibly charming.

Neal lived and wrote without structure, sometimes frantically, getting in every detail and including every colorful facet of his adventures.

Neal's life was interesting. Neal was interesting. Reading the letters, you can't help but get sucked in, finding yourself in a drunken conversation with a legless wino, or simply lingering with him over coffee at a truck stop at 3 a.m. on California's 101 freeway, waiting for the sun to rise and shine the way to Los Angeles.

It is no wonder that when a young man named Jack started reading these letters, he was fascinated. Jack had grown up in Lowell, Massachusetts, in a religious, working-class French Canadian family. At the age of twenty-eight, Jack was living with his mom, exploring his prospects as a writer. He'd been toiling away at a novel, but when he began corresponding with Neal, his life—and his writing—changed. Jack became captured by Neal's stories, and the crazy, enthusiastic way Neal wrote them. To Jack, Neal was a living force and a mystery. He represented the allure of the unknown and he embraced life like no other. Neal was the most engrossing, most fascinating person Jack had ever encountered.

Jack Kerouac went on to tramp with Neal, and he wrote his most influential novel, *On the Road*, about these adventures. *On the Road* crystallized the relationship between the two, but most of all captured Neal's spirit and the ways in which it captivated Jack. Neal's life sparked Jack's attention in the way that interesting things do. *They capture you, engage you, and make you want more.*

Jack started by hearing about Neal's adventures and later joined them, but one gets the sense that even when he was traveling alongside Neal, he was still a vicarious participant. Jack was along for the ride. It was Neal's adventure, and Jack rode shotgun, taking in Neal's spirit in the way a child takes in their first TV show—unblinking, rapt fascination, no hesitation. Neal's adventures, as chronicled by Jack, became the impetus for the Beat Generation, the first countercultural movement within the United States. One decade later, Neal's adventures would also become a foundational impetus for the sixties countercultural movement. We see his influence continue well into the twenty-first century with the rise of Van Life, a social movement of folks embracing a nomadic lifestyle, sacrificing the comforts of home for life on the road, searching for something, the way Neal always was.*

Think about this. One man, with no "real" contributions or achievements, has shaped not one but two and maybe more counter-cultural generations. This guy's value? People were intrigued by him. He didn't follow norms, any of them. He lived his life solely with zest—a zest for experience, and a zest for words. His way of existing in this world was unparalleled. For sure, Neal drank a lot, ingested every drug he was offered, and had a lot of sex, much of it under questionable circumstances. His life was not lacking in pleasure. But what made him unique, what made him stand out to Jack Kerouac, and to so many who have written about him, was the way he captivated people's attention. Neal Cassady was not only the hero of the Beat Generation, occupying starring roles in both Kerouac's *On the Road* and Allen Ginsberg's poem "Howl." He was also at the center of Ken Kesey's acid tests as the driver of the school bus made infamous through Tom Wolfe's *The Electric Kool-Aid Acid Test*. Even the Grateful Dead sang about him.[1]

He didn't catch people's intrigue by discovering a new planet, or by helping the homeless, or by spreading love. It was, simply, his mode of existence that caught their eyes, that stimulated their thoughts. It was how he talked, how he drove, how he walked. Everything about Neal, from his stories, to his choice of words, to the way he always seemed in motion, engaged the people around him. He was interesting. And you know what? The interesting spreads, nowhere as clearly as the way people's interest in Neal spread.

Neal died, by an overdose, on train tracks in Mexico at the age of

---

* Although in the twenty-first century, the nomadic lifestyle offers much more comfort and also the possibility of maintaining gainful employment through remote work.

forty-one. He never compromised his lifestyle or his zeal for interesting experience. And yes, he died young. The point here is not that Neal lived a model Good Life, not at all. But he is a rare example of someone for whom the guiding force of life was not pleasure, or fulfillment, but the interesting.

I know all of this because I am among the many who discovered Neal through Jack. It was a discovery that sparked my interest in, well, a major way. I shared in Jack's fascination with Neal. I read with endless intrigue story after story. I was captivated by the words, the momentum, all of it. I was captivated most of all, though, by Neal's legendary status. Here was a guy who by all traditional markers was not very special. The only thing that stood out about him was his spirit and the way he saw and embraced the world.

Even a quick look at a legendary letter he wrote to Kerouac—the Joan Anderson letter—shows the novel, exhilarating, emotionally charged perspective through which Neal viewed the world.[2] Every detail is noticed, and every detail stimulates something within him, be it a random connection to some obscure fact, or an insightful diatribe. A conversation/argument with his girlfriend MaryLou, who sits on a three-legged stool, thirteen inches high, invites him to think about the eighteenth-century milkmaids who made the stool famous, while the disdain he observes in MaryLou's eyes becomes a look of "exhausted murder."

It took me awhile to understand what made Neal so memorable to so many, but right now it is crystal clear: He had seized on the missing piece of the Good Life.

THE MISSING PIECE

So many of us have been struggling to live Good Lives, striving to be happier, and striving to find some kind of fulfillment through our aims and pursuits. And too often, we react to this struggle by thinking along dangerous "if only" tracks. *If only I made more money, I'd be happier. If only I could quit my job and find myself, I'd be fulfilled. If only I didn't carry around so much baggage from my childhood, I'd be happier. If only I were smarter and more organized, I'd accomplish something important. If only I could develop more optimism, I'd be happier.*

I could go on like this all day. Maybe you could too. But "if only" tracks serve no purpose here (or anywhere, really). It's time to consider a different reason that explains why you might be struggling to live a Good Life. This is because the things you are probably striving for—pleasure and fulfillment—simply do not and cannot play the role you want them to. We can go for more happiness, but we can't change the reality that sustained happiness is impossible. We can go for more fulfillment, but the weak link between accomplishing and feeling fulfilled makes it unwise to prioritize it too heavily, and the rationally loaded nature of fulfillment makes it especially unwise to make significant sacrifices in its name.

If you've been struggling to live a Good Life, it probably has nothing to do with you and much more to do with the imperfect nature of what you're going after, of what you've been led to believe the Good Life looks like. But you're ready now to shed this baggage and see your Good Life with fresh eyes, on your terms. You're ready to move out of the happiness/meaning dichotomy and see what else life has to offer.

I'm here to show you: There is so much more to living a Good Life than happiness and meaning. A life that includes psychological richness as well is a Good Life, the Good Life you've been struggling to find. Now that you've found it, your struggles can start to lift. You can stop struggling for more happiness and meaning. And you should, right now. Take that energy and use it to start appreciating the interesting in your life. Use it to start inviting the interesting into your life. Let the interesting infuse those spaces inevitably left behind by pleasure and fulfillment.

It sounds so easy, and with a couple of tweaks, it really is! The interesting is something that you can create, without struggle. And, while you are welcome to do so, you don't have to change a damn thing about your life to make it more interesting. Because unlike happiness, which depends on external forces (reward); or meaning, which requires transformed actions and life circumstances (sacrifice), the interesting depends only on your mind. All you've got to do is learn to recognize the interesting when it arises, to feel and appreciate the value it brings to your life, and to open your mind to having interesting experiences. The rest falls into place.

Through coming to understand deeply what the interesting is, we can begin to appreciate the unique value it delivers to our lives. We can begin to recognize where our lives already contain this value, and where our lives will benefit from more of the interesting. We'll see why psychological richness is important to the Good Life, and how developing the practical mindset and skills discussed in part 2 will enrich your life, immediately.

Learning about the interesting is the first step toward cultivating the art.

INTERESTING EXPERIENCES ARE UNIQUE TO YOU

As you wrap your head around the interesting, it's good to keep in mind one of its features: Interesting experiences are unique to you. While it's true that they share core features—and we'll go into detail on those in a moment—chief among them is their individuality. Your mind is as unique as you are. Embrace it and you'll be one step closer to the art of the interesting. Don't find Neal Cassady that interesting? Then think about what does it for you. What was your first experience of being captivated and engrossed?

The vicarious experiences offered by books, films, video games, blog posts, and more provide some of our most memorable and earliest interesting experiences. They change the way we see the world and they have the power to change the way we live in the world. I didn't need to meet Neal or Jack to catch their interest. I really, really wish I had, but I didn't need to in order to engage with their interesting experiences. Meeting them probably would have delivered something more like fulfillment—that was largely what I felt when I met Allen

Ginsberg. But without my ever meeting Neal and Jack, their interesting experiences became my own, and a source of the interesting. All I had to do was open the book.

My earliest, most memorable interesting experiences were the vicarious ones I got through reading Kerouac. For some it was reading the flirtatious back-and-forth between Darcy and Elizabeth, revealing a world of rules to jump through and identities defined by how well you jump. And for others it was reading about a magical closet door, revealing a world with brighter colors, with more experiences, with more to discover every time, from talking lions to ice witches. Many of us found ourselves pretending that those were our very own worlds. And for some of us, just maybe, every time we open a new door there is still a glimmer of hope that a more magical place awaits.

We're all different. What we find interesting is different, too. Lots of people found Neal interesting, but of course not everyone did or does.[*] Often, we can appreciate what others see without seeing it for ourselves. It doesn't click. We are not alone in this experience. What resonates with me and stimulates my mind has everything to do with who I am and what's going on in my mind. Our minds are unique. They are structured by our thoughts, memories, fears, hopes, and beliefs. These make up a package that is unique to us, making our minds so much more distinctive than our bodies.

Things that give us pleasure are relatively common across individuals. Food, sex, massages, love have predictable effects on the body. Yet what cognitively arouses us—what arouses our unique minds— really does vary between people. It even varies within one person. What engages us one day may not do so the next.

This may sound complex, but our sense of what's interesting to us is as innate as our sense of pleasure. Don't believe me? Let's try something together...

---

[*] And don't worry—as my editor made very clear on earlier drafts of this book, I get one Kerouac story only.

WHAT'S ENGAGING YOU TODAY?

Read each of these statements and notice what sparks your attention, makes you curious, and gets your thoughts to ripple. Note the feeling of engagement kicking in—this is the start of the interesting!

- Hawaii has the most beautiful rainbows.
- Lemons float, but limes sink.
- Before becoming an actor, Christopher Walken was a lion tamer in the circus.
- Mount Everest is taller now than it used to be.
- The circulatory system of a human being is more than sixty thousand miles long.
- Steve Martin was a philosophy major.
- Tiger shark embryos start attacking each other while in their mother's womb.
- Actor Daniel Radcliffe broke more than eighty wands while filming the Harry Potter movies.

Did you notice that "ooh!" moment? That flicker where your eyes got wider or you cocked your head in disbelief or fascination, or reached for your phone to double-check what you'd just read? That, my friend, is the interesting. Whatever sparks it for you, relish in it.

CORE FEATURES OF THE INTERESTING

While hopefully reassuring, it shouldn't be too surprising to hear that interesting experiences are unique. All our experiences are unique. Think about what happens whenever we experience, anything—say, reading a book. When we read, we don't just passively take in information. Even if we try to do that, what we take in depends upon what was already in our minds. We may not always realize it, but our starting points impact and direct what we take in. If we're engaged with the book, we do more than passively take it in. We react to it, we think about the ideas offered, we question, and we feel. How we react, think, question, and feel all depends upon what's already going on in our minds—the thoughts, emotions, past experiences, memories, phobias, whatever. This is the stuff that shapes our experiences, that makes our experiences our own.

We never go into an experience with a completely blank slate.* We always experience things through our minds, which are loaded with other thoughts and emotions. So, whenever we experience, the nature and quality of that experience are determined just as much by what we bring to that experience as by the features of what we are doing. The interesting arises from this synthesis between our thoughts and emotions and the activity we're engaging in.

While what we find interesting is thus, always, unique to us, any interesting experience shares five core features. Let's take a closer look at each of them, along with some suggestions for testing them out on your own.

1. *The interesting describes the value attached to our experiences of psychological richness.* It is correlated with novelty, challenge, and complexity, which suggests that these are the conditions that stimulate the interesting.

    Test it out: Choose one of these conditions and think about the last time you engaged with something novel, challenging, or complex. What was it? What did you do? And how did the novelty/challenge/complexity shape your experience?

2. *The interesting is a quality of our experiences.* This means that the interesting describes how certain experiences feel. In this sense, the interesting is like pleasure: It derives from a characteristic range of experiences that deliver the same feeling.† I'll use a lot of words to explain this feeling, but ultimately, you've got to feel it to know it. That's why I'll encourage you often to try it out, to

---

* Except maybe birth, at least according to John Locke's theory where we are all born with a "tabula rasa," a blank state of mind that gets filled through experience.
† Philosophers call this *phenomenology*: It's what an experience feels like.

harness the interesting when it arises within you, so that you can connect the words to the feeling.

Test it out: Reading a book can be interesting or boring—it's the same activity, but one that feels very different to experience. Try to rehearse your experiences of both in your mind now. Zero in on the feelings: of the interesting arising and of boredom looming. These are the qualitative features of our experiences.

3. *The interesting arises from cognitive engagement.* This means the interesting arises from our minds. While we're used to thinking of our minds as rational, it'll help to reserve the word "rational" for a particular kind of cognitive engagement, structured by plans and purposes. This helps us to see that we can use our minds in ways that aren't always rational, and that the interesting captures a different way of using our minds. Because the interesting arises from cognitive engagement, which is internal to the mind, our experience of the interesting doesn't depend on anything external to the mind. Lots of stuff out there can and does prompt our minds to engage in ways that stimulate the interesting, but so, too, can our minds alone, even in the absence of any external stimuli. This means that experiencing the interesting is completely within our control. It doesn't depend on achieving or accomplishing something, nor does it depend on others' affirmation, as so many of our experiences of fulfillment do. It doesn't depend upon our physiology, either, so it isn't limited in the way our experiences of pleasure are.

Test it out: We've already practiced noticing the feeling of the interesting clicking in, which arises whenever something engages us. Build on this and see what happens when your mind starts to engage, without purpose and structure. You'll find yourself thinking new thoughts, which is the mark of engagement. Our minds like to engage! Once something flips the switch, they'll naturally take off. The interesting arises when our minds engage without the rules of rationality, which direct our thoughts and tell us what to think next. So, shake off that rational side, those urges to evaluate, to plan, to control, and just let the mind do its thing. That's unstructured cognitive engagement. That'll beget the interesting.

4. *The interesting is prolific in more interesting experiences.* Once cognitive engagement takes the shape of the interesting, it takes on a life of its own. When we let our minds wander, they'll take off from one thought to the next. And they'll keep taking off, for once we feel the interesting kicking in, we'll be moved to keep it going. Since the kind of cognitive engagement that produces the interesting is unstructured by plans and purpose, once we've become engaged, our thoughts will start to ripple. Where? Who knows! Better still, the destination isn't the point. The point is to let one thought spark another. Interesting experiences take off in our minds, leading them to places of wonder and intrigue, where the thoughts keep coming and the mind is engaged. Unlike pleasure, which can last only so long, the interesting doesn't have this kind of shelf life. It can keep going, building in complexity, even changing the architecture of our minds. It can't keep going on forever—our minds do have limits, after all—but the interesting is not limited to our physiology and is prolific in nature, which means it can fill and enhance our lives robustly.

Test it out: There are all sorts of ways the interesting stimulates more of the interesting, but one cool way is by reliving it. Call up the most interesting experience you've had—maybe it was reading a book, maybe it was a trip to Mexico, maybe it was the time your car broke down in Albuquerque, leaving you stuck for days. Do you have it? Are you reliving it all again? Are you having an interesting experience just by thinking about an interesting experience? I hope so.

5. *The most interesting experiences impact the emotions.* One of the distinctive aspects of psychological richness is the experience of a variety of emotions, emotions that the other dimensions of

the Good Life simply don't include. Happiness comes with only the positive emotions associated with pleasure; and meaningfulness is independent of the emotions or, worse, exclusive of the emotions—that rational part of our minds has no patience for them.* This is kind of crazy; we are emotional beings, subject to a range of complex emotional responses, but we're told to shove them away. The cost of doing so should be coming into the picture. Our emotional responses are just as important as our thoughts, and are inseparable from them. Thoughts make us feel things, and feeling things makes us think new thoughts. When we allow our thoughts to land and impact our emotions, we engulf ourselves in a richness that begets the most interesting experiences. When our emotions are aroused, they give momentum to our thoughts, creating those little ripples of *Why?*, *Really?*, and—the best—*Wow*. When we let them, emotions infuse the connections we make, making them vivid and impactful. And when we let our thoughts impact our emotions, a robust form of cognitive engagement emerges...often to the point that we find ourselves changed afterward. This change of perspective, also distinctive to psychological richness, changes the ways we experience things, presenting an internal source of novelty prolific in more interesting experiences.

Test it out: Pick out a memorable experience, maybe a "first time." The first time you rode the subway. The first time you rode the school bus. The first time you left your town. The first time you saw the ocean, the snow, or the leaves change. If it's a memorable one, it's likely an interesting one, and it's one that impacted you. What do you remember? Is it the thoughts you were thinking or the emotions you felt? Or are they inseparable, leaving you only with a charged, complex, yet indescribable memory? Now think

---

* Remember? They are among the things we are told to sacrifice in the name of achievement, purpose, meaning.

of how that experience left you. It's likely it changed you, left you never again to look at the subway, the bus, your town, in the same way. That's the change in perspective that happens when we let our thoughts land and impact our emotions.

With these core features in hand, you can notice and identify the interesting. And when you do, you can play around with it. Keep noticing how it feels, and what's going on in your head. Practice becoming more comfortable with the range of emotions your experience generates. See how it feels to give yourself over to the magic of unstructured cognitive engagement. And see how it leaves you even just slightly changed. The more you practice, the easier it'll become to have interesting experiences when you want them, and to enrich your life with them.

TAKING BABY STEPS WITH WORDLE

In 2017, a young developer named Josh Wardle designed an interactive website for Reddit he called "Place." Place was essentially an open whiteboard where internet users from all over the world could draw something. Wardle's ambition was to see what would happen and his hope was to provide a safe outlet where people could come together, interacting through their creative contributions.

Wardle quickly realized the need to establish *some* guidelines and direction. Blank, open spaces are just too daunting. The magic of Place began to happen when Wardle set up rules forcing some structure: Participants had to wait five minutes between contributions so that others could collaborate. They also found themselves in a different, random spot each time, a nudge Wardle put in place to help them contribute something *new*, rather than to add on to whatever lay at the center of Place.

The result was amazing. Over seventy-two hours, a million people from across the world participated. They formed teams; they made unique contributions and collaborative ones. A drawing of Mona Lisa emerged, apparently the product of hundreds of people. How did it emerge? Someone started with the face, hoping that others would recognize the mysterious smile and then turn toward sharpening the nose, adding the long, dark hair. It worked. Recognition of the drawing emerging stimulated people to engage and to contribute.

Sometimes we need to be stimulated. Trust me, there can be nothing more daunting than staring down a blank page in front of you. How do you begin? Where do you begin? What do you begin with? Nudges help.[*]

Place was a success and Wardle went on to think of more ways to engage people safely. Many of us know all too well the dangers of the internet: the places we can find ourselves; the people on it waiting to take advantage, to enter our homes and bank accounts; the never-ending rabbit holes YouTube invites. *How did I end up here?*

It is hard to truly let go—to open one's mind in the sense that invites the interesting—when dangers loom. Taking away some of those dangers encourages us to challenge ourselves. Wardle's genius lies in recognizing that once we remove the dangers surrounding challenges, people will challenge themselves. Sure, removing the dangers makes it *less* challenging, but baby steps.

Wardle's latest creation, Wordle, provides a very structured challenge. We still start off blank, but it is a blank *grid*. Six rows, five squares. One row at a time. The goal is to guess a word. In six tries. Even better, we can play *only* once a day.

I don't know about you, but in 2022, I'm talking about Wordle with my mom friends, with my fifteen-year-old son, with my eighty-year-old dad, and with my college students. Everyone's finding something in it. Why? Because Wordle gives us a safe,

---

[*] I refer here to scholars Richard Thaler and Cass Sunstein's somewhat controversial concept of Nudging, which involves arranging features of a person's environment in a way that encourages them to make choices that will promote their well-being. See Richard H. Thaler and Cass R. Sunstein, *Nudge: Improving Decisions About Health, Wealth, and Happiness* (New York: Penguin, 2009).

easy way to challenge ourselves. We don't have to find or create the challenge; it is right there waiting for us. We don't have to worry about getting overwhelmed by the challenge or getting sucked in. We know we've got only six shots. We know we can only play once a day.* It's a safe venue to challenge ourselves.

But what are people finding in Wordle? What does this well-defined challenge do for them? It's not just pleasure, even though, of course, there is pleasure that comes from posting your two-shot win on Facebook. It's not just fulfillment, even if you are on your best streak ever. It taps into these values, but they don't hit the mark completely; they don't explain why we Wordle. No, we Wordle because it's interesting. It gives us five, ten minutes to engage. And in those minutes, it offers the whole package. Challenge, engagement, a full suite of emotions—stress, triumph, disappointment. Wordle stimulates new thoughts: It leads us to see the patterns between words and to exhaust the uses of "x." And I know I've gone on from Wordling to look at words in new ways, even if the shift is ever so subtle. Wordle even leads us to have this new perspective on words.

That's the thing. When we challenge our minds, we're forced to have new thoughts. We're forced to make new connections. Embracing challenges provides us with the opportunity to experience the interesting. While the popularity of Wordle testifies to the appeal of challenging opportunities when they are made safe, we can learn from this, and learn to approach challenges with a different mindset, one that helps us to see challenges not as opportunities to conquer, but rather as opportunities to explore.

Structure can ease us along, but we can find ways to challenge our minds without any structure. We can find a way to be comfortable with the blank piece of paper and turn it into the most interesting experience we have. It's all about recognizing the value at stake. It's all about recognizing how much the interesting can enhance our lives and then going for it.

---

* Although one of my students filled me in on the loophole here, which I share with reluctance: Create different accounts so that you can play more.

THE MISSING PIECE, NO LONGER

The interesting has been there all along. But now we know how it fits into the puzzle of the Good Life, and we have the language and research we need to go after it. Some people don't need to see the interesting as part of the puzzle to appreciate it. They are those lucky folks, like the Beats, who have escaped the Cult of Happiness and the pressures toward meaning and found their Good Lives simply by following their passions—without ever reading an article, much less a book, on how to live a Good Life. A lot of us, though, do benefit from explicitly seeing how the interesting fits into the Good Life, and from appreciating the distinct value it brings.

I know I do. I've always been attracted to psychological richness and to the interesting, way before these words were ever at the tip of my tongue. Back when I was in my early twenties, and full-on obsessed with the Beat Generation, I recognized right away the inordinate influence Neal had had over this group, over the Ken Kesey crew, over the Dead. It stuck with me. I couldn't think of a single other person who'd had such an influence on others while seemingly doing nothing, and certainly not accomplishing anything, on his own.[*] In that moment, I labeled Neal as completely unique. Even as my obsession faded, I held on to this belief for decades, always thinking how singular the impression he'd made upon American culture was, insofar as it rose independently of any accomplishment. It was a belief I couldn't explain, though; one I couldn't really say any more about. I believed it, I knew that, but, really, I didn't know what to do with that belief, and never took away any deeper insights from it.

It was only just recently, as I began to think about psychological richness and to develop my ideas about the interesting, that I realized: This is exactly what Neal had going for him. This is what he brought

---

[*] Muses might do this. But being a muse seems to involve standing in a particular relationship with an artist while being concurrently aware of their influence. Cassady just doesn't strike me as a muse. He lived and played, even wrote, as an active and equal player within the circles of writers and musicians he hung out with. It's just that most everyone in these circles went on to succeed, while Neil did not. He should have been the black sheep, the weak link in these circles, but the opposite seemed to be the case.

the world, and this is why he inspired. My internal "aha" moment was never stronger.* Suddenly, it all made sense. And more than that, my own life started to make more sense to me. I began to see clearly the same spirit in my now husband, Jody, whom I was just beginning to fall in love with. The more I realized how much of the interesting Jody was already bringing to my life, the deeper my attraction to him became.

The importance of being able to make sense of one's attractions in ways like this is drastically underrated. Labeling an attraction to the interesting validates it and helps you connect components of your life that otherwise might not make sense. Labeling it allows you to appreciate it more and so experience more of it. And labeling it gives you something to go for.

The same can happen to you. You've got the language. See the interesting in your life. Name it, relish it, and own it. See what more of the interesting you can add to your life. Recognize its indispensability. Label it as the missing piece.

Now that we've got the piece and know just how much the interesting adds to our lives, let's think about how it makes the puzzle of the Good Life complete by filling in the gaps left by pleasure and fulfillment. Let's think about how and why it fills those gaps, making the Good Life—at long last—complete.

Take a look at what the interesting has going for it. Because the interesting arises in virtue of cognitive engagement that stimulates new thoughts and emotions, experiencing the interesting is prolific in more interesting experiences. This is how the interesting spreads and builds. Every turn of thought, every "why," every "wow," ripples into new "whys" and "wows." In this respect, the interesting functions in exactly the opposite way of pleasure. It doesn't fade away or disappear like pleasure, leaving you there, wanting more, to no avail. And that makes it so much better than pleasure.

---

* And, trust me, the relish I take in being able to draw on this deeply ingrained and somewhat random belief about Neal's status, which I really have carried with me for decades, and to be able to explain it in my own work, is beyond compare.

The good stuff	Duration	Nature	Likelihood of experiencing it when you want it
Pleasure	Short. Circumscribed to moments.	Bounded by physiology.	Completely random.
Fulfillment	Unpredictable.	Elusive and never as good as you expect.	Zero.
Interesting	As long as you want, almost.	Prolific and limited only by your mind's stamina.	100% within your control.

Whoa! Is the unique promise of the interesting clear enough yet? OK, here's one more.

The good stuff	Why is it like this?	Upshot 1	Upshot 2
Pleasure	Some things deliver pleasure reliably, only if they are available. But then we start to adapt to those things and have to figure it out all over again.	Embrace it when you've got it, because pleasure is short-lived.	A life of sustained happiness is not possible.
Fulfillment	Depends on other people and on external stuff going your way.	Do not prioritize it at all costs.	A meaningful life is an impoverished one.
Interesting	You can create the interesting, even without changing anything around you.	Go for it!	Psychological richness pays off big.

Because the interesting immediately and concurrently arises along with the cognitive engagement it's attached to—it's that qualitative feature of our experience of cognitive engagement—the interesting pays off immediately and reliably. When you've got an interesting experience, you've got it. You don't have to labor at something else, sacrificing and sacrificing, hoping you'll be rewarded at the end of the day. You don't have to struggle to predict how accomplishing something is going to make you feel. You're not going to find yourself feeling oddly and disappointingly flat even though you've accomplished something. No way. That's the way of fulfillment, but not of the interesting. The interesting delivers value in the moment. It depends on your mind, yes, but that's it. If you're a gambler, it's not even a question of what to go after. You go after the interesting. You learn the skills and then you go after the interesting and stop wasting your life working and sacrificing in the name of fulfillment and the meaningful life. You're not a philosopher-king, right?* Then no need to act like one. Don't mistake their Good Life for yours.

THERE'S JUST ONE CATCH...AND IT'S NOT THAT BAD

Is the interesting really as easy and attainable as I'm claiming? Yes. This is its unique promise, and it is encapsulated by the fact that interesting experiences are solely the product of our minds and can be created using our minds alone.† There is a catch, though. Our minds do have limits, which means that we'll burn out at some point. We can't keep up the requisite kind of cognitive engagement forever. At some point, those damn mortal limits of our minds will get us, and if we push ourselves too long and too hard, we'll end up fried, barely capable of

---

* Trust me—you are not a philosopher-king.

† I get that all this emphasis on "the mind" and "cognitive engagement" sounds a little weird from someone who has just bashed the philosopher-kings for prioritizing a life of reason. The key is to remember that there is a lot more going on in the mind than rational thought. Minds house totally random thoughts, with no structure or built-in trajectory. They house emotions. They do a lot, including housing and producing the interesting.

piecing together a sentence, much less sparking a new idea. It's a good idea to take a break before you get to that point.

As a philosopher, I'm familiar with the feeling of frying my brain: thinking so hard, for so long, that I exhaust my brain. I even love to threaten my students with this on the first day of class: "This *may* be a class on happiness, but my goal is to make your brain hurt." It's not just philosophy that does this. We all have seen a kid emerge from gaming looking like a zombie. We all have found ourselves somewhere online, wondering how we got there. We got there because we kept clicking even after our minds stopped engaging. And maybe we all haven't done this, but some of us walk away from a long day of writing about *the most interesting things* unable to put words into a coherent sentence.

The interesting does have its limits, and they stem from our capacity to engage. All experiences may have the potential to be interesting, but in order to find them interesting, we've got to have the resources to engage with them. If we're burned out, we'll still experience something. We just won't experience the interesting.

This is the limit of the interesting: Our minds can burn out. It is one you can learn to avoid, though, by recognizing the signs and giving yourself a restorative break. Whatever we do, we can't stay locked up in an apartment by ourselves, so scared of going overboard that we never step outside. Even if the interesting comes with some risks, it is worth it.

———

We'll live better lives when we make them more interesting and prioritize psychological richness. No longer will our Good Life teeter-totter on a shaky stool. But what exactly will your stool look like? What does a life full of psychological richness, meaning, and happiness look like to you? We've got the clarity we need to start building our Good Lives. We know it's going to include three legs, but it's time to think more individually about what *your* Good Life looks like. We do this by thinking about our passions and the degree to which the values driving Good Lives resonate the most with us.

KEEPING IT INTERESTING

Through understanding the nature of the interesting, we find our missing piece to the Good Life. The interesting is what we feel when we experience a robust form of cognitive engagement, full of those ripples of thoughts and emotions, that evokes a variety of emotions and that is itself prolific in more interesting experiences. It'll fill in the gaps inevitably left behind by pleasure and fulfillment, and—even better—it depends only on you!

Chapter 5:

Passions and Values

OLIVER SACKS IS ONE OF THE MOST UNIQUE PEOPLE TO HAVE left a detailed record of his life and of his mind. A neurologist by training, he wrote books on topics as diverse as Alzheimer's patients, ferns, music, and his own life.

Sacks's life story isn't one of success, although the *New York Times* described him as "a kind of poet laureate of contemporary medicine."[1] He wrote and published thirteen books over the course of his lifetime and received numerous grants and honors through the years. It isn't a story of triumph over turmoil, although he certainly enjoyed his fair share of both triumph and turmoil. Instead, it is a story of his life. It's a story of a life that seems to have no rhyme or reason and runs from one adventure to the next.

Sacks grew up in a British family, full of medical doctors, in the 1930s. His brother suffered from schizophrenia, which took its toll on the Sacks household. Oliver describes the "sense of shame, of stigma, of secrecy" his brother's episodes delivered to the family, a burden he most certainly felt.[2] Oliver's formative years were made even more difficult by his increasing awareness of his homosexuality in a time when this also was shamed by both the culture and his own family.

Oliver discovered—or rather, channeled—his passion for understanding the diverse workings of the mind when he first entered

university. The passion itself took root much earlier, no doubt stem-
ming from his early interactions with a brother whose mind worked so
differently than did Oliver's own. Upon receiving his degrees, Oliver
went on to jump from one position to another, seizing the opportunities that were offered without consideration of the things like tenure
and prestige that typically define the life of the academic. He wrote of
an odd moment toward the end of his career, catching up with a former mentor who expressed astonishment at the work Sacks had done:
"But you have no position!" his mentor—a professor of neurology at
UCLA—exclaimed.[3]

One thing is clear: No mold could quite capture Oliver Sacks. His
was a life of motion. His preferred vehicles were motorcycles, journaling, and swimming. During his residency at UCLA, he'd spend his
weekends on his motorcycle, riding upward of one thousand miles over
the course of two days. "Saddling his horse," as he put it, was a form of
freedom: "I felt that I was inscribing a line on the surface of the earth,
at other times that I was poised motionless above the ground, the whole
planet rotating silently beneath me."[4]

He noted with irony the hidden nature of his weekends and how he
would return to work Monday mornings for rounds with the rest of the
residents, with "hardly a sign" of the adventures he'd had.[5]

This isn't to say that Sacks didn't care about his work, or that he lived
for the weekends, like so many of us do. Sacks was deeply passionate
about his work, most of which involved engaging with and trying to
understand the minds of those with severe and little-understood cognitive impairments. His patients fascinated him. Of his postencephaletic
patients, he wrote, "What fascinated me was the spectacle of a disease
that was never the same in two patients, a disease that could take any
possible form—one rightly called a 'phantasmagoria.'"[6]

He published the story of his life, *On the Move: A Life*, in 2015, a
signal he was becoming increasingly comfortable sharing his detailed,
colorful observations of himself in addition to sharing his observations
of so many others.[7] By that point Sacks had established himself as both

a cutting-edge neurologist and a remarkably popular author given the obscure subject matter he often wrote about. He was a natural writer, obsessively keeping journals loaded with details, nuances, and wonder about the world and events around him.

I describe his story in terms of an observation of himself for a reason: His storytelling doesn't seek to show the overarching meaning of his life, nor does it strive to paint his life as more than it was. He writes the story of his life as he writes his journals, with the primary aim of organizing his thoughts into a story seen through real time as opposed to telling them retrospectively or imaginatively transformed through some narrative.[8] His scientific eye and instinct for details, combined with his passion for keeping track of those details, simply depicts his life as he lived it. This is not a guy writing to promote his way of living. And while his end-of-life reflections express an awareness and deep gratitude for being able to live the life he had, it isn't even clear that he thought his life was an admirable one.[9]

I imagine Sacks was surprised by the kind of praise the story of his life generated. Review after review of *On the Move* uses words like "extraordinary," "exciting," "amazing," "inspiring," and pretty much every other possible superlative to describe both his life and the feelings one gets when reading about it. It's hard to look at them and not to wish to live the kind of life that generates such awed praise.

Taking in the big picture of Sacks's life, its ebbs and flows, its contradictions, and its robust authenticity, it is clear that Sacks led a Good Life—even if it is not clear what *kind* of Good Life he lived. What made his life a good one was that it worked for him. Given his passions, and given what he valued, his life was his best possible life.

———

No matter who we are, our passions and values form the foundation of our Good Life. Our passions push us toward having certain kinds of experiences and pursuits and so inform the content of our Good Lives. And reflecting on our passions allows us to see which values (pleasure, fulfillment, and the interesting) resonate most with us. It's the degree to which each of these values resonates with us that informs the specific shape of our Good Life. We all need the three legs (happiness, meaning, and psychological richness) of the Good Life, but each of our stools is unique, made distinct by our passions and values.

It's time to begin building your unique stool, your Good Life. You've gotten a feel for the nature of each leg, and the values at play that make those legs good. You are well positioned to take charge of your Good Life and shape it in the way that, well, feels good to you. Here's how you do it.

PASSIONS AND VALUES: A METHODOLOGY

Thinking about our passions helps us to give content to our Good Lives, and it also helps us to understand the shapes of our best possible lives. Your Good Life probably doesn't look like Sacks's life. But it might have the same shape as Sacks's life, which psychologists would describe as overwhelmingly, psychologically rich. Recognizing this connection allows us to make use of the increasing amount of psychological and philosophical research about how to live a Good Life.

We make even more progress in coming to understand the shape of our own best possible lives by thinking about the values that make them Good Lives to begin with. The value of a Good Life explains why it's a Good Life and what makes it good for the person living it. It's that *prudential sense of value*: the value of our life as we experience it. Good Lives have lots of prudential value, which is why we want them. Bad lives lack prudential value, which is why we avoid them.

What are the values at stake in the Good Life? We answer this question through philosophical analysis of the dimensions of Good Lives identified through psychological research. Psychological research identifies *happiness, meaning,* and *psychological richness* as distinct elements of the Good Life. This doesn't mean they are exclusive of one another, but simply that they track different dimensions of the Good Life, that each delivers something unique to our lives. When we consider philosophically why each is good, it becomes clear that happiness is good because it delivers *pleasure*, that meaning is good because it delivers *fulfillment*, and that psychological richness is good because it delivers *interesting experiences* that generate free-flowing ripples of thoughts and emotions. (Want some practice wrapping your head around these different values and their relation to the Good Life? Check out "A Primer on the Good Life" at the back of this book, page 247.)

Unless you have some reason to think your mind is completely unique in its basic structure and unlike any mind previously studied (then why are you reading this book?), your Good Life contains each of these values: the *interesting*, the *pleasant*, and the *fulfilling*. It's the nature of and the degree to which each of these values contributes to your Good Life that is unique to you, because the degree to which you respond to these values depends on the nature of your passions. It depends upon what you are into and what kinds of things resonate with you.

THE VALUES

The word "value" can be a little heavy, and depending on the kind of value we are talking about, it can be daunting. Reflection on moral values? Daunting as fuck, often involving some of the most difficult forms of abstraction. Reflection on prudential values? Those things that have value to you, personally? So much easier. You just need to start paying attention to the shared features the good things in your life have in common.

Waiting for me to tell you what the good things in your life are? How could I do that? I've never met you! I can (and will) tell you the kinds of things that typically make people's lives go better, and I will tell you why the good things in your life are good. But you are the ultimate authority of determining what the good things in your life are—that's part of the magic of this category we call prudential value. It's all about what benefits the person.

THE GOOD THINGS IN YOUR LIFE

Here's some of the good things in my life: My job teaching philosophy to bright young minds. My latest publication. Arguing about philosophy. Skiing with my family. Sailing. Paddle-boarding with my husband. Friday night happy hour with friends. Staying connected with my teenage sons. Watching those same boys become men. Cuddles with my dogs. Sex with my husband. Driving my stick shift on windy country roads. Traveling in any and all forms.

Are you making your own list right now? Go ahead. Write it down. It's kind of fun. Just identify the good things in your life. That's it. Now, notice the clusters of things that seem to go together: the accomplishments and the things that make you proud; the meaningless but pleasurable stuff that makes you feel good; and the things that are on the list but stand out from the others. Maybe there are things that challenge you. Maybe there are things that have opened your mind and left a dent. Maybe you don't really understand why some thing are on the list. That's okay. You don't need to know why those things are on your list to know that they are good. You're the authority, remember?

Coming to learn and to know why the good things in your life are good puts you in the position to get more good things. And this is why thinking about values helps. Values explain why good things are good. They explain what the clusters of good things in your life have in common and, by extension, how you can add more good things to your life. They teach you the shape of your best possible life.

Pleasure. I'd be shocked if your life didn't include some things that are clearly valuable only for the pleasure they bring. What else explains why we cuddle with our dogs, why good sex makes the list of good things, and why we enjoy happy hours? While all these things factor into our lives in dynamic ways, there's no denying that the pleasure they bring benefits our lives. Good sex may contribute to a rewarding marriage full of opportunities for personal growth, blah blah blah...but on its own good sex adds value to our lives because it brings pleasure. There doesn't have to be more to it, and we should resist any urge to look for a deeper explanation. The value of pleasure lies solely within its experience.

Pleasure arises in us as a physiological response to things that are evolutionarily advantageous to us, although the way things work, this connection often becomes less transparent. The point to keep in mind is that human beings experience pleasure as a reward: When that dopamine hits, it feels good. Those good feelings add value to our lives. They add value in the form of pleasure.

It's the value of pleasure that makes happiness important to us. Happiness is a state of mind that accompanies our feelings of pleasure. We want to be happy because happiness feels pleasurable. It's easy to lose sight of this very simple fact. Reminding ourselves of it helps us to understand the role that happiness plays (and doesn't play) in our Good Lives. Does anyone really want a life full of pleasure and nothing else? Then why do we talk as if happiness is the be-all and end-all of our lives? At the same time, wouldn't a life of no pleasure seem just as impoverished?

We see here the advantages to be had by focusing on values, rather than on the states that reflect those values. (Looking for a more concrete way of laying this out? There's a worksheet at the back of the book, on page 255, that will help!) It's one thing to know that happy lives are Good Lives. But it's so much more important to know why.

Fulfillment. I would not be shocked if your list didn't include things that are valuable because they are fulfilling. It's a sad fact of so many of our lives that fulfillment is elusive. So often we strive to accomplish things and fail. So often we end up with jobs that are not fulfilling. I'm guessing, though, that if your list doesn't include things that are valuable because they are fulfilling, you are already painfully aware of this fact. Experiencing fulfillment may be elusive, but we are trained to seek it nonetheless. We're also trained to think that fulfillment has to come from something lofty, something that contributes to the world. This just isn't true. Break free of these expectations, and maybe you'll uncover some good things in your life, like the fulfillment to be had on that day you finally get around to taking a shower.

Fulfillment is something we experience internally. It's a form of satisfaction, or of being content. And we should let ourselves experience it whenever it arises, whether that's from taking a shower, writing a book, or getting the kids on the school bus that morning.

The value of fulfillment explains why accomplishments consistently make our lists of good things. How else can our accomplishments add value to our lives, except by being fulfilling? I guess some accomplishments (very few of mine) deliver financial rewards. Money makes life easier, and provides access to lots of good things, but let's agree right now not to mistake financial gain as any kind of proxy for a Good Life. It's instrumental to lots of good things, so it has *instrumental value*, but when we are talking about what makes for a Good Life, we're looking for the values that make it good, period.

Fulfillment is one of these values, valuable on its own, whose presence in your life makes life better. (If you are tempted, call this an *intrinsic value*.) And it's the value of fulfillment that explains why meaningful lives, driven by purpose, are Good Lives. The rational part of our minds seeks out purpose and strives to find meaning. Fulfillment is the reward. Its value to us explains why accomplishments, contributions to the world, and the like make our list of good things. And its value explains why, when our efforts are not successful, we feel its absence like puncture wounds. It's the difficulties involved in finding fulfillment that make it so important to ensure our Good Lives go after more than just fulfillment.

The interesting. You know those good things in your life that you know are good—they are on your list—but that you cannot explain in terms of pleasure or fulfillment? Maybe it's the heated arguments you always end up having with a friend. Maybe it's books you like to read that leave you unsettled...but eager for more. Maybe it's your passion for documentaries. These kinds of things share one thing in common: They stimulate our minds in ways that create little ripples of thoughts, that penetrate our emotions and change our very outlook.

That's what we're after when we find ourselves mentally engaging in something for no other purpose than the engagement itself. And that's the bonus that comes from engaging in things that might also be fulfilling or pleasurable. The interesting is compatible with these other values, for sure. Yet it's easier to identify when it's on its own. Have you ever been so captivated by a book, movie, or TV show that you find yourself thinking about it the next day? Have you ever been so passionate about something that the wonder and the whys simply penetrate your mind? Have you ever walked away from an experience so moving, so complex, that something in you has shifted forever? Then you know the interesting.

And if you don't? That's OK. Keep reading. It will come quickly. Even though our capacity for psychological richness is innate, after years of beating down the impulses of our minds in favor of happiness and meaning, we could all use some pointers on how to harness them again. That's where we're headed in part 2. It'll show you exactly how you can bring more of the interesting to your life, and help you awaken your capacity for it.

The interesting has a lot in common with pleasure. They are both features of our experiences, and their value lies solely in their experience. While pleasure has its basis in the body, the interesting has its basis in the mind. This explains why something can be interesting yet not pleasurable, and vice versa. Its basis in the mind makes it more impactful on our lives. Pleasure comes and goes, but the interesting sparks new thoughts and begets new emotions, all of which penetrate our perspective.

The interesting also has a lot in common with fulfillment. They're both *cognitive*, which means they are both based in the mind. Both values reflect the trajectories of our minds. Just as a part of our minds strives for purpose and meaning, a part of our minds strives to engage. That's why we need the interesting in our lives. Becoming engaged in something helps us find fulfillment. But engagement itself adds independent value to our lives, regardless of what we are engaged with or what we are after. This makes the interesting much more accessible than fulfillment.

Our attraction to the interesting explains why the cluster of things that make up a psychologically rich life are good. The more we pay attention to the value of the interesting, the clearer it becomes that interesting experiences are the missing piece of the Good Life. And the more we learn about the interesting, the more we'll be able to enrich our lives with lots of it.

BUILD YOUR FOUNDATION

The values of pleasure, fulfillment, and the interesting explain why certain activities and experiences enhance our lives. Our *passions* inform how we realize these values. My passion for philosophy explains why I find arguing about philosophy interesting. My passion for my sons explains why I find it fulfilling to watch them grow into kind, honest men. My passion for adventure explains why I find battling with the wind on my sailboat so interesting, and why I find so much pleasure in skiing with my family.

Passions aren't *desires*, although often they feel the same. We can desire all sorts of things without any passion. I desire to pay my taxes on time, but, umm, I'm not passionate about doing it. Our passions reflect instinctual drives in us that point us toward the experiences we will go on to find interesting, pleasant, or fulfilling. We can spark new passions within ourselves, but we can't force new passions on ourselves. There's got to be some kind of seed within us that responds to something, something that resonates with us, for passion to take hold.

This is why passions and values form the foundation of our Good Lives: Our passions point us toward the things that add value to our lives. Our passions teach us how to pursue lives full of pleasure, fulfillment, and the interesting, and can help us understand the degree to which our lives need these values to be Good Lives. This is the stuff we need to know in order to live our best possible lives.

At the back of this book on page 248 you'll find a quiz titled "What Does Your Best Possible Life Look Like?" It will help you identify your passions and the values those passions direct you toward. It will also help you identify the current gaps in your life, or the values that you may be neglecting. Maybe you've been so trained to think in terms of purpose and meaning, you'll find your answers clustering heavily to fulfillment at the cost of no pleasure. Or maybe you've been completely schooled in the meaning/happiness dichotomy to the extent that nothing lights up for the interesting. These results show where you might strive to spark passions that ignite the values you've been missing out on. Whatever you find out about yourself, use it. Use it to build a foundation for your best possible life.

BUILDING BETTER FOUNDATIONS

Our starting points tell us a lot, if we're honest about them. None of us have been raised in a vacuum. We've been raised by other people and shaped by our societies. Our current passions and values no doubt reflect these influences. These influences can be helpful when they've served to spark passions that tap into all three legs of the Good Life in a combination that works for us. But they're unhelpful when they've sparked only one kind of passion and stamped out others. They're unhelpful when they leave us with passions and values that don't lead us to Good Lives.

It's downright unreasonable to expect that our current passions and values provide the foundation for our best possible lives. Being honest about ourselves means being honest about both the influences others have had on our passions and values and the quality of our current lives. That you picked up this book suggests that whatever your current foundation is, you're interested in building a better one.

WHAT'S INFLUENCING YOU?

It's actually pretty easy to identify the major influences on our attitudes toward the Good Life, the passions we let ourselves embrace, and the values that we experience most regularly. And it's an important exercise, too. Once we know how we've been influenced, we can think about which influences are helpful and which aren't. We'll be on our way to living better lives in no time!

In this context, your "society" and your "family" is whomever you consider it to be. Don't overthink that part. And please, don't start to judge. This is an exercise in understanding.

My society	My family
Holds up as role models:	Thinks it's most important to be:
Prioritizes leisure time:	Does this regularly together:
Expects me to:	Vacations tended to be:
Makes me feel bad when I:	Expected me to:
Thinks these values are most important:	Encouraged these passions:
Thinks these passions are not important:	Discouraged these passions:

Better foundations make for better lives. We aren't completely stuck to what we are given, and thank goodness for that, as so much of what we are like is based on what we've been trained to value. We can ignite new passions, and we can harness or redirect old ones. And we can shape our values, as well. We can recognize the limits of what we go after in life, and we can learn to find value in new sources.

Your best possible life is grounded in *your* passions and your values—not society's, not your mom's, not of that friend on Facebook who is so clearly living her #BestLife. Find your best possible life by finding your passions for all the good things in life: the pleasant, the fulfilling. And the interesting. You need all three. But you need them your way.

KEEPING IT INTERESTING

We live our best lives when we follow passions that lead us to experience pleasure, fulfillment, and the interesting. While our current passions and values no doubt reflect outside influences, taking stock of our starting point allows us to see which values we need more of and which passions may need more fuel. We're aiming to find the unique combination that works for us as individuals and leads each of us to our best possible life.

PART 2

CULTIVATING THE INTERESTING

Chapter 6:

Stepping Away from Pursuit Mode

WHEN MY AND OISHI'S FIRST PAPER ON THE PSYCHOLOGI-cally rich life came out in 2020,[1] a journalist from *Science News* reached out to me to learn more. She thought it would be fun to have an interesting experience together. She happened to live nearby, which was helpful as this was deep in the pandemic and, well, options were limited. But we'd just had our first shots of the vaccine and were eager to get out, so I agreed, albeit with some hesitation. What were the odds we'd pull this off? That we could successfully plan to have an interesting experience?

We did our best. She had read about the fairy houses an architect had randomly built around South Hero, Vermont, an isolated island in northern Lake Champlain. We drove the loop of the island, past the long stretches of farmland, scouting, looking for these fairy houses. We had no idea what we were looking for and missed the first couple. Then, boom, we started recognizing them. They were a trip. Scattered all over the island, in different people's yards, in different states of repair. But the most interesting thing about that afternoon? When we stumbled upon literally hundreds of wooden birdhouses, each painted in bright colors, bringing the swampy forest of someone's property alive. Even better? Scattered among these trees, brown at the end of the dreary winter, lit up only by the neon colors of these birdhouses, were full-sized dinosaurs. *What?*

The afternoon was a success in the end, but it highlighted a critical challenge of the interesting. There's no one path for the interesting. We'd thought the fairy houses would be interesting, and they kind of were. But they would have been more interesting had we stumbled upon them without looking, planning, just as we stumbled upon those dinosaurs amid the birdhouses.

Novelty is a mark of psychological richness; novel experiences force us to engage, to think. Unfortunately, planning takes away from the novelty. We'd already googled and read about the fairy houses, so we knew what to expect. Planning also has a way of forcing us to put all our eggs in one basket, directing our attention exclusively to the plan. If we'd been too stuck on the fairy houses, there's a good chance we would have missed the dinosaurs!

Scientific research identifies the kinds of things that are correlated with psychological richness (i.e., complex activities, novelty, and challenge), and we're learning more and more every day, but even with the best possible scientific research at our hands, there's no guarantee that any one activity will be, for any one person, an interesting experience. What I can tell you, though, is that the surest way to miss the interesting is to chase it head-on.

PURSUIT MODE AND ITS LIMITS

We know by now that the Good Life can't be all about pleasure and fulfillment. These values won't fill out our lives on their own. The more we attempt to model our lives as happy lives, or meaningful lives, or lean into that tempting combination of weekdays for fulfillment and weekends for pleasure, the more impoverished our lives start to look, and the more emptiness we may feel creeping in.

In the face of that emptiness, a lot of us try to fill the time with more pleasure or more fulfillment or more pursuits. Surely, the way to fill our lives, to make them the best they can be, is to add more ways to feel fulfillment or to add more sources of pleasure! But if it is emptiness we are feeling, more of the same is not likely to cut it. And here is the big problem with this line of thinking: The more we try to fill it with the same, the more we get locked into a pursuit mode that ends up making it harder to enrich our lives.

I know this might sound counterintuitive. After all, we've been taught that the best possible way to get something is to go after it with single focus and relentless tenacity. And there is some truth to that. The power of pursuit mode got me tenure during one of the most difficult years of my life, when my first marriage had fallen apart, leaving me on my own to raise two very young boys. I'd be crying on the way up the hill, across campus, to teach a class where, I knew, colleagues were waiting to evaluate me. And then, bam, pursuit mode would kick in, distractions would go out the window, and I'd bring it. Pursuit mode helps us get what we want. It helps us accomplish goals. It helps us move forward.*

Yet the kind of emptiness that arises when life lacks the interesting isn't one that can be filled by pushing forward. Pursuit mode might distract us from the emptiness, but there is a good chance the emptiness arose in the first place *because* we were in pursuit mode. Pursuit mode leads us to see the things around us in terms of what they can *do* for us or what they can *give* us. Everything becomes a goal. Everything becomes a single-minded quest to achieve, to get somewhere or something. Everything becomes about one thing. Anything that doesn't contribute gets filtered out.

---

* Philosophers highlight and describe pursuit mode in terms of exercising agency—our capacity to use our minds to govern our actions. Within psychology, pursuit mode is often framed in terms of goal pursuit and of self-regulation. My own work on virtue highlights the importance of self-regulation, which is our ability to regulate ourselves by goals. Self-regulation is an important skill, but the point here is that sometimes we need to let go of goals and allow ourselves just to experience. See Lorraine L. Besser, "Virtue of Self-Regulation," *Ethical Theory and Moral Practice* 20, no. 3 (2017): 505–17.

WHAT DOES PURSUIT MODE LOOK LIKE FOR YOU?

In what area of your life do you feel pursuit mode kicking in? Identifying the areas where you tend to find pursuit mode can help you slow down and break free from it.

Maybe pursuit mode kicks in as soon as you clock in to work and lasts until you leave. Could you broaden your focus just a little during the workday? Could you pause to pay attention to the little things going on, such as the sun shining through the clouds, or the group of people gathered outside your window, or the outfit your coworker has chosen that day?

Maybe your pursuit mode kicks in in smaller bursts, such as at the grocery store, or on the commute to work. Can you step back and take in the walk? Can you smile at the people you pass? Can you notice the people you pass? Who knows what you will see if you try! You'll still get the shopping done, and you'll still get to work, but maybe you'll also have an interesting experience along the way.

WHAT WE MISS WHEN WE'RE IN PURSUIT MODE

Interesting experiences capture and stimulate our minds. They engage and arouse, generating a sense of intrigue or a sense of fascination. They linger, they develop their own momentum, and they take on lives of their own. The catch is that we must be open to them. If we're always pursuing a goal, we're cutting ourselves off from engaging the interesting when it arises. It's not that these values can't overlap and be found within the same experiences. They can. The problem is that focusing on pleasure or fulfillment leads us to overlook the facets of our situation that might spark the interesting.

When we're locked into pursuit mode, we become so intent on achieving or accomplishing that we forget to play in the nuances. It's like those times in high school when you're cramming for a big test—maybe a history test. Your eyes are on the prize: learning the stuff that you know will be on the exam. You read and study for the test—looking at the dates, the major players, the wars, the policies. To succeed, you've got to keep focused on these things. You can't let your mind drift too far. To stay on track, you've got to silence the wonder and the whys. It's like this whenever we are pursuing something, whatever it is we are pursuing. But the wonder and the whys are the good stuff! If we're always in pursuit mode, or if we let it take up more space than it warrants, then we inhibit the range of value life can have.

The interesting promises to bring out all we're capable of experiencing. It promises to enhance and enrich our lives in a way that doesn't cost much but pays off beyond compare. But we're not going to find the interesting when we are in pursuit mode. It might be possible to experience the interesting when we are pursuing things, but it's more likely that the interesting things are the ones that get filtered out, left in the dust, judged to be distractions interfering with what we really want. This is a mistake. Taking in the interesting requires stepping back or away from pursuit mode.

Pursuit mode is effective when you know what you want and how to get it. It follows a well-established model of desire satisfaction. If I want to get tenure, I need to publish a lot and teach well. And if I want to eat a delicious meal, I know what to do: call my friend Zoe. I know that Zoe, a wonderful cook, will deliver what I want, especially if I bring the wine. So, calling Zoe makes sense. I can predict that her meals will satisfy my desire and I can plan around it.

The interesting works differently. Having a desire for the interesting doesn't, on its own, point the way. It doesn't inform me of the steps to take in the way my craving for delicious food tells me to call Zoe. In fact, having a desire for the interesting, on its own, won't even make it more likely that I will have an interesting experience.

In philosophy-speak, having a desire is neither necessary nor sufficient for the experience to be interesting. Need convincing? Think about the last time you turned on a movie, thinking it would be interesting, and found yourself surfing your phone within fifteen minutes. We can want to find something interesting with great willingness, but whether we will succeed depends on how our mind reacts to it—how we respond to it—and this isn't entirely under our control. A lot depends upon what we are trying to engage with, especially before and as we are learning the art of the interesting.

There are three important points here. First, wanting or desiring an interesting experience won't make whatever we go on to do interesting. No, just like a meal, the experience has got to be a certain flavor for it to be interesting. And the flavors of experiences are often hidden, especially if it is our first bite. It might look like chocolate but end up being a peppermint stick.

Second, notice how hard it is to predict what we'll find interesting. How many times have we each picked up a book we thought would be fascinating and then been disappointed? This is commonplace. It is hard to predict how we will respond to something or, specifically, whether something will engage us, in that moment. Every day we learn more and more about the errors we make in predicting how anything will make us feel. This is the problem of affective forecasting we talked a little bit about in chapter 3. Dan Gilbert's research shows this convincingly through a series of experiences gauging a subject's predictions of how they will feel if they get something, such as a good roommate, versus how they end up actually feeling when they get it. It turns out we worry a lot about the impact of things, like having a good roommate, for no reason, and the impact turns out to be much less than we thought. The technical language for this is that we have difficulty in affective forecasting, which is predicting the impact an event will have on our affective states. This is why Gilbert argues in favor of stumbling upon happiness rather than actively pursuing it.[2] It is just flat-out hard to predict in advance how something will impact our experiences.

Third, since it's hard to predict what we'll find interesting, it is hard to *plan* for it. Obviously. How can we plan what we can't predict?

Wanting, predicting, planning—these are all features of pursuit mode. But they aren't a recipe for the interesting, and they can even make it impossible to access.

Think about it. Did we all end up majoring in what we thought we would? And if we did, did we do it because we found it just as interesting as we thought we would? Or did we stick with the major even though we did not? More often than not, what sparks interest is the class we took because of the time slot (see: me) or because it was the only one we could get after our computer crashed during course registration. Preconceived thoughts about what we will find interesting rarely pan out to be true.

PURSUIT BY ANY OTHER NAME

At this point you might wonder: *What's the point of thinking about this new form of the Good Life if we can't pursue it?* The answer is complicated. It is not that we can't pursue interesting experiences. We can. But we'll need to step away from our old standby (pursuit mode) and instead create circumstances for ourselves in which the interesting can emerge through a combination of action and holding space.

Just do something

There's a caricature of the depressed and downtrodden teenager, sitting in her room all day, becoming more and more depressed with each day. She wants desperately to be happy. But her want leaves her frozen, for she has no idea what to do to become happy. She just knows she wants her life to be better.

She's not stuck in pursuit mode, but she's stuck nonetheless. She's stuck because she's waiting for a plan and isn't sure what to do without one. She's got a target without a plan motivating her to get there.

If this teenager is lucky, she has a parent who has read the philosopher and bishop Joseph Butler and will simply kick her out of the house with the advice of "Just go do something."* Butler preached to the folks of

---

* Although, trust me (or my kids?), being that parent makes one's children unlucky in other sorts of ways.

eightenth-century Britain about the nature and importance of self-love, which he took to be a robust and general desire for a Good Life. He made a fundamental observation about self-love.[3] This is that self-love is empty absent particular passions. If we just try to pursue "self-love" (or "happiness," or "the Good Life," or whatever placeholder does it for you), we'll get nowhere. What we need to do instead is focus on our passions.

It's a technical but intuitive point, true of many targets, including the interesting. We can't pursue it directly, but we also can't sit around wishing and waiting to have an interesting experience.

There's a lot of things in life that work this way, that we've learned are better off pursued indirectly rather than head-on. We learn quickly that the best way to make use of a reading light isn't to shine it in one's eyes, but to angle it at a corner so that it lights only the words. We learn that the most effective paths wind up the hill rather than veer straight up it. We learn that sometimes, and for some people, the best way to get what we want isn't to ask directly for it, but to rather proceed more coyly, making our need clear without ever asking the question. Some of us (but, really, not me) learn to look at the tiny red dot on a camera while taking a selfie, rather than staring into the screen head-on.

We're used to making these adjustments in all kinds of areas. It will help us all to recognize that pursuing the interesting is also an indirect kind of thing. It's best achieved by doing and experiencing, rather than planning.

This is why the teenager gets nowhere moaning about how she just wants to be happy. She's got an empty target, and her focus is on that target. It's a standoff, with no movement and no resolution. Paradoxically, the only way to get movement is to shift away from the target. We shift away by getting out of bed and trying some new things. Through experimenting, we'll learn what we are passionate about, and we'll start to fill in the target.

TRY SOMETHING NEW

When's the last time you tried something new? Has it been too long? Reading books about the Good Life is a great, important activity—obviously. But it'd be a little insincere for this author not to tell you to put down the damn books every once in a while and go out and try something new.

What can you try? (Make a list.)

What's holding you back? (No, seriously: Make a list.)

Are any of those good reasons not to try it?

The answer is no. If you can try it, you should. While no doubt there are things that are holding you back—time, fear of failure, embarrassment— these aren't good reasons. You know that. So just try something. It's your Good Life. It is worth the time. And failure? Who cares? Success is not the point. The point is to try something new. There's nothing that should hold you back.

Remember the unique life Oliver Sacks lived, which broke every rule of "the Good Lives playbook" yet turned out to be a very Good Life, full of one interesting experience after another? Sacks clearly didn't sit around reflecting or thinking about the nature of the Good Life. He just lived. And he lived his best possible life because he knew, embraced, and followed his passions. He was one of the rare few who so clearly know what they are passionate about and embrace their passions without hesitation. His ability to follow his passions without evaluating, without planning, without pursuit, took him from one interesting experience to another.

For example, Sacks didn't pause to reflect on whether his passion for ferns fit into his idea of a Good Life; he just set out with the American Fern Society in 2000 to fulfill a lifelong goal to see his beloved whisk fern in the wild. He dove wholeheartedly into wherever his passions led. Perhaps this explains why the fern-loving, motorcycle-riding neurologist is also a record-breaking weight lifter, once known by Los

Angeles's Muscle Beach crowd as "Dr. Squat," who in 1961 set a California record by performing a full squat with six hundred pounds.[4]

While it is natural to wonder exactly how Sacks managed to develop such a wide range of passions, even a quick look at any one of his books makes it clear. The common theme between them all is the ways in which they show Sacks's distinctive curiosity and the wonder by which he guided his life.

The number of times the words "wonder" and "curiosity" appear in his book *Oaxaca Journal*, for example, to my expert count, is *huge*. Sacks sets up every move and juncture in terms of the curiosity that drove him to whatever particular object/experience/person he goes on to detail, noting that "the point of wonder is not to answer but to notice and to ask."

He wonders whether the twenty types of chilies are "separate species or varieties produced by domestication." He wonders why chocolate should be "so intensely and so universally desired." His wonder at a fellow traveler's story leads him to think about "our primordial need to organize."[5] He treats wonder the way others might treat money, something whose importance and relevance need no justification whatsoever. He praises his traveling group for its "sweet, unspoiled, preprofessional atmosphere, ruled by a sense of adventure and wonder rather than by egotism and a lust for priority and fame."[6]

Wonder was Sacks's way of fueling his passions, of turning their sparks into a blazing fire. Wonder led him, and can lead all of us, to notice the nuances and to respond with more wonder. Wonder begets wonder and sets passions aflame. Whether it is wonder prompted by the vastness of the world, or wonder prompted by the perfect formation of tiny ants on our countertop, if we embrace its tug, we'll find ourselves operating on passions. Big or small, wonder helps us discover our passions and can make the whole project one interesting experience to boot.

As you stop focusing so much on targets and focus more on experiences, do so with a sense of wonder. See what happens!

Practice holding space

Trying things out will help us learn what we're passionate about and will put us on a path toward living better lives. But as we step away from pursuit mode, we also want to strive to become more comfortable just sitting with our minds. Our minds, remember, can stimulate the interesting on their own! This is a remarkable power that the depressed teenager mentioned earlier in this chapter obviously lacks. And it's one that most of us could use some practice with.

Most people hate to be alone with their thoughts. We're much more comfortable when we have something to do that engages us and gives direction to those thoughts. One notorious study on boredom forced people to be alone with their thoughts for all of fifteen minutes.[7] Beyond squirming in their chairs, the only thing available for them to do was to press a button and shock themselves. Two-thirds of the men and one-fourth of the women shocked themselves. Pain, apparently, was preferable to sitting alone with nothing to do but think.

It is not easy to be alone with our thoughts. But it is not rocket science, either. We've just got to let our minds go. They'll go somewhere. Find the stimulation if it is needed. I imagine the three-fourths of women who did not shock themselves thought instead about how weird it was that there was this button available to them and about how many people may have pushed the darn thing and about how silly they were. They thought about what the purpose of this experiment was, anyway, or they thought about their toenails. Whatever. Thoughts happen. We should let them, without worrying about where they go.

Find yourself thinking about your toenails? Great! Find that thinking about your toenails makes you cringe? Great! Find that cringing makes you think of your colleagues complaining on Facebook about students' rampant use of flip-flops? Great! Find that thought makes you think about Teva tans? Great! These are the ripples of the interesting building. We should let them penetrate our emotions. We should embrace the circle of thoughts and feelings and let the interesting spread, doing its thing, building and rippling.

When we sit with our thoughts, we turn our minds into playgrounds. We create a space to see what comes along, to feel the tug of curiosity arising and creativity blooming. And when we feel the tug? We should follow it. It's the white rabbit that'll take us straight to Wonderland.

The concept of "holding space" is helpful to think about in this context. Psychologists invoke it most often in the context of relationships. "Holding space" describes the importance of simply being with someone in the moment, hearing them, letting them feel, and sharing in their feelings. When we're holding space for a friend, we're giving her a shot to flourish—to let her personality shine, in whichever ways it does. We're not controlling, dictating the terms of our interactions. We're not setting standards she needs to live up to. We're giving her the room to let the nuances of her personality shine through, to be who she is, in the way that she wants. We're putting the spotlight on her, without any expectations. And ideally, she's holding space for you as well, giving you the opportunity to express yourself however you want, giving you the space to be who you are. That healthy relationships offer each party this kind of space is one of the reasons why relationships are so important, for they allow—no, encourage—you to flourish and grow.

Holding space within our relationships allows us to enjoy our relationships, the people we're with, and ourselves. But to hold space we've got to hold back from judgment, from giving advice, from dominating the scene with our own opinion. We've got to resist the urge to control the scene and instead let the goods of that relationship flourish—whatever that happens to look like.

We can hold space for ourselves, too, and we need to. We need to let ourselves off the hook and stop holding ourselves to whatever preconceived notions we may have about who we are, what we should be doing and thinking, and so on. We can sit with ourselves, nonjudgmentally, without purpose, and simply listen to our thoughts and feel our emotions. When we do this, we'll tune in to our responsiveness and learn to recognize the interesting clicking in. The open mind holding space sets itself up for unstructured cognitive engagement—the crown jewel of the interesting—for there's no judgment or purpose lingering, ready to stifle the free flow of thoughts and emotions that comes with engagement, that creates the interesting.

I get that this is a hard ask for many of us, even a painful one. Many of us feel anxiety at the very thought of being alone with our thoughts. And many of us already battle the script of self-criticism providing constant narration of all we do. These are difficult, painful emotions that too often hold us back. It might help to hit them head-on, to ask yourself, in this instance, *What am I really so fearful of? What is there to lose by holding space for my thoughts and seeing what crops up?* You see, the thing is, just like meditation, there's no way to do this wrong. Are you worried about what might come out? Why? Remember, there's no sense that whatever happens *can* be good or bad. They are just thoughts, thoughts that might lead to feelings, that might lead to new thoughts, that might lead to...anywhere. That's the point! To free yourself from the fear, and to see what happens. To notice. To feel the tug of curiosity and to see where it leads. To let your creative self out of its pursuit-mode handcuffs. There's no way to go wrong here, except to not try in the first place.

If it's not the fear holding you back, maybe what's holding you back is the thought that holding space for yourself is just a waste of time. I'm guessing that holds a lot of us back. But that's pursuit mode speaking up, trying to kick into overdrive. Identify it as such and stamp it down. Developing your capacity to create the interesting is not a waste of time. It's your ticket to living your best possible life. Press pause on pursuit mode. Give yourself the space to do it.

We could all benefit from holding space and the essential lesson from it: Simply take the moment for what it is, with no judgment, no analysis. If a thought comes to you, let it. See where it takes you. If a feeling comes to you, embrace it. If it starts to ripple, let it. The bottom line: Holding space for yourself opens up the space for the interesting. It gives the seeds of the interesting room to grow. And if you find the interesting growing, don't question your response. Just go with it. But, please, step away from pursuit mode as you let yourself go. There's no room to hold space when you are in pursuit mode.

COUNTING BLADES OF GRASS AND
OTHER SOLITUDE SKILLS

Does the thought of sitting alone with your thoughts make you want to shock yourself? It's not often these days that we hold space for our minds, allowing ourselves to just be. The ubiquities of technology make it rare that we must sit alone with our thoughts. We can always just pull out our phones, right? Actually, there's a better way.

One of the most influential philosophers of the twentieth century, John Rawls, writes of a grass counter who finds pleasure in counting blades of grass—in fact, this is his only pleasure: sitting around on the most manicured of lawns, counting its blades.[8] Rawls brings up the example to prove a point: Clearly the grass counter is not living a Good Life; therefore, any theory that suggests he is, is wrong.

A lot of philosophers find Rawls's argument completely compelling. There's no way the grass counter could live a Good Life, they believe, because no real value derives from something so tedious and so unattainable. I, on the other hand, find the example fascinating. For one, it's clear that the grass counter has a special skill. And while this language wasn't on Rawls's radar—or, in 1971, on anyone's radar—it's clear that the grass counter finds counting blades of grass interesting.

Maybe I resonated with Rawls's example because it reminds me of that one summer day before fifth grade when my best friend Laura and I decided to look for four-leaf clovers in her yard. We did it for hours. We found some. It left an impression.* I tried to do it again, briefly, just a few days ago. The grass counter example had been on my mind,

---

* I ran into Laura's older brother Andy recently and told him about this story. His reaction fascinated me: (1) He remembered very clearly, "You and Laura used to do that all the time." (2) He told me his twenty-one-year-old-daughter (Laura's

and I was sitting around, waiting for something, staring down at the grass. It was pretty well-manicured grass, suggesting little chance of finding a weedy four-leaf clover in it, so I wondered how and whether it would be possible to start counting the blades. I saw a clump of it, slightly longer than others. I dug around and saw a cluster of clumps. I realized that by sectioning off the area into clusters of clumps I could make some progress, one clump of grass at a time. I thought about that grass counter, and the skills and techniques he'd have to develop. It all seemed like one interesting project. Also, though, a very daunting and time-consuming one.

Now, I'm not going to recommend you try counting blades of grass (although if that is your thing, you know what to do). But I am going to encourage you to think about the value of developing these kinds of skills, skills you can use, all on your own, in almost any context, to stimulate the interesting. They'll help you learn to be alone with your thoughts—and turn that time into an interesting experience.

One of my Middlebury colleagues, Virginia "Gina" Thomas, happens to be doing some cutting-edge psychological research on solitude skills, the skills conducive to having rewarding experiences while alone. Her focus is on any kind of rewarding experience to be had in solitude, not just the interesting ones, although she is one of the first to study the correlation between spending time alone and psychological richness.[9] It makes sense that there would be. When we're alone with just our thoughts, opportunities are ripe for interesting experiences—that is, if we can harness those thoughts.

Practicing some solitude skills can pay off in critical ways for your mental health and, more generally, will help you create more positive experiences in your life. For one, solitude skills will help you become more comfortable holding space, sitting with your thoughts and harnessing them, generating those ripples of the interesting. Consider

---

niece) does the same. I was shocked! And gratified that there is at least one member of Generation Z counting four-leaf clovers.

Diana, a self-described "solitude expert" Gina interviewed who claimed, boldly:

> I'm never, ever bored in solitude...because in solitude I can follow whatever is interesting. I find my thoughts interesting, and if my thoughts aren't interesting, well there's always a book...and if I'm not in a reading mode, well I can take a bath, or I could, you know, dance, or water the plants. I mean...there's nothing about being alone that is boring.[10]

While she may not realize it (yet), in being an expert at solitude, Diana is also an expert at the interesting thing. In fact, Gina's analysis of Diana and other solitude experts reveals the skills and characteristics that lead them to have rewarding, constructive experiences alone, which she clusters into three themes: connecting with oneself, protecting one's time, and finding balance—all of which bring us closer to conditions in which we'll encounter the interesting.

Connecting with oneself

Perhaps the most fundamental component of spending time in solitude is connecting to yourself. Solitude experts enjoy solitary activities, and it's not at all misleading to think of the requisite skill here as forming a relationship to yourself. When we've got a relationship with our self, we embrace, rather than resist, the thought of being alone. We're curious about our own emotional and cognitive states, just as we'd be curious about what's going on in a good friend's mind. We feel and regulate our own emotions, never blocking off some as being "too much," and never worrying about getting swept away by moments of sadness, distress, or anxiety. When we're tuned in to our own emotional lives, we're able to experience our emotions as they come and regulate them on our own, oftentimes simply by being aware of them. And, last, we can connect to ourselves through introspection—through checking out what is going on in our heads and bringing a little reflective spirit to them.

Protecting time

The next big thing solitude experts do is recognize the value of solitude and prioritize it in their lives. While it's inevitable that we often find ourselves alone, alone time isn't necessarily solitude time. Solitude doesn't just happen anytime we are alone. Solitude describes time willingly spent alone, for the purpose of engaging in activities alone.

Solitude experts go after solitude. This means both that they assert their needs for solitude and that they use their time alone to engage in constructive activities—they approach solitude with intentionality.

This one hit home to me. I'm comfortable being alone and enjoy doing a lot of things alone. But often I find my alone time gets wasted, and rarely do I conscientiously decide I need it. Gina's research shows that solitude doesn't just happen. It's intentional. We've got to willingly embrace the time and flip the switch, therein activating solitude.

Finding balance

As good as solitude can get, it's also all about balance. We are not meant to be solitary creatures, connecting only with ourselves. Solitude experts find the balance. They recognize when they need solitude, and they recognize when they've filled their cup with it and are ready for social engagement. These particular skill sets are all about learning one's own internal cues. Gina's experts know to enter solitude when they feel overwhelmed, irritable, or overstimulated. And they know to leave it when signs of loneliness or boredom loom. This is where those introspective skills pay off big-time. Through connecting with our self, we become more aware of our internal states and more reflective about our own needs. These skills snowball, helping us to learn what we need and when we need it.

PRACTICING SOLITUDE

Need a little help sitting with your thoughts and learning to hold space for yourself? The next time you happen to find yourself alone, make the intentional choice to turn that time into solitude: to use it to connect with yourself, and to engage in an activity on your own. Don't let the time waste away by scrolling on your phone, or distracting yourself through the news or whatever happens to be on TV.

A time-honored approach to cultivate interiority is to try journaling. Journaling is a wonderful opportunity to force some self-reflection and develop the powers of introspection. And if, as you write, you notice emotions bubbling up, stop and listen to them. Let yourself cry, cheer, or embrace whatever comes. Never underestimate the cleansing power of a good cry or a good laugh. Let your emotions engulf you.

Need a prompt? Try this one on: *What am I thinking right now? Why? How does this make me feel?* Follow the threads of your own thoughts, and notice when you stumble onto something interesting.

Whether you've got to fake it until you make it, or you've already got a leg up on this whole solitude thing, through practice you can open a range of experience that is all yours, and yours to enhance.*

We can't pursue the interesting the way we pursue good grades, but that doesn't have to leave us stuck in bed. By learning more about our passions, by bringing a sense of wonder to them, and by practicing sitting with our thoughts, we, too, can activate the playgrounds of our minds and encounter the wonderland of the interesting.

---

* For a directed practice of solitude skills, check out Dr. Thomas's Embrace Solitude program online: www.embracesolitude.com.

KEEPING IT INTERESTING

We don't get better at predicting what we'll find interesting by thinking about what we *want* to find interesting. We get better at making these predictions when we think about how we *experience* the interesting. We get better when we pursue the interesting indirectly—not through chasing it down, but by giving it space to appear naturally in our lives, minds, and experiences.

Chapter 7:

Developing an Interesting Mindset

W E'VE ALL GOT THAT CRAZY FRIEND WHO IS TOTALLY INTO something for reasons we just don't get. And we've probably got some of that craziness within ourselves. I certainly do. Like most philosophers, I thrive on critical debate. We cherish the times when we gather, share the views we've painstakingly developed, often over years and years, and then proceed to critique the hell out of one another. This is not everyone's cup of tea. Direct, face-to-face challenges? Confrontations and critique of someone's deeply held views? Not the kind of thing most people seek out. But these things mean something different for philosophers, whose curiosity and intellectual ambition transform those experiences into ones of insurmountable value.

I also really, really love to scuba dive. For me, being deep underwater, enveloped and lifted by the cool sea, engulfed in complete silence, interrupted only by the gurgle of a regulator, is one of the most comforting experiences I've ever had, that I can only describe as womb-like. Again, this is not everyone's cup of tea. Many people think I'm crazy. Why? Among the reasons they've offered (repeatedly): "Humans aren't meant to breathe underwater." "There's no sense of relaxing when you are hooked up to all of this apparatus in order to breathe." And, of course, "Sharks."

To a diver, there's nothing more exciting than encountering a shark.

It's almost indescribable, the pull that these encounters have. You see a shark while diving and your instinct is to swim after it. The peace of the water invites this reaction, which really is so very different from what you'd expect it to be. Don't get me wrong: I'm scared of sharks. The thought of seeing one while snorkeling or paddle-boarding terrifies me.* But when I'm underwater, swimming in tune with them, it's a completely different experience.

What we bring to our experience changes everything. It especially changes the value we get from that experience. And here's the prize when it comes to the interesting: By shifting our mindset ever so slightly, we can make the world more interesting. And the shifts here aren't anything liable to get called "crazy," ones that make sense only given a particular and distinctive frame.† We are talking about developing a mindset defined by creativity, curiosity, and a form of mindfulness based on noticing. There are kernels of each of these traits within all of us, just waiting to bloom. (Yes, even you.) It turns out that our minds strive toward this mindset naturally, that our minds drive us to see the world as more interesting. We've just got to let them.

OPEN UP TO THE INTERESTING

We've seen already the ways that the interesting is self-stimulating. One interesting experience begets new thoughts and emotions that generate more interesting experiences. The trick with these cycles is figuring out how to break in—how to get the cycle going. But it isn't really a trick. We can change our experiences simply by changing the way we look at them. We can shift our mindsets so that they beget the good stuff.

Fundamentally, to experience the interesting and to create the interesting on your own, you've got to be open to it. You've got to be

---

* The number one rule of swimming with sharks: Stay low. They always attack from below, which is why being on the surface of water around sharks is terrifying, while being underwater is not.
† Not that there is anything wrong with crazy.

comfortable opening your mind to new thoughts and emotions. Once you open your mind to the interesting, the rest of the art falls into place.

Of course, depending on where you're starting from, opening your mind to the interesting may take some effort. This is because adults have tendencies that close their minds off from the interesting. But these tendencies aren't anywhere as strong as those deeply rooted, physiologically based tendencies to adapt to pleasure. We can avoid these tendencies just by being aware of them.

While adults often get stuck with closed minds, kids simply have it made. Their minds are completely open to the interesting, making the world their oyster of interesting experiences. Try to remember what it was like to be a kid in the world. (If that is too difficult, you're probably old enough to remember the movie *Coming to America*, and Eddie Murphy's face when his character takes in New York City for the first time. Same thing.) Everything is new. Everything forces the mind to engage, triggering new thoughts, new emotions. And everything is a challenge. When you don't have expectations to guide you, every experience is an experience into the unknown. Everything is a challenge in this way for kids, which is why it's important for kids to have loving adults to guide them and keep them from being too overwhelmed.

By the time we've grown into adults, though, our relationship with novelty and the challenges that accompany it has changed. There's less of it, for one thing. When we're older, things are more familiar. Our minds are less open because they are full of beliefs and expectations built from past experiences. Adults don't tend to get stuck in the cereal aisle for hours, distracted by the colors on the boxes. No way—we've learned to filter out those distractions, especially when they interfere with a plan or purpose. We can run straight to the cereal aisle, grab a box, and go to the checkout. Because things are more familiar to adults, we face fewer challenges than we did when we were kids. But here's the sneaky thing: The more familiar something is, the harder it becomes to engage fully in the details of the world around us.

There's an important scientific reason for this: Our minds can only take so much active engagement, and thus they quickly make automatic as many things as possible.* This is why we don't have to think when we drive a car or walk. The new driver and the toddler must think hard about these things, yet once they've learned it, and the practice becomes routine, the mind will take over. And thank goodness it does. Can you imagine having to think out every step of driving a car every time you get in one? Or having to think about lifting your legs, placing your foot on solid ground for only a millisecond before placing another foot eight inches in front of it? It would be as exhausting as it sounds. If we exhausted our minds on the little stuff, we wouldn't be able to use it in the moments that count, when we are faced with a new decision to make.

And this is where the downside of being an adult comes in. We become so adept at familiarizing, we get lazy and miss out on a lot of the little stuff. When was the last time we let ourselves notice the colors of those cereal boxes? The many different shades the flavor of "honey nut" can give rise to? The contrasting textures between the shredded wheat and the frosted shredded wheat? The pale tone of the crunchy-looking marshmallows against the grain-laden shapes?

Our brain's ability to automate mental labor is beautiful and powerful, but the obvious drawback is that, to some degree, it encourages us to check out and to disengage. And, let's face it, the more we get used to checking out, the more daunting it becomes to check in, especially to check into anything that might challenge our minds. Our attitude toward challenge shifts from that childlike openness wherein everything presents an opportunity to engage, to that adult-like closed-mindedness of seeing challenge as a hindrance and something to be avoided.

* Psychologist John Bargh's influential line of research on automaticity highlights this tendency. It's a tendency the philosopher John Doris worries is so strong, he thinks it calls into question whether we have the kind of agency over our actions that we think we do. See John A. Bargh and Tanya L. Chartrand, "The Unbearable Automaticity of Being," *American Psychologist* 54, no. 7 (1999): 462–79; and John M. Doris, *Talking to Our Selves: Reflection, Ignorance, and Agency* (New York: Oxford University Press, 2015).

But we can shift our ways of seeing the world by learning to use our minds in ways that bring the interesting. By practicing being mindful of our environments, being curious about, well, everything, and embracing our creativity, we can start to open our minds. We'll develop a mindset that brings the interesting.

MINDFULNESS 2.0...NOT THE USUAL KIND

You've no doubt heard about mindfulness before. In some circles, the very word signals The One Thing We Are Missing That Can Save the World! Being mindful helps us do anything and everything better, we are told. Struggling to get your coworkers to engage after forcing them to come back into the office? A mandatory session on mindfulness sounds right. Struggling to learn in the classroom? A few minutes of mindfulness before class is just what you need. Struggling to lose those last ten pounds? Mindful eating will do the trick. Struggling to parent your twin toddlers? Here's a book on mindful parenting. Struggling to not tell everyone around you to fuck off? You know what to do.

As with all cure-alls society tends to cling to,* there's a solid foundation driving the mindfulness craze. Mindfulness describes a form of attention to what's happening in your mind. The technical term for this is metacognitive awareness of your mental states. Its classic form is found within meditation practices, wherein meditators learn to focus on something internal to the body (such as breath) through developing first awareness of when the mind takes off and ultimately command over the trajectories of their thoughts. The process of learning and exercising this kind of mindfulness is a nonjudgmental one; the point is to notice where our minds are going and to bring them back without judgment.

To be clear, depending on what's going on in our head, developing mindfulness can be an essential tool—a lifesaver, even, for those of us with tendencies toward anxiety and depression, which lead us to evaluate and judge, well, everything. But amid all the talk of the powers of

---

* Optimism and gratitude, anyone?

mindfulness to save us from whatever we are struggling with, though, we can lose sight of the lurking power of mindfulness, which serves to allow us to engage. Too often we think of mindfulness as a tool to detach from our thoughts and emotions. But when we develop mindfulness of our environments—by which I mean an attentiveness to the nuances and details of what we are doing, unclouded by preconceived judgments and notions, we open our minds up to the ripples of thoughts and emotions that bring the interesting. We'll call this Mindfulness 2.0.

The legendary art critic Jerry Saltz has some apt pieces of advice for this venture—for how to shift our mindset so that our Mindfulness 2.0 blossoms into robust, emotion-fueled engagement. Saltz is well known for explaining art in a way that allows others—even those who never stepped foot in an art history class—to appreciate it. He does so by encouraging us to use and embrace our *imagination*, untainted by beliefs, prejudices, and anything else, really.

The first step? Just looking and noticing. Here's Saltz trying to explain to a journalist how to take in Vincent van Gogh's *Starry Night*:[1]

SALTZ: What do you see? What's the subject matter?
SIMON: It's the sky.
SALTZ: The sky, a cypress tree, an evening.
SIMON: Mmm-hmm.
SALTZ: OK, now stop seeing the subject matter. And what do you see?
SIMON: Swirls.
SALTZ: Swirls. So, you see shapes…
SIMON: Colors.
SALTZ: …Colors, brush strokes…
SIMON: Brush strokes.

The brushstrokes, the colors, the swirls, it turns out, are everything. The lure of *Starry Night*, Saltz argues, is simply the way in which Van Gogh brings these together while preserving their individuality. Van

Gogh invites us to see these different components simultaneously. But to see this, we've got to get concepts out of our mind. We don't see the brushstrokes when we see the sky. We see the brushstrokes when we shed our mind from the thoughts it is so laden with, and when we allow ourselves to simply notice.

Saltz's lesson reminds me of the first time ever I put on a pair of glasses. I was young, maybe ten. My vision had dropped so sharply, my mom thought I was faking. But I wasn't faking. Things were blurry. I couldn't see the blackboard. Yet I had no idea *what* I was really missing until I put on that first pair of glasses, complete with thick, bulky lenses and frames that overwhelmed the chubby cheeks they rested upon.

Wow. It was the trees that stood out. Suddenly, I could see the pine needles, hanging together in clumps of sap. I could see the bare sticks turning brown, strips of old bark clinging, hanging sickly from the tree's bare base. I could see the leaves, some bendy, some basking tall in the light.

Wow. It was the details, the nuances that had been there all along, simply waiting to be seen. It was as if those glasses delivered me into a secret world, one that was way more interesting than the blurry one I left behind.

Maybe you've had this same experience. I'll admit some kind of perverse excitement I had for my younger son the first time he had to put on a pair of glasses. His world was about to be opened. "Whoa" was his response.

We forget the magic of such small moments. The feeling of being able to see something that was right in front of you all along in new, glorious detail. Moments like this connect you to the world around you, making you less of a stranger, less of an observer, moving absently from day to day, immune to the nuances of the world you are moving through. When we see, we inhabit the world. We make it our oyster of interesting experiences.

This may not be how we are used to thinking about mindfulness, but it is mindfulness at its core. Mindfulness, fundamentally, is an ability to be present in the world. Its most basic contrast is distraction.

When we're caught up in our own stuff—in our own cycles of thoughts and emotions—we're distracted. We are not present. And when we're not present, we move through the world. We don't inhabit it. We don't experience it.

The promise of mindfulness lies in its reminder to be present. It's a reminder to put on your glasses and to open your eyes to what is right in front of you. To see the pine needles covered in sap, to see the brushstrokes, to see the swirls. To see before thinking. When we see first—tuning in to the details of what exists already in the world around us—we open up our minds to having an interesting experience.

GIVING MINDFULNESS 2.0 A SHOT

Mindfulness 2.0 is all about bringing fresh eyes to your day-to-day. You can give it a shot by picking one routine aspect of your day. Maybe it's the rush to get the kids to school on time, or the subway ride into work, or the dog walk. Anything will do.

If it is routine, chances are high two things are happening in your mind. First, you've blocked out a lot of the details regarding your surroundings. You focus only on the central aspects you need to get through it. You see only the big clock ticking away in the subway station, and you look past the unhoused people. You see the lunches that need to get made, and not the cool color combination your kid picked out to wear today. You see a dog that needs to pee, and not the way his pant looks just like a smile, just for you. Second, your mind is primed to evaluate every step of the routine. Your dog is taking too long to pee. (Or, great, he's done already!) Your kids are being pains in the ass and making you late. (Or, miraculously, they are cooperating! Yay!) The subway smells, again. (Or it doesn't. Yay!)

Try to notice these two things about your routine: what it is that you see (and don't), and how you evaluate it. Now you are primed to bring fresh eyes. Bring them! See the colors, the dog smiles, the unhoused, and whatever else comes at you. Hold back from judging anything, and instead allow your thoughts to take off. That everyday routine will become more interesting.

The danger of mindfulness lies in its suggestiveness that being present means being detached from one's emotions. That is, that the goal somehow is to be aware yet not emotionally invested. That's where the turn toward mindfulness starts to get…boring and overrated.

After all, the interesting is found and reinforced in the ripples between thoughts and emotions. And the best ripples start from Mindfulness 2.0. It's a position of being present, of seeing the world, and of inhabiting it. When your mind starts to take off from a place of Mindfulness 2.0, the ripples that follow make you feel connected to the world rather than disengaged from it.

Whatever the world around us looks like, being mindful of it positions us to make it more interesting. So be mindful. Be present. Notice. By paying close attention to your experiences, you'll find opportunities to spark the interesting. Let Mindfulness 2.0 be your launchpad for the interesting, and allow yourself to take off.

CURIOSITY

Whoever said that curiosity kills the cat was just wrong. We all know cats have nine lives, so they don't just die from curiosity alone. And trust me, as the owner of far too many cats throughout the years, they die because of cars and other animals. Their curiosity, however, does bring them their joy. Have you ever watched a cat staking something out? So present, so intense, so aware of the moment. I guess maybe their curiosity also brings them across the road or leads them to wander alone through fields in the middle of the night, but that's the price of joy.

Curiosity can make us alive. Curiosity can fuel our adventures. Curiosity can stimulate the ripples of the interesting. While developing Mindfulness 2.0 primes us to take off, curiosity fuels the launch. And it just involves asking why.

That may sound too easy to be true, and I get it. A lot of us are less curious than others. Some of us may have a hard time simply allowing ourselves to be curious. It's a trait we are quick to encourage in children but forget about as we get older. Things get more familiar. And many of us find that there is simply less to be curious about. Even worse, we may start to think we *know* everything already. Curiosity arises only when we think there is *something to learn*. If we don't think there is something to learn, we'll never be curious.

One of the most important things I've learned as a philosopher is exactly how harmful this perspective can be—how harmful it can be to think you know it all. The most important piece of advice I give my students? "Never pretend you know more than you do. Never think you know it all." There are very few things I will say with such certainty, but the reality is that the smartest people are the ones aware of what they know *and* what they don't know.

Plato makes this point so clearly in *The Apology*. He depicts an encounter between Socrates (his teacher) and a friend. The friend tells Socrates he has just heard from the Oracle of Delphi—aka the voice of the gods—that Socrates is the wisest man in Athens. "What?!" Socrates replies. "That's crazy." There had to be someone smarter than him. So, he goes off looking. He quickly realizes that those around him don't know all that they claim to. The only difference between Socrates and the others turns out to be that Socrates knows he doesn't know anything. And this little piece of information, Plato suggests, makes *all* the difference. The mark of the wise person is that they know their limits. They do not pretend to know what they don't. The greatest piece of knowledge we can have, it turns out, is knowing that, really, in the big picture, we don't know much.

Plato's right about this. But the reason why sometimes gets buried behind the (very entertaining) drama of Socrates running around town making fools of everyone, as he proves they don't really know what they think they do. It's important to be aware of our limits, and to know what we don't know, so that we can learn. If we think we know it all, we have nothing to learn and we close our minds. This helps us believe we know it all—because we've cut ourselves off from the factors that might lead us to question our beliefs! But, gosh, we can never know it all. There is always something more to learn. And no one should be threatened by this. The greatest minds were not. Neither should we.

Accepting some intellectual humility is part of becoming curious. Curiosity arises in conditions of uncertainty, and uncertainty forces the mind to engage. Sure, from a functional perspective our curiosity allows us to conquer uncertain conditions. That is why we encourage it in children. "Put yourself out there! Learn something new," we say. But the experience of curiosity has independent appeal. It isn't just a tool for our conquests, good only insofar as it is helpful. Nor does curiosity arise *only* in response to conditions of uncertainty. Curiosity can generate uncertainty and encourage our mind to engage.

Curious George, as depicted in the Margret and H. A. Rey classics, is a little monkey, living in the big city with his friend, the Man with the Yellow Hat. (We'll bypass the traumatic part of that story where George's "friend" rips him out of the jungle, throws him in a bag, and tries to leave him locked up in a zoo.) Even with such a traumatic history, George is unscarred, eager to explore the new world that lies just outside his friend's apartment. Curious George doesn't sit back and wait for his curiosity to click in. His curiosity takes him out of his friend's apartment and leads him to break the rules and to have one interesting experience after the next. He gets himself in trouble, breaks his bones, eats puzzle pieces, scares his loved ones, but no matter what, George keeps getting out there. Why? Because allowing curiosity to bloom *feels good*. It does not feel good in the way that eating ice cream and getting massages feels good, but it feels good in the active way, distinctive to our minds. It's that feeling we get from Wordling, listening to a particularly stimulating podcast, learning a new knitting pattern. And it's a good one. So why limit it to these small, individual pursuits?

The great television series *Only Murders in the Building* is about exactly what the title suggests: a murder in a residential apartment building. Or rather, it is about a death that *some* neighbors think must have been a murder, even though the police claimed otherwise. The neighbors—

previously just strangers in the elevator, with nothing in common other than the fact that they each lived, alone, in the same building—come together, fueled by curiosity. Could a murderer really live in their building? How else could we explain the guy's death? Maybe this explains the weird looks constantly coming from the neighbor in apartment 5? Who is the neighbor in apartment 5, anyway?

Their curiosity feeds off one another's, amplifying, beckoning for more. They begin an investigation. Or rather, they create a murder mystery to solve. It's Hollywood, so the possibility is that there really was a murder. Whether or not there was is beside the point. What brings the group together is the mystery, the investigation. And they find that this adventure fills holes in their lives they had barely recognized were there. They've found intrigue and excitement. They've developed friendships that grew solely from their shared pursuit. They act in ways they haven't in years.

They find their lives are transformed—not because of any actual event that did or did not happen, but because they came together, driven by the moment, embraced their curiosity without hesitation, and created a mission. Through being curious, they created the interestingness that goes on to enhance their lives.

The season 2 premiere finds them briefly considering taking a break from their investigations and letting their curiosity fizzle out. Selena Gomez's delightful character suggests, tentatively, "We could just live normal lives...we could just be boring?" To which Martin Short's snappy character exclaims: "I'd rather be dead than boring." That's all that needs to be said. Without another word, their adventures go on.

We see this kind of thing all the time in TV shows. A group of friends, or strangers who become friends, pursuing some kind of mystery that very well might have been made up. They are interesting to watch, for sure. But why limit ourselves to experiencing their interestingness vicariously? Why not create *our* own interestingness, our way, in our worlds?

OPTIMAL AROUSAL

Part of the reason curiosity is such a powerful fire starter for the interesting is that it represents what psychologists call a state of "optimal arousal." Their idea is that our minds can be understimulated, such as when we never feel the urge to ask why, and rather just keep moving on. That's probably a familiar mode of operating for a lot of us, yet it's not good for our minds, which strive for stimulation and thrive when stimulated. Yet just as important is the corollary—which is that a state of overstimulation is just as harmful as a state of understimulation. When our minds are too stimulated, they shut down. They can't process the fundamentals of their experience, much less find the space to ask why.*

A state of optimal arousal, in contrast, describes the place where our minds are stimulated to a degree that doesn't overwhelm. It describes the place where something engages, just enough to allow our minds to take off and do what they are designed to do: to think, create, and feel, on repeat. These feelings of interest both sustain and motivate the engagement, creating the spirals of thoughts and emotions distinctive to the interesting. It arouses us in ways that feel good.[2]

How do we know when we've reached optimal arousal? It is an individual thing, but, really, we know it when we've got it. We're at optimal arousal when we feel the engagement clicking in, when the wonder and the whys start to fuel that engagement, taking our minds to places unknown but welcome. We also know when we've gone too far—when we've passed the point of optimal arousal and begin to feel less of the wonder and the whys, and more that our minds have been hijacked. We've gone too far when our brain starts to hurt from the engagement, when we no longer feel engaged but instead feel sucked in. We've gone too far when those feelings of interest start to fade away and yet we're still pushing, seeking, overaroused. We may sense that things have started to go downhill yet we arc so stimulated it's

---

* Realistically, a young monkey, raised in the jungle and then thrown into a modern city, is going to be too overstimulated to do, well, anything.

hard to pull back. Other times, we may realize it only later, after we've crashed and burned.

DISCOVER YOUR STATE OF OPTIMAL AROUSAL

If you've got a mind, you know what it feels like to be under- and over-stimulated. It's time to zero in on those states so that you can better predict where you'll find your state of optimal arousal or, in other words, learn how to set the state to engage the interesting.

Pick your favorite leisure activity that uses your mind. Is it playing a video game? Reading a book? Trivia night? Listening to a podcast? It doesn't have to be anything lofty, and it certainly does not have to be intellectual but something that requires thought, and something that you tend to enjoy.

Now try to carve out instances—reading particular books, playing particular games, et cetera—when:

1. This activity left you completely unengaged. You may have done it, but you got nothing from it. It was understimulating. Boring, even.
2. This activity overwhelmed you to the point where you couldn't engage in it. Maybe you gave up, or maybe you pushed through—only to find yourself worn out.
3. This activity felt engaging, activating, and invigorating—leaving you wanting more, in a good way.

These are your states of under-, over-, and optimal arousal. Notice how they make you feel, especially that state of optimal arousal. If you can take this one step further and identify what it is that triggers these states in yourself, you get bonus points. And if you can't? Don't stress. It's the states that count, and the more familiar you are with them, the more you can recognize how to shape your activities so that they deliver optimal arousal.

There's a learning curve here. Exactly what counts as optimal arousal varies from person to person. It's worth listening to your instincts to discover your optimal state. Maybe the *New York Times* crossword puzzle is simply too much—in which case, why not Wordle instead? But maybe Wordle is not enough. Maybe it was at one point, but the allure drifted away with the challenge as you started getting better and better yet. That's exactly why the Wordle phenomenon blossomed into Absurdle, Kilordle, Mathdle, Octordle, Star Wordle, and who knows what else. Harder and harder instantiations of basically the same thing.

Curious George sometimes got tired, and often got injured, but his appetite for the interesting was insatiable. He could never be content just sitting in his friend's apartment, zoning out on cartoons. He needed to be stimulated. He needed engagement, and his curiosity showed him the way. While we aren't all little monkeys, we are all like George. We have minds that strive for engagement. We have curiosity that can show us the way. Our natural curiosity drives us to explore and to engage our minds in ways that feel good and that benefit us. Curiosity *sparks* the interesting. And we can be smarter than George. Curiosity wasn't his downfall—knowing his limits was, which is why we should experiment and learn what works for us individually. So, let's open up our curiosity and allow it to encompass our minds, to drive us. We just don't want to forget that puzzle pieces are not meant to be eaten, even if they look like candy, and that if we are light enough, helium balloons can take us far, far away.

CREATIVITY

If you are anything like me, creativity is daunting. As a kid, I was the reader, *not* the drawer. As a mom, I was also a great reader, yet I could never encourage my children to engage in imaginative play. As a teacher, I've had to turn my dismal artistic skills—an inability to draw so much as a circle—into the running joke of our classroom. But as I've grown older and learned how to be nicer to myself, I recognize there are all sorts of ways to be creative. Creativity isn't just about artistic talent, or imagining you are surrounded by pirates in your yard. It's about being able to go beyond where you've started. It's about being open to experiencing things in a new way. It's about creating new solutions to problems. It's about using all your mind's powers and developing new lines of communication between them.

Interesting experiences are expressions of creativity: The ripples of new thoughts and emotions they beget move us away from our starting points and leave us in new positions, begetting more ripples. That's creativity, and it is within us all.

At least when I was growing up, we used to divide people by their brains. "Left brain" people were good at the analytical stuff, the straightforward problem-solving. "Right brain" people were good at the creative stuff, the drawing, and the imaginative play. That made it easy to identify with one part of the brain and not with the other. It made it easy for me to see myself as good at philosophy yet bad at anything creative.

I was wrong. We've all got right and left hemispheres in our brains and, thanks to our advanced ability to conduct brain imaging studies with the use of functional MRI, what we know now is that creativity involves making connections between these sides, not necessarily feeding only one side.[3] We can stimulate these connections by developing an openness to experience, by looking for new ways of solving a problem, by being aware of our routine thought patterns, and by being willing to disrupt them.

This all feeds into the importance of opening our minds. Our minds offer us so much potential, but we so often close them off and keep them focused on the tasks at hand, sticking to the routines we know will work. That's where, after we step back from pursuit mode and hold space for our thoughts, Mindfulness 2.0 comes in—it allows us to press pause on these routines and to stop the automatic thoughts that simply click in and direct us along the same path, leaving our minds in the same place. Pausing gives us the space to be curious, and—if we are open to it—offers creativity its chance to bloom. Pushing forward stifles everything. We shouldn't worry about what will happen if we press pause or worry about how to redirect attention so that it becomes more creative. If we trust our minds and give them the space to do their thing, the rest will come.

Creativity comes in all forms, but what unites forms of creativity is that they push the boundaries of the status quo. Creativity often sets apart those who excel in their fields. The best lawyers come up with new arguments, new frames for seeing the case, and new avenues for resolving it. The best cooks are the ones who tweak the recipe, who are willing to add the smoked paprika, or to replace the vanilla extract with almond. This is creativity. It's not always about creating something new out of fresh air. It's about moving forward.

But we don't have to be the best to be creative. We can be creative simply by choosing to explore a new recipe. We can be creative simply by choosing to read a new book. Or by trying a new color of toenail polish. Whatever. Whatever takes us somewhere new. A new thought, a new feeling, a new outlook, a new perspective.

We can start small if needed, but we should aim high. When we allow our minds to engage in their entirety, we become more creative. Of course, we always were creative, so it's better to think of this as embracing the creativity we've always had. As long as we're moving, there's no chance of failure.

But whatever we do, we should try our hardest not to embrace creativity for the sake of something else. We shouldn't go about trying to "harness" or "master" our creativity. That's not being open. To paraphrase Saltz's top tips for becoming an artist: It's all about the doing and the experience.[4]

The more we build up our creativity, the more prone our minds become to having interesting experiences, especially when we layer it onto Mindfulness 2.0 and curiosity. The mindfulness gets us to notice details and gives our minds something to work with. Curiosity and creativity prime our minds to take off from this point. Curiosity gives us a trajectory to explore, while creativity pushes us to go beyond what we're given. Both encourage our minds to engage, rather than to digest, and all three are parts of a mindset that, quite simply, will bring more of the interesting to our lives.

TAPPING INTO YOUR CREATIVE SELF

It can be hard to wrap your head around the role of creativity, especially if you, like me and so many, grew up believing you were not creative. One of the most enhancing things I've done for myself over the past few years has been to attend a weekend-long women's retreat. It's organized by a woman who knows all too well the importance of pausing, and of taking the space to let your mind bloom. She and her husband have found their best possible lives through running a family camp nestled in a remote, beautiful spot in the Northeast Kingdom of Vermont, where not even reliable cell service exists to distract you from the task at hand: being open and free to explore. There are no rules or structure, just opportunities.*

A treasured, always optional, event is the art workshops. One year my friend Emily—who is analytical and creative, with a fine arts degree and careers in music and finance to boot—led a print-making workshop. Most of us there did not think we were creative. Yet, wow, we all created some very cool prints.

Emily taught us this trick that apparently real artists do to center themselves and to harness their creative spirit. It's easy. Grab a pencil and a blank sheet of paper. Now, look up and find any object around you. Maybe it's the kitchen table, the TV stand, whatever. Without looking at the paper, start to draw what you are looking at—without ever letting the pencil leave the paper. Try to find as much detail as you can. Look and draw.

Emily had us do this in pairs, where we each looked at and drew our partner's face. That introduced a somewhat hysterical dynamic. But I've since found it helpful to draw my couch, my window, my TV stand. It really does help you to center, to draw out your creative self, and to feel more peaceful. (It's also a lot more fun than trying to meditate.)

Give it a shot—can you tap into your creative self? If you do, when you are done, follow Emily's next tip: "Artists sign and number their work." Signing and numbering really does have the magical effect of turning doodles into art.

---

* True story: During one retreat, falling into typical patterns, I was giving a friend a hard time for leaving the dance party. Lilly—who runs the retreat and is literally the nicest person I know, a woman surrounded in a halo of loving-kindness—overheard me and chastised me: "Lorraine! There are no rules and no pressure here!" Seriously, where else in the world can you find such a place?!

Once you release your powers of creativity and layer it with Mindfulness 2.0 and curiosity, you're primed to make your life more interesting. And you should! There's a variety of ways to personalize the world around you, making it more textured and ripe for the interesting.

On a recent trip to India, being mostly a pedestrian competing on streets overflowing with about a gazillion rickshaws, cars, bikes, and cows, I often found it all but impossible to cross the street...until I turned it into a game. I pretended like I was playing *Frogger*—you know, that video game from the early 1980s where the task was to get frogs to jump through traffic, moving safely across the road. Playing *Frogger* was way more entertaining—and effective—than standing there completely overwhelmed. This little game, in my head, transformed the entire experience.

What little games can you play to transform your day-to-day into one interesting experience? Can you create an adventure, even if just in your mind?

THE POWER OF A NICKNAME

My husband, Jody, and I love to ski. It's one of our shared passions, through which we found each other. We also have the good fortune to live super close to our small but mighty ski resort and to have flexible jobs that allow us plenty of time on the mountain. There's nothing like being on the mountain, especially ours. It's like we disappear from our regular lives and become part of a secret community where no one knows what we really look like under our helmets and goggles and where no one cares or talks about their jobs and families. It is not a place where everyone knows our name, but it is a place where everyone around us is just *so* damn happy to be there, even when the wind chill is well below zero and the sun hasn't shined in days. It's like being part of a family we only see five months a year and never have to feel guilty about not reaching out to during the other seven months, yet whose simple presence brings us comfort.

And Jody and I? Well, we built up that family. We created that community. How? Not through throwing potluck dinners or apres-ski parties. Not even through introducing ourselves and asking others about their jobs and families. Rather, through the very simple process of noticing the people who are always around us and giving them nicknames.

Nicknames transform strangers into a cast of characters. I don't know the real name of "Yellow Raincoat," but gosh, it makes me feel good to see him there, along with us, in the most frigid of all weather. (And I cannot begin to describe the excitement I felt the day I realized I was riding up the chairlift with Yellow Raincoat, disguised in his new blue coat.) We don't know a single personal detail about each other, outside of our shared passion. But he's part of our crew, along with "double coat," "the gladefather," "the influencer," "red coat," "green helmet"...the whole gang.*

Calling everyone by a nickname adds a layer of interest to our experience. It connects us to those around us. It gives us a cast of characters to engage with. It solidifies the real bond we have—regulars with a shared love for our mountain—which would have otherwise just drifted into the background. It certainly makes those cold rides up the same damn chairlift that much more entertaining. And, sometimes, it seeps into our regular life as well, such as when I realized that I'd unknowingly become friends with...the glade daughter!

So, childlike, yes. But so harmless. And such a source of interest that has its roots in mindful, open awareness of the people around us. Creating little layers like this is like sprinkling flakes of gold on the mud, an ever-so-subtle overlay that introduces a hint of glitter into what could otherwise devolve into a bland and forgotten backstory. The more we can build and develop this capacity to add layers of interest to our ex-

---

* There are some obvious limitations to our nickname system. When red coat changed coats, my son Beck tried to teach me (and make me use) the kid's name. I refused. He will always be red coat. In defense of our system, I should note that it helps that the place is so small, we know them also simply by the way they ski or ride.

perience, to color our own worlds, the more rewarding those experiences will be.

So, try it out. The next time you find yourself alone someplace, boredom looming...look around. Give people some nicknames. Invent stories in your head. See for yourself how easy it is to create the interesting!

THE POWER OF A MINDSET

There are so many valuable aspects of the interesting, it can be hard to rein in its praises. Yet the point we've seen here—that shifting our minds to be more Mindful 2.0, curious, and creative positions us to develop and create interesting experiences—cannot be emphasized enough. As we struggle to live Good Lives, it is so tempting to fixate on our circumstances, and to think that whether or not we can live a Good Life depends on the stuff around us. We think the grass would be greener if we could change our jobs, that our lives would go better if only we could make more money, or were more talented, or had better luck.

Life can be tough. There are lots of shitty, horrible circumstances that can and do hold us back from living the Good Life: illness, poverty, imprisonment, oppressive laws regulating what we can and cannot do. These conditions make it very hard to find fulfillment and, likewise, pleasure. The production of pleasure and fulfillment depends upon one's surroundings being a certain way and upon having the freedom to pursue what one finds valuable. Of course, we need food and basic material comforts to feel pleasure. But the interesting? We just need our minds.

No one can take our power to create the interesting away from us. But we hold ourselves back when we forget this and fall into a mindset fixated on the external stuff, the mindset that tells us, *If only I could change [my job, my partner, my life], then I could lead a Good Life.* So, let's get rid of that mindset, for good. And let's replace it with the mindset of the interesting, which embraces our powers of Mindfulness 2.0, of curiosity, of creativity—powers we already have—and allows us to make the new connections that are so conducive to the interesting. This is the mindset that will get us to live better lives.

The British author Alan Sillitoe illustrates this point so very well in his short story about a young man, Smith, growing up in a British reform school post–World War II.[5] The environment was oppressive. Basic freedoms—autonomy, privacy—were removed for the sake of reforming troubled young men. But Smith manages to escape, to find a place where he can freely experience. Where and how? Within his own mind.

> They can spy on us all day to see if we're pulling our puddings and if we're working good or doing our "athletics" but they can't make an X-ray of our guts to find out what we're telling ourselves. I've been asking myself all sorts of questions and thinking about my life up to now. And I like doing all this. It's a treat.

The impenetrability of our minds allows us to live freely within them. Smith finds these powers of the mind and comes to cherish the inner life of his mind, through long-distance running—a pursuit he's permitted due to the administration's interest in their school winning an upcoming race. He finds rich enjoyment in the thoughts he's able to develop. He finds a place where he can think, where he can engage, and where he can live freely. And this place is always available because it is within his own mind.

The lesson here is so important. Whether we find ourselves stuck by oppressive conditions, by illness, or simply by the weight of our everyday routines, learning to find the interesting within our own minds is a skill that can transform our lives. And it's based on the capacities we already have. The trick is to allow it to flourish.

KEEPING IT INTERESTING

Our minds are primed and ready to find interesting experiences if we let them. This is the superpower of the interesting, and all it takes is shifting our mindset. Really! Allowing ourselves to be mindful of our environments primes us to inhabit and engage with them, and opens up the space for curiosity and creativity to do their things, moving us from places of stagnation to places of engagement, wherein the interesting beckons at every window.

Chapter 8:

Finding Your Zone of the Interesting

M Y FRIEND ANDY LEADS ONE OF THE MOST FASCINATING lives of anyone I know. He is a documentarian, photographer, and all-around storyteller. Animals are his specialty, especially the biggest, scariest, wildest animals. He's photographed gorillas in the Congo, filmed great whites in the deep waters of False Bay off the tip of South Africa, and recently won his third Emmy for his work on whales. If you're a fan of *Shark Week*, you've probably seen his work.* His life is one adventure after the next. He's managed to pull off the ideal: Find something you love and get paid for it. That he loves the adventure is clear. It is no doubt a necessity for his chosen path. He was made for a psychologically rich life.

What's unique about Andy, though, isn't just that he leads a psychologically rich life. It goes deeper than that. His stories are one thing (one super-entertaining thing). But Andy is also a creator. He's excelled in his career by capturing his experiences in ways that bring them to life for others and that allow them to become a source of interesting experiences for others. This guy has a special talent for the art of the interesting.

---

* And, maybe, the tip of his pinky floating away in the stream of the ocean. Oh wait, that was the dolphins, not the sharks. See?! Sharks are not scary.

One evening I grilled him, trying to figure it out. I pushed. I prodded. "What are your secrets? How do you *see* things? How can you know what makes a good shot?"

He sees, he knows. And he knows better than to plan or predict. Instead, he feels. He feels the stimulating features of wherever he happens to be, he notices and responds to them, and he engages with them. He can't tell us his secret because he doesn't have one. He simply experiences.

While a little frustrating—"Really? You don't have *any* tips?"—our conversation came to be reassuring because it affirmed in every way what I'd already come to believe about the interesting: There is no one-size-fits-all formula. Nothing in the world is, in itself, ineffably and essentially interesting on its own. Finding something interesting is a response, which means that the art of the interesting lies not in discovering the perfect list of things and circumstances that are interesting to us, but rather in cultivating this responsiveness.

You've already done the prereqs for this one: You've ditched pursuit mode and have stopped the endless cycle of predicting, planning, and evaluating. You've recalibrated your mindset so that it's prone to respond in ways that will bring the interesting. All of this is essential. But it's not enough. Remember those markers of psychological richness? Psychological richness is significantly correlated with novelty and challenge. This is because new and challenging things force the mind to engage in ways that beget the interesting. But if we haven't cultivated our responsiveness to these things, chances are that new and challenging things will have the opposite effect: They can overwhelm and shut down our minds.

Andy's responsiveness to new and challenging things allows him to have such interesting experiences. More generally it's Andy's responsiveness to his instincts, and an unwillingness to be held back by plans and conventions, that's allowed him to build his unique Good Life. And this is what we can learn from him. We can cultivate our responsiveness by learning to listen to our instincts. Our instincts play vital roles in our mental lives. They point us toward certain experiences, making us prone to engage in ways complementary to that experience, much like how Andy captures so many images, so well, on film. And they direct us away from certain experiences, most often the dangerous ones. Learning to trust our instincts allows us to avoid the dangerous experiences that shut down our minds while also feeling safer in the face of new or challenging experiences.

LISTENING TO OUR INSTINCTS

I'll admit that I was surprised at my conversation with Andy. Part of me thought he'd have some great formula of capturing the light, the action, and the textures in a way that made them look interesting. That's how photographers are trained, right? To measure the light, to shoot at the right speed, at the right moment, and so on. And this is how many photographers produce beautiful, captivating images that may or may not be interesting, and that may or may not have been an interesting experience to shoot. That's the thing about formulas: They present the steps necessary to get to a desired end. They give us something to follow, a surefire recipe that anyone can follow—as long as they've got the requisite skills.

In many aspects of our lives, we rely on formulas to do things we lack the instincts to do (or rather, that we think we lack the instincts to do). We've all heard, or maybe said ourselves, "I can follow a recipe, but I can't cook." That's just shorthand for saying you don't trust your instincts in the kitchen. And maybe that's a good thing, if your instincts in the kitchen lead to salt-laden, soggy, or otherwise inedible food.

When we're after a specific goal, like making an edible meal, or taking a shot of Mt. Washington at sunrise, formulas help, especially if we are learning. Our instincts may not naturally get us to our targets. But, as we know already, the interesting isn't like this.* At all. There's no specific target to be had other than the interesting experience itself—which

---

* You know this. This is why we ditch pursuit mode, practice holding space, and develop a taste for the interesting by embracing Mindfulness 2.0, curiosity, and creativity. These are steps, yes, but they are steps aimed at developing the open mindset from which we'll experience the interesting.

emerges from a cultivated perspective. This means we aim to cultivate the perspective, but that's it. Once we've cultivated the perspective, the interesting simply arises.

HOME IN ON YOUR GUT

Now may be a good time to do some soul-searching. Learning to trust your instincts and to tune in to your responsiveness to experiences is a crucial part of the art of the interesting. Yet I imagine a lot of us don't do this or, worse, have trained ourselves to ignore our instincts. Have you ever trusted your gut? What happened? If you haven't, what has held you back?

One helpful, low-stakes way to learn to trust your gut and tune in to your responsiveness is to pay attention the next time you surf the internet or scroll through the daily news feed. The internet is built to capture our attention, and it can do this so quickly we aren't even aware of it. But if we pay attention to what's happening inside us as we read the headlines, or scroll through a Google search, we can tap into our instincts and learn what responsiveness feels like.

So go ahead and pull out the phone or the laptop. Open the news feed or type a random word into Wikipedia. See what you are drawn to. See what sparks your attention. Go ahead and click that link. While you do it, focus on the feelings of being drawn to something, of having your attention sparked. Notice if any new thoughts or questions arise. Notice if you start to feel any emotions rising—anger, shock, intrigue, whatever. Experiencing new thoughts and new emotions signals engagement. It signals the interesting beginning to bubble.

And if it doesn't happen, if you just find yourself bored and are mindlessly clicking, then focus on those feelings instead. They may be more familiar! And while they are the opposite of what we are looking for, they can be equally instructive. Notice that when you are bored and are mindlessly clicking, there is no spark. There is no responsiveness. There are no new thoughts. There are no new emotions. There is nothing. Recognizing the feelings associated with boredom, the feelings that arise when you're not engaged, is just as important as coming to recognize the feelings associated with the interesting and with engagement.

So far, we've talked a lot about how planning, predicting, and evaluating inhibit our experiences of the interesting, and how being mindful, curious, and creative helps us to stimulate the ripples of thoughts and emotions that beget the interesting. It's now time to talk about how to listen to our instincts and home in on our guts.

Our minds strive. They strive to engage. Our instincts point us toward where our minds will engage. If we are after the interesting, we should listen to them. We should learn to recognize our instincts cropping up within us, whispering: "This."

LETTING YOURSELF RESPOND

We've all got instincts. Even if they aren't going to lead us to make the perfect chocolate soufflé, we've all got instincts. And once we've learned to identify their whispers, the next step is to follow those instincts along.

Andy has mastered following his instincts. He's learned to trust his gut and go for it. If you push him further, he'll self-deprecate: The academic life never clicked with him; that way of thinking, of researching, of learning through books and so on, never felt comfortable for him. He made his way through college, through life, learning instead how and when to trust himself. He never got caught up in pursuit mode. What perhaps first or at some times felt like his only option—to go with the gut—became his strongest asset. Case in point: the story he tells of how he and his now-wife, Lisa, ended up moving to our small town in Vermont, where they've lived happily for almost twenty years. They were living in Washington, DC, and were fed up with life in the city. They realized they could do something about it. A week later, they moved to Vermont and never looked back. They never second-guessed.

Most of us have been taught to question our instincts. We're schooled from a very young age to think before deciding, to weigh the consequences, to predict, to plan. And while important, this schooling can lead us away from our gut. It leads us to evaluate one's gut—my gut instinct may be to move away, but does this make sense in the long run?

Andy doesn't question his gut. Maybe there's some sense in which he should, and he'd be the first to say so, but trusting his gut has delivered him one interesting life and afforded him the embarrassing riches of interesting experiences. He keeps a list of the most memorable experience of each trip. Reading just one line from the list will trigger for him the trip in its entirety—the smells, the feelings—leading him to relive those interesting experiences all over again. It is an understandably private list. And he's self-conscious about the privilege of being able to rack up such a list, especially as he's gotten older. But he shouldn't be: It's not the privilege that gave him his Good Life. It's his ability to follow his instincts.

Too often we shy away from following our instincts, especially when they're pointing us to something new or unknown, to deviate from the expected course. Staying on course, following a well-known formula, sticking to the plans and expectations, is the safe route. It's reliable, and for many of us, that counts for a lot. The problem is that there's no formula that can lead you to your best possible life. Certainly, there's no formula that will lead to a psychologically rich life, full of the interesting. This may make learning to follow your instincts feel like a gamble. But it's not a gamble. At all. To allow yourself to listen and respond to your instincts is to open yourself up to interesting experiences.

One thing that's going to help a lot is to reframe your perspective on challenge. Formulas tend to mitigate challenges—this is one of their strengths. It is also one of their weaknesses, especially in the context of the Good Life. Formulas make things easy on us. Cling too heavily to them, and they'll lead us to an unhealthy perspective on challenge, wherein we start seeing challenges as threats to be avoided at all costs. This perspective holds us back from following and responding to our instincts.

"A Good Life doesn't mean an easy one."[1] This was how author and psychologist Alison Gopnik described the central takeaway from our research on psychological richness. She knows what she's talking about:

Her life is one we highlight as a psychologically rich one, and it hasn't been an easy one. Instead, it was full of challenge, like many lives are: divorce, existential life crises, difficult professional navigations. And even so, it was a good one.

WHAT'S YOUR PERSPECTIVE ON CHALLENGE?

This is a quick and important check. We're not all starting with blank slates here. It's likely that your current perspective on challenge has been shaped by your friends, family, and past experiences. Figure out where you are starting from to get a feel for what you might work on.

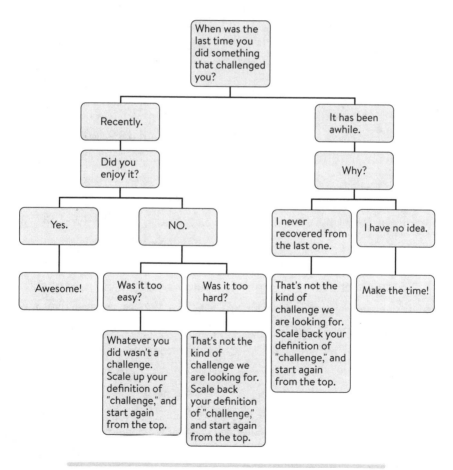

Our research shows there are a lot of people like Gopnik who choose and laud the challenges of life. And it shows that embracing challenges can transform our perspectives, suggesting that we'll all live better lives if we do. Why? Because embracing challenges opens the interesting.

This speaks against the mythology that the Good Life looks and feels like easy street, where we get (and have the resources for) everything we want, and our problems and conflicts simply fade away. Easy street isn't just a hopeless ideal, although of course it is hopeless to think we'll ever get there. It's worse: Easy street won't deliver a Good Life. Living on easy street is a recipe for boredom and a truly impoverished life. If you're on easy street, start opening your eyes for the exits that will challenge you and take you on the road to the Good Life. Your instincts will point you right to them!

FEELING SAFE

Don't let all this talk of embracing challenge mislead you into thinking it's not important to feel safe. Challenges are about degrees of difficulty, about being hard or easy. Just as it's wrong to think of challenges as threats, it's wrong to forget about the importance of feeling safe as you take on challenges. Too often, those comfortable with challenge forget about this very important factor, and they may find themselves threatened in a misguided pursuit of challenge, their minds shut down as a result. Here again, we learn from Andy.

Andy may not be able to pin down how or why he experiences the interesting, but he can describe it.* He's got the stories and they spill quickly. Among the most interesting was a photo shoot he did in the Congo. He and his crew were filming gorillas. One night, after a long hike back to camp, they stumbled upon a handful of forest elephants:

---

* This is an essential tool. As you learn to trust your gut and feel your responsiveness, keep the emphasis on how the experience feels for you, not *what* that activity is, nor *why* it interests or bores you. This is not to say that it isn't an interesting experience to wonder about what you find interesting and why. But that's the advanced stage, after you've gotten the rest of this down.

magnificent beasts emerging from the forest, their huge ears dragging behind their tiny eyes, their tusks dropping from the corners of their smiles, balancing out the drag of the ears.

Andy immediately felt safe. *What???* "I feel safest knowing I'm not the strongest predator," he admitted. "Humans scare me *way* more." His comfort in the wild, being the tiny fly among some of the largest animals known to exist, allows him to see the things most of us would lose sight of, for we'd be frozen in terror, staring at the mammoth size of this animal, scared for our lives. Absent such fears for his own life, Andy is able to hold space for the interesting to flourish, to open that wonderland. He is able to engage, to play with the elephants, to capture their ears wrinkling, their trunks flying up and down as he shoots away.

Interestingly and importantly, this experience was not interesting to *all* the parties involved in that shoot. (Remember, it's the subjective experience that is interesting, and each person experiences the same situation differently!) Andy learned later that his guide for that shoot, a native to the area who'd been showing them around and making these encounters possible, had been terrified at the sight of those elephants encroaching on their camp because the guide's mom had been killed by a forest elephant years before. Andy's guilt at this rises to the surface even (or especially) now, decades later. He feels remorse—stupidity, even—at his obliviousness to the fact that while he was playing with the elephants, trying to get closer and closer, his guide had been struck by fear the whole time, likely traumatized by the very experience Andy found so interesting.

There are probably a few lessons here, but the most salient for us is this: Tuning in to our guts, following our instincts, and embracing challenge help us find the interesting. But to experience the interesting, we've got to feel safe. We can't experience the interesting when we're frozen in terror, when we can't prevent our own thoughts, fears, beliefs, traumas from coloring our experience.

This is Andy's most important lesson for us all. He lets himself respond to the challenges. He follows his gut, rather than back away from the challenges it points him toward. And he's able to do this because he's found his sweet spot, wherein he challenges himself without challenging his sense of safety.

Andy's guide did not have the interesting experience with the forest elephants that Andy had, because his sense of safety was threatened. His fear and his grief made it impossible for him to find the experience interesting. Andy had none of this fear. He felt safe enough to immerse himself in the experience. Perhaps unwisely so, given the male elephant's known tendency to act with such intense aggression during puberty, this aggression has its own word—"musth"—but that's beside the point.

We're all bound by our central nervous systems and the unique ways each person's has developed. Our nervous systems are designed to keep us safe, and through the course of our development we form ways of responding to threats to our safety. Perceived threats trigger the sympathetic nervous system, producing some combination of a fight-flight-or-freeze response.* Our hearts beat faster, our pupils enlarge, our digestion slows, and neurotransmitters fire, all to better equip our bodies and minds to think and act in ways that protect us. We feel one emotion—fear—or none. When our sympathetic nervous system is activated, it dominates. For good reason—to keep us safe—but it does this by inhibiting our mental capacity to do anything else. All of this means we're not going to be able to experience the interesting when our sympathetic nervous system is activated. This is why Andy's guide could not possibly have had an interesting experience. There simply wasn't room within his mind to make it a wonderland and to engage in the ways that stimulate the interesting.

As the differing experiences of Andy and his guide show, each of us develops a unique sense of what constitutes threats to our safety and when our sympathetic nervous system is going to take over. Sometimes

---

* Conversely, the parasympathetic nervous system helps us relax.

these are pathological, as in cases of trauma, wherein a person's central nervous system (CNS) misfires, seeing as threats things that do not currently threaten. But whether pathological or not, if that CNS is screaming "threat," the sympathetic nervous system will kick in, and a physiological reaction will follow that incapacitates one from being able to hold space for the interesting.

Thankfully there is a sweet spot, unique to each of us, but one for all of us. Here's the thing: We know psychological richness involves challenging experiences. We know that to find the interesting we've got to put ourselves out there, and that too much safety can hold us back from experiencing the interesting. Yet we know that if we go too far, and take on too much risk, too much challenge, we are more likely to end up freezing, fighting, or fleeing than having an interesting experience. This is why we should go back to the baby steps. Start with the small challenges, those embedded in an otherwise safe context for you. Then push it out carefully, looking for indications that you've gone too far and the challenge has overwhelmed any chance of finding the interesting.

The circumstances that bring us to that zone of the interesting—the sweet spot of challenge without triggering our nervous system—will be different for everyone. They may even be different for the same person at different times in their life. Our job is to experiment, to learn about ourselves what provides a space safe enough so that we can hold space to engage and to experience the present moment.

Andy's interesting experiences are his. They are unique and not ones we can all experience, nor that we'd all want to experience. We've all got to find our own paths to the interesting, but we can learn from one another. We learn from Andy how important it is to follow our gut, to learn about ourselves and our responsiveness. We also learn just how important feeling safe is to the experience of the interesting. Even though pushing our boundaries helps us find the interesting, we need to learn when we go too far.

SAFE CHALLENGES

As you reorient your perspective toward challenge, it helps to think about the areas in your life where you already do challenge yourself—and enjoy it. Enjoyment arises when we're engaged in an activity that is personally rewarding (for whatever the reason). That you voluntarily take on a challenge and enjoy it tells you it's a safe challenge.

Take a minute to think of the kinds of books, movies, or documentaries that challenge you, but that you enjoy. Maybe it is the movie *12 Years a Slave*, forcing you to confront the realities of racism and feel the pain of the slaves. Or maybe it's the documentary *Conversations with a Killer: The Ted Bundy Tapes*, which simultaneously stimulates disgust and fascination. Or maybe it's an old-fashioned Freddy Krueger–style horror film, putting you on the edge of your seat, or those very scary Gremlins, or Guy Sajer's autobiographical account of his time as a German soldier during World War II. These kinds of media press buttons, but if you enjoy them, that's because they haven't triggered your sympathetic nervous system. This means you feel safe taking them in—even though they challenge you. Can you place yourself now, pull up some of those scenarios in your mind, and feel your mind activating without shutting down? That's a safe challenge, presenting conditions ripe for the interesting.

Now think about the kinds of books, movies, or documentaries you do not enjoy because they are too violent, scary, or depressing. These are the ones you avoid. (For me, this includes all horror movies, especially *Gremlins*.) Just for a second, can you place yourself in one now, and feel its impact on your mind? That's danger bubbling up. Let's not even call that a challenge. That's just the shit we should avoid.

All of this doesn't have to be done solely by trial and error.* We can do a little introspecting to help us along. Start by thinking about your comfort zone. And of course, sorry, its nasty nemesis: your danger zone.

* Although, why not? It could be interesting.

COMFORT ZONES AND DANGER ZONES

While we don't have to jeopardize our safety to find the interesting, we do need to loosen our grip on our safety nets and be willing to move out of our comfort zones. Why? Think about what makes something a comfort zone. It's not just safety. What makes something a comfort zone is that it is familiar. It doesn't challenge or confront. It doesn't force us to think or engage. It doesn't force us to do anything, really. Things are easy and safe. Those pleasant feelings can emerge and flow freely. We can rest in comfort, without a new thought ever entering our mind. Comfort zones feed and restore, stimulating pleasure, perhaps...but that's about it. Staying put in our comfort zones, never finding or pushing our boundaries, is a surefire recipe for a life of boredom.

But look at what happens when we start to move around in that comfort zone and start to push its boundaries. Things become less familiar and comforting and start to feel more laden with uncertainty. Things start to challenge us.

Challenge provides conditions ripe for the interesting, but we are creatures built first and foremost to survive. In the face of uncertainty and challenge, all kinds of mechanisms crop up within us to help us cope. At a biological level, anything new presents a threat, a challenge we must overcome to survive. When we perceive something as a threat (be it consciously or unconsciously), our minds naturally respond by focusing on the sources of the threat, which allows us to reduce it or to remove ourselves from it. Our minds are primed to conquer new situations. This means when faced with any new situation, our tendency is to focus on the novelty to reduce the uncertainties embedded in it. Focusing on novelty triggers cognitive engagement, which is essential to our success in conquering. It is also essential to our experience of the interesting.

Uncertainty triggers focus and engagement but hinders feelings of pleasure. This is one reason why safety and security are so highly correlated with happiness, but not with psychological richness. Safety and security present conditions conducive to feeling pleasure. We give in to the deeply intense and pleasurable sensations of a massage only when we feel safe on the table. If we don't feel safe, maybe because we get a bad vibe from the therapist, or because there is a lot of noise in the hallway and we worry that someone might interrupt and find us naked, we're too activated to give in to the pleasure. These kinds of considerations activate us with the purpose of pointing us back to safety. *Don't give in to the massage,* our body and mind scream. *You are too vulnerable here. You need protection from this stranger, from the strangers outside in the hall.*

WORKSHEET: COMFORT, CHALLENGE, AND DANGER

The only way to learn your zone of the interesting is to start recognizing what it feels like. Luckily, it's the sweet spot between two things we're probably familiar with: our comfort zone and our danger zone. Recognizing what these zones feel like alerts us to when we are in the zone of the interesting and especially to when we've pushed too far and gotten into that danger zone. Remember: Nothing good happens in the danger zone.

The zone	Common descriptions	Good for...	Feels...
Comfort	Your "safe place" "Home" Your "person"	Happiness and pleasure	Relaxing Familiar Restorative [Boring?]
Interesting	An adventure "Pushing the boundaries" "Open your eyes to the world around you" "Follow your instincts wherever they lead" Unusual	Psychological richness and the interesting	Stimulating Engaging Captivating Intriguing Memorable

| Danger | "Do not go / Do not interact"
"Nothing good happens here / from interacting with this person"
The place or person you are only tempted to go to when intoxicated or peer-pressured | Nothing | Threatening
Anxiety-provoking
Heart beating too fast
Can't breathe
Must. Get. Out. Now. |

Now, begin to think about the spaces, places, and interactions that make up your zones. Begin with the descriptions above but try to make them your own. Discover your zones and what they feel like to you!

The zone	Your go-to example	How do these spaces, places, and interactions make you feel?	What other spaces, places, and interactions make you feel like this?
Comfort			
Interesting			
Danger			

Now let's think about your tipping points.

Can you think of a time when your comfort zone morphed into an interesting zone?

Can you think of a time when your interesting zone morphed into a comfort zone?

Can you think of a time when your interesting zone morphed into a danger zone?

How did you know (or how can you know now) when these shifts happened? What are your indicators of the tipping points between your comfort zone and your zone of the interesting? Between your zone of the interesting and your danger zone?

Note that we don't morph or shift anywhere from the danger zone. We can escape the danger zone only by removing ourselves from it. It won't morph into any zone. Do not bother trying. Nothing good happens in or comes from the danger zone.

In response to uncertainty, we develop a heightened awareness of the risks we face. Depending on the degree and nature of the risk, we trigger our nervous system and experience many of the physiological effects associated with anxiety and fear: Our heart starts pounding and sweat starts to trickle. Too much risk and we find ourselves in the danger zone. Nothing good can happen here, for when we're in the danger zone, our nervous system dominates, overriding our cognitive functioning. There's no space to notice, to engage, to explore. Instead, we can only focus on getting back to safety.

But in between too little risk and too much, there's a sweet spot where we can hold space for the interesting. This is where conditions of uncertainty take us out of our comfort zone, yet not to the point where we are in our danger zone. This is the zone of the interesting, where uncertainty comes with enough safety that we can dig our minds into it and start to engage.

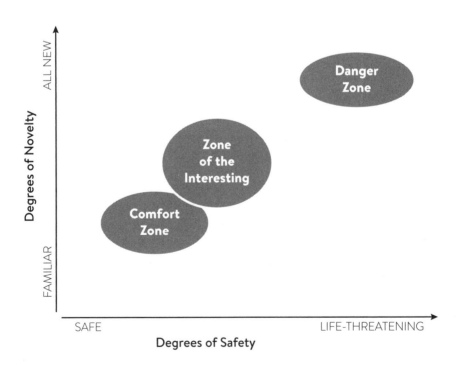

To experience the interesting, we've got to be open to pushing our comfort zone. We need to find a way to be comfortable embracing novelty, challenge, and uncertainty. We can do some of this within our comfort zone, but getting out of our comfort zone offers so much more. Moreover, it doesn't always require us to engage in activities that present actual physical risks. That's one way to bust out of our comfort zone, but it isn't the only way. We bust out of our comfort zone anytime we do something different, even if we don't take on any physical risks. We could go from reading beachy romance novels to reading novels about Charles Manson. We could learn a new language. We could ask a new colleague out for coffee. The point is to try out new territory, even if it presents risk, and to not cling so much to our comfort zones that we never get to the zone of the interesting.

As we challenge ourselves, it helps to be clear about what we're after. And because what counts as a challenge is unique to each of us, there's no one-size-fits-all prescription that will define this for us. Instead, what we've got to do is focus on our feelings. By learning to recognize when we're within our comfort zones, and when we're in our danger zones, we'll make progress on finding our zones of the interesting.

EMBRACING THE ZONE OF THE INTERESTING

On the Adirondack shores of Lake Champlain there lies the scary-as-shit Rattlesnake Mountain. On this mountain, massive black timber rattlesnakes enjoy protected, free rein. And, yes, they have rattles and are just as poisonous as the rattlesnakes that hang out in the desert.

Snakes are by far the scariest thing for me to even think about. Yet sometimes I can't stop thinking about those damn rattlesnakes. I've only seen one once, and it was dead—roadkill so dark, textured, and bulky that it looked from the distance like a torn tire abandoned in the road.

Every spring, the rattlesnakes come down from the mountain, toward the lake, to find a sunny place to warm their bodies after the long winter hibernation. There is some unofficial boundary in the area the rattlesnakes are known to respect, a line they haven't yet crossed. I wonder: *How can snakes respect a boundary? And, please, please, how can I help them?*

My friends Chris and Lexi live within their boundaries and occasionally find these huge beasts in their lawn, or in the compost bin. One spring Chris noticed something swimming and caught on video footage of a rattlesnake swimming to shore. Rattlesnakes aren't supposed to swim, but there's no question this is a rattlesnake in the video. He zoomed in on its little rattler, announcing to all the havoc and terror it was ready to wreak.

I have watched that video too many times. It scares the living shit out of me. It makes me look differently at the water on my beloved lake. It makes me wonder how they float, and how they swim. Could humans do a similar stroke, just wiggling their bodies? Watching that video, and thinking about these rattlesnakes, hidden in the woods or, so much worse, swimming along in the water with me, remains one of the most interesting and most unpleasant experiences I've had. I'm reliving it now, even as I write.* I'm wondering, again, how snakes can respect a boundary and if learning to swim might make their reach greater. I'm one step away from physically shaking...But my mind is on fire. The intrigue catches every time.

Our most interesting experiences do often involve unpleasant sensations and the emotions they are associated with—anxiety, fear, shock. The ripples of the interesting involve thoughts that stimulate new emotions and new emotions that stimulate new thoughts. The ripples aren't always comfortable, nor pleasant, and there's no guarantee when we start where we'll end up.

I can get my thoughts rippling by thinking about rattlesnakes from my desk, tucked safely away across the lake in Vermont, but there is

---

* Even as I revise and reread. Every time.

no way I could feel anything but terror if I saw one stretched out in front of me.

By coming to understand the boundaries of our individual comfort zones and of our danger zones, we learn how to find our zones of the interesting. I learn that snakes can be in my zone of the interesting only if they are not physically present. My comfort zone? Dominated by dogs, teenage boys, classrooms, arguments, and water. My danger zone? Snakes, very high cliffs, and packs of toddlers. Identifying the boundaries distinctive to our zones helps us see where we can push them, and what to avoid, as we find our zone of the interesting. I can push out of my comfort zone by reading one of my husband's favorite travelogues from sixteenth-century explorers. He could push out of his by reading some of the books I've written. I push myself out of my comfort zone when I give a talk to a public audience full of adults. I'm pushing myself out of my comfort zone right now in writing this book, my first for a truly public audience.

I know better than to push my comfort zone by volunteering at my children's former childcare center, which is raging full of needy, wild toddlers. I know better than to push my comfort zone by hiking Rattlesnake Mountain in the spring, or, let's face it, by ever stepping foot on that damn thing. You can take a second to think through your comfort and danger zones. Where can you push your boundaries? Which boundaries are you better off respecting than pushing? What does your zone of the interesting look like?

In this chapter we've learned how much more interesting it can be to follow your gut, rather than always stamping out its whispers. And once you've mastered your zone of the interesting by pushing out of your comfort zone, while always keeping a fair distance from the danger zone, there's no reason to hold back. When you're in the interesting zone, you can embrace fully and engage with challenge, feel the thoughts ripple and your emotions arise, over and over again. You're becoming the master of this whole enterprise.

KEEPING IT INTERESTING

Learning how to hone our guts and letting ourselves respond to them is key to developing the art of the interesting, but too often many of us shy away from our instincts, held back by the threat of challenge. The upshot of this is that we stay in our comfort zone, where life gets boring. Reframing our perspective on challenge allows us to experience more of the interesting, but only if we've tapped into the feelings of safety and of danger, and of the tipping points between our interesting zone and our danger zone.

Chapter 9:

Harnessing the Power of Novelty

IN COLLEGE I HAD THE GREAT FORTUNE TO STUDY ABROAD ON A ship that took me and my shipmates—some three hundred of us— around the world, literally, in one hundred days. It was the opportunity of a lifetime. The sheer mass of valuable experiences I collected during that time sometimes leaves me in awe.

Yet the thing about sailing around the world is that there's a lot of time in between, spent on the ship, with nothing to do. And then there would be *the* most exciting thing to do ever. As I think back on this time, it's the extremes that stand out. The thrills of walking along the Great Wall. A crazy flight from Odessa to Siberia, during which we drank vodka and smoked cigarettes with Russian flight attendants in the cargo area of the plane. A solo retreat at a monastery in the hills of Taipei, reachable only by foot. The insane glory of seeing the stone "jail" near the Acropolis—more like a cave—where Socrates spent his final days before drinking the hemlock that killed him. And then, the boredom of spending day after day on the same ship, looking out at the same horizon, for days on end, often with nothing to see but the same open water. The endless card games of War I played with my new friend Kate, one after the other, after the other, after the other. We all had our own tricks to pass the time while we waited for the next adventure. Kate and I went on from that trip to become lifelong friends and travelers. When you can sit with someone for hours, spending easy time, day after day—well, that means you're with someone you should be with.

The first stretch at sea was the longest: a two-week journey across the Pacific Ocean, from Vancouver, BC, to Kyoto, Japan. To prepare for our arrival in Japan, my friend Sarah (not a new friend, but a childhood friend I was shocked and delighted to see on the ship that first day) and I were determined to become expert chopstick users, having both grown up in the same small town, which, at the time, offered zero opportunities for chopstick use. We spent two weeks using chopsticks to eat everything from salads to Jell-O. We couldn't wait to get off the ship and show off our chops. And we were so disappointed when the waiter at the first sushi "train" we hit handed us plastic forks.* What did we look like, after all? Two white college girls who'd just stepped off a ship, I guess.

It seems so silly that we did that. It seems silly that we thought learning to eat with chopsticks would help us feel less like tourists. And that part *was* silly. But what wasn't silly, and what *is* an important lesson, is how trying to eat with chopsticks for two weeks made that time so much more interesting than it would have otherwise been. And decades later, I will never look at Jell-O the same way. Trying to scoop up this jiggly, bright red substance with two sticks taught me more about the nature of substance than years of reading Descartes.† I remember the delicate precision it required to gently press on the middle without breaking it apart. I remember how, when it inevitably did break apart, two new shapes would form, amazingly just as contained in themselves as the first initial blob.

It's not that I had never eaten Jell-O. I was born in the 1970s, after all, and spent more than a decade at summer camp. I knew Jell-O. The

---

* Sushi trains are restaurants that serve sushi, on small plates, on conveyor belts. You grab what you want and pay per plate.

† Descartes believes that substance can be material *or* immaterial, and famously maintains that our minds are immaterial substances, while our bodies are distinct, material substances.

point is that changing one little thing can transform your experience of something entirely. It can make eating Jell-O, even for the billionth time, an interesting experience. And it's crazy, isn't it, that I've just sat down, raided my mind for the most interesting memories of this amazing adventure, and landed on eating Jell-O with chopsticks.

What makes something novel for any one person depends entirely on their past experiences. Fall foliage—not at all novel for someone raised in New England (although still interesting to experience and to think about), but so very novel for many others.* Novelty presents whenever you do/encounter/explore something you're not familiar with. Maybe you haven't experienced it before. Maybe you have experienced it before but not noticed it.

While everything new is novel, something can be novel without being new. In classrooms we often talk about taking a novel approach to an old text. It's the same thing as having "fresh eyes." When we take a new perspective on something familiar, we make it novel. Fresh eyes erase the familiarity, transforming it into a novel experience.

And if that Jell-O story didn't make this clear: Novelty comes in degrees. Things can be totally and completely new, such as visiting Japan for the very first time, or just kind of new, like returning to Japan and staying in a new part of the city, or even just barely new, such as when you take fresh eyes to a favorite old film and notice a new sentence, laugh, or outfit. When it comes to the interesting, it doesn't matter whether novelty is big or small, just that you've noticed it.† Whatever its size, whatever its degree, it'll prompt the interesting.

You see, novelty puts you on the autobahn and takes you quickly and easily to interesting experiences. At this point, that shouldn't be entirely surprising. Novelty functions in our minds much like challenges: stimulating, forcing ripples of thoughts and emotions. And while we all get in those ruts where it feels like nothing is new, everything is familiar,

---

* We call them "leaf-peepers" who take over during "leaf-peeping season."
† This is one reason why Mindfulness 2.0 is so important. Without it, your mind is going to shoot right past those little bits of novelty.

boring...well, that's rarely actually the case. Novelty is at the tip of our fingers, no matter where or what we are doing.

You've already ditched pursuit mode, mastered the mindset of the interesting, and discovered your zone of the interesting. And I know you are revved up and roaring to go. You're ready to get on the autobahn.

NOVELTY AND PSYCHOLOGICAL RICHNESS

Novelty is a marker of psychological richness and presents one of the clearest correlations we see. Novelty goes hand in hand with a psychologically rich life but isn't a distinctive aspect of either meaningful lives or happy lives. A quick look at the values driving these lives explains why. That something is new doesn't have any bearing on whether it is fulfilling. Feelings of fulfillment derive from reflection concerning the relationship between your pursuits and the objective value they add to the world. Sure, there's a sense in which novelty offers the opportunity for accomplishment: Sarah and I felt a fleeting sense of accomplishment when we mastered the art of eating Jell-O with chopsticks, but neither one of us would ever claim this as a source of fulfillment.

That something is new does have bearing on whether it delivers pleasure. Seeking new sources of pleasure can help block the nullifying effects of adaptation. After bingeing on chocolate ice cream for a month, vanilla starts to taste pretty good. These kinds of changes help to keep pleasant feelings flowing. But as you'll remember from chapters 2 and 8, in the long run, happiness is more strongly correlated with safety, comfort, and security than it is with novelty. It is easy to see why: Safety, comfort, and security provide us with a base from which we can increase and broaden these feelings. Take away that safety net, and it's quite simply that much harder to *feel* the good feelings, to allow them to develop and expand so that they shape our life. That's why comfort zones are comfort zones. They block out the novelty, preventing those feelings of uncertainty, of risk, from ever cropping up. Yet, of course, in blocking out novelty, comfort zones make it that much harder to find the interesting.

Think, for a second, about what happens when you experience something new—anything new. Yesterday, I was playing tennis with (the creative and analytic...and fantastic tennis player) Emily, and met a new person, Don, who was playing on the courts next to us. At first, I was nervous. I've been playing for only a few months, and he'd talked us into a doubles match with his friend Ron, which I was convinced would be, well, very embarrassing for me. But we had a great chat about philosophy, psychology, yoga, happiness, grief, Martin Seligman (of the positive psychology movement), and William James (a philosopher or a psychologist, depending on whom you ask)—all in the course of five or ten minutes. Even as we were talking, I felt my mind shift. The nerves faded away. I was excited. And my mind was on fire.

"Ohh, I should get him to teach/lead a section on yoga and happiness in my class!"

"Yes. I need to finally get into William James."

As I wake up this morning, it feels like meeting Don was the most memorable part of my day, even though it was the shortest and least "important" part of my day. And I'm having such an interesting experience right now remembering it.

How is it possible that Don has lived here for four years, and I have not met him?

Maybe my town is not so small after all.

How many more people are there in this town with so much to contribute to my thoughts on happiness and well-being?

I've been down on my town lately, and all of this makes me optimistic. I feel rejuvenated. I wonder:

How can I find them?

How can I turn finding them into an adventure?

Whether novelty arises from a short encounter with a new person, from sailing around the world, or from using new utensils to eat your lunch, novelty activates your mind. And if you run with it, novelty activates the interesting.

PLAYING WITH NOVELTY

Can you mine your mind for something new that happened yesterday? Don't overthink it. Don't bypass the little things. Something new happened yesterday. I promise. New construction on the drive to work? New pen to write with? New lunch spot? New record temperature? Start small. Then let your mind make it big. See what thoughts come up. See how they make you feel. Notice how you are different afterward. Pretty cool, huh?

The powers of novelty to beget interesting experiences are remarkable. And to take advantage of it? Sometimes, all you have to do is use that Mindfulness 2.0 to notice it.

NOTICING THE NOVELTY

There are all sorts of ways to embrace novelty. One way, as we've seen, is simply noticing it. Change happens all around us, in big and little ways. And change, well, changes things. It makes them new. We can stimulate the interesting by witnessing the change and appreciating the novelty it introduces.

In my part of the world, we have not four, not five, but six distinct seasons: winter, mud, spring, summer, fall, and stick. Stick season crops up after the leaves fall, but before the snow comes. It's the worst, next only to mud season. Mud season crops up when the snow melts and, yes, *everything* turns to mud. Vermonters argue about whether there's a second stick season around mud season, and I personally deny there is ever a spring season in Vermont, but you get the idea. Every few months, the weather turns drastically, making everything around you remarkably different. The very same drive goes from glorious green to bursts of red and orange popping like fireworks. Then, in the blink of an eye, there's just brown. Everywhere. Finally, the snow comes, painting the brown sticks, carpeting the dead hay fields, and all is right with the world. At least that's how it goes for me.

Lots of people resist the changing of the seasons. It's totally understandable. They cling to the last day of summer or begrudge those first beautiful snowflakes and prepare to shut down for the next five months. I get it. I often find myself clinging to those last days of summer. Hard. But there's no good to be had by resisting the change of seasons. When things are changing around you, and are beyond your control, you've got a choice. You can fight it or you can embrace it. Fighting it won't change anything. Embracing it can change everything.

Near my old house, there's a chunk of forest littered with different trails—little offshoots that have been created over the years by hikers and mountain bikers. I've done dozens of trail runs in these woods. I can't even begin to describe the number of times I've gotten lost in these woods. The woods are so dense that you can take off on one random trail and suddenly have no idea where you are. The chunk of forest is small—probably no more than two square miles in all—but the trails work like a labyrinth, winding with no reason. Running those trails is an adventure, and every time is different.

What's most magical about experiencing these trails, though, is taking in the impact of the seasons. By the end of the summer, maybe, I've developed confidence in my routes. I've formed some signposts in my mind to look out for. I've become light on my feet, easily able to avoid the rocks and crevices begging to trip me. Once those leaves drop? The experience becomes completely different. The forest becomes carpeted in brilliant red, yellow, and orange leaves. All the trails are hidden and whatever sign points I'd grown used to become useless. The leaves make it more slippery and hide the rocks. I need to think about every step. Fall brings hunting season as well, and there's gunshots in the distance. The dogs wear bright orange vests, and I must keep them close. Over the next few months, we develop new routines, signposts, running styles. And then the weather changes again, making everything different. The experience starts anew, over and over.

It's all the same woods. It's all the same trails. But the changes force me to engage, presenting different challenges that generate different emotions.

The seasonal changes are so drastic where I live, they force confrontation. That's helpful. It leads us to notice the differences. And if we don't let the changes hold us back—keep us in our houses and on our treadmills—they offer opportunities to experience the interesting.

Changes happen all around us, though, wherever we are. The sun sets at different times during the year, lighting up different areas with its glow. By being aware and present within our surroundings, we can make sure we notice the novelty change brings. And by embracing rather than resisting the changes, we set ourselves up for a range of interesting experiences that we would have otherwise missed.

THE TRAP OF SENSATION

Noticing novelty enriches our everyday lives. Yet we don't always have to sit around and notice changes to find novelty. We can create novelty within our lives, and we can pursue novelty. Both set us up for the interesting. As we get on novelty's autobahn, though, it's going to help to keep in mind the features and nature of interesting experiences. We're not after novelty for the sake of novelty. We're after novelty for the interesting experiences it prompts. If we lose sight of this, our pursuit of novelty may veer off course, and we may very well find ourselves in a sensation-seeking trap.

Novelty, risk, and openness to experience are all significantly correlated with psychological richness. Yet they are also correlated with sensation-seeking. Sensation-seekers consistently pursue bigger and bigger risks for the sake of the adrenaline rush they deliver. On the outside, a life of sensation-seeking may look like a psychologically rich one. Sensation-seekers prefer to live outside their comfort zones, and their lives are chock-full of novel, varied, and complex experiences. A life of sensation-seeking can easily be confused with a psychologically rich life. If we're not careful in our efforts to introduce psychological richness to our lives, we may find ourselves sensation-seeking instead of experiencing the interesting.

Risk-taking helps to bring the interesting by introducing novelty and challenge, and sometimes may even be necessary to experience the interesting. But those prone to sensation-seeking take risk-taking overboard. They become propelled by the risk itself and start to seek out risk for its own sake. Their risk-taking becomes sensation-seeking. The problem with this is that sensation-seeking doesn't make for a Good Life. Sensation-seeking leads people to drive fast, have risky sex, and to abuse alcohol and drugs. Sensation-seeking becomes addictive, to the point that sensation-seekers create stress and tension in their lives, for that's how they thrive.

There's a fine line here, but it's a hugely important one. It again goes back to the values at stake in life, and the importance of understanding what we are after in our pursuit of a Good Life. When we look at things from this level, we see that sensation-seekers are not searching for psychological richness, nor are they experiencing the interesting. This is because sensation-seeking tracks pleasure rather than interest. To develop psychological richness within our lives, we want to pursue feelings of interest, not sensation.

Remember those studies of boredom that left subjects alone, bored, and with the opportunity to shock themselves? Lots of folks, especially the men, chose to give themselves electric shocks in the face of boredom. That's a classic sensation-seeking response to boredom. It alleviates boredom through introducing sensations. Whether those sensations are positive or negative, the stimulus they deliver occupies one's attention. It takes one's focus away from the boring environment and toward the sensation. Because it solves boredom by taking the focus away from the environment, it is a disengagement strategy.

As a coping mechanism for boredom, sensation-seeking works…but only in the short term. What happens is that sensation-seeking becomes addictive, in much the same sense that drug use can become addictive.

The person starts to depend on stimulation and the adrenaline rush that it brings. They recalibrate their expectations. Boredom, for them, starts to consist in the absence of sensation. And to avoid boredom, they seek greater depths of sensation. They begin to approach their activities for the sake of the rush they bring them and introduce greater and greater levels of danger to maintain the rush. They'll start arguments around them and begin to prefer chaos and stress for the challenges they bring, challenges that come with the elusive promise of that rush. They'll overbook their schedules, running from place to place, to keep that adrenaline pumping.

Many of us know what this feels like and the temptation it offers. There's certainly been times in my life when adrenaline was the only thing sustaining me. In my case, I don't think it was because I was deliberately seeking sensation, but for complicated reasons I ended up in this place. It's not a good place. Adrenaline drives you, stimulating and sustaining you at a high pace, but it doesn't feel good. The sensations never really settle. It's almost as if they promise pleasure and never deliver. I can see how easy it is to get caught up in this cycle. And I've learned the hard way how important it is to avoid. Our minds and bodies just aren't meant to always operate like this. Adrenaline rushes are meant to save us; they aren't meant to sustain us. When we rely on adrenaline to sustain us, we set ourselves up to crash and burn.

How can we embrace novelty and risk without falling into the addictive cycle of sensation-seeking? We do this by keeping in mind that what we're after is something that stimulates cognitive engagement. The interesting arises within our minds. It impacts how we feel by stimulating new thoughts. When we're sensation-seeking, we're guided by our bodies rather than our cognitive engagement. By paying attention to the difference between the physically based adrenaline rush that often rewards the pursuit of novelty and the cognitive nature that engagement with novelty brings, we keep ourselves on course.

ENGAGEMENT STRATEGIES

Novelty generates the interesting through stimulating cognitive engagement, which begets new emotions. Novelty can also generate new sensations. If this sensation-seeking stuff sounds all too familiar—a trap you know is set for you—then it'll help to keep your focus on the cognitive side as you seek to embrace novelty. We want to find novelty within our experiences to help us engage more robustly, rather than using novelty to disengage from those experiences.

We find loads of examples of this difference in orientation within research on coping with boredom. One classic study examined long-haul truckers, stuck alone on the road for hours and hours at a time.[1] They found, consistently, that those best at coping with boredom did so by using engagement strategies, rather than disengagement strategies. For example, rather than daydreaming about beaches and sun, they noticed deer on the side of the road, signaled to other drivers, made observations and comments about other drivers, or pointed out changes in the roads and updates to construction projects.[2]

Engagement strategies are all about interacting with the environment in ways that introduce subjective variety into one's experience. We enrich our experiences by finding the variety within them, even if this happens by engaging with or introducing into the mix features otherwise irrelevant to the task at hand.

Looking again at the truck drivers, each of the engagement strategies the drivers turned to introduced things that are largely irrelevant to the mechanics of driving a truck, but they each have the effect of introducing variety to the driver's subjective experience, thereby preventing the monotony that leads to boredom. Were the driver instead focused narrow-mindedly on a single aspect of the task—say, delivering on time—he'd be blocking out these sources of variety, leaving him very much bored and disengaged from his experience overall.

This observation is consistent with related research on workplace boredom, which finds that the most significant factors influencing boredom are not objective ones, such as how monotonous the task is.

Rather, it turns out that our subjective perception of the situation has more influence on our levels of boredom than do the objective features of the situation. It's not what we are given, but how we perceive what we are given. Once again, we see the power of a mindset.

HOW CAN YOU ENGAGE?

So much depends on our ability to see the novelty around us, and to allow it to stimulate our minds. We learn from the truckers, though, just how helpful it is to be active in this enterprise. Active engagement strategies help us find and embrace variety in our experience.

Dr. Jason Duvall, who's done a ton of research on experiences in nature, describes engagement strategies in terms of "awareness plans": specific strategies we can invoke to become more aware of our environment, thereby facilitating our engagement.[3] It's a cool approach we can use in any context. The engagement strategies follow a formula, which is essentially adopting another perspective or way to view our surroundings. Try one out now!

1. See with your senses: Pick one sense to focus on—for example, sound. Focus in on the sounds around you. Are they different? Is it quiet?
2. Pretend you're in a different role and look around from that perspective. What would an artist choose to paint here? What would a spiritual person tap into right now?
3. Make guesses or predictions. "If I changed this little piece up, what would happen?" Or, "What will this space look like in twenty years?"
4. Think beyond what is possible. "If I had a magic wand, what would I change right now?"

The best tricks are those that allow us to engage with the context of what we're doing rather than disengage from it, either by focusing very narrowly on just one aspect of what we're doing, or by removing our focus on what we're doing entirely (such as by shocking ourselves). When we're engaged with what we're doing, we're priming the interesting to take off.

RISK-TAKING, THE INTERESTING WAY

We want to avoid the trap of sensation-seeking, and we do this by approaching novelty in the spirit of cognitive engagement, with that mindset of the interesting in place. But we don't want to shy away from risk entirely. Developing a healthy attitude toward risk-taking is essential to the art of the interesting. Taking risks allows us to get out of our boring comfort zones and find novelty. All of this sets us up for the interesting to arise.

What does a healthy attitude toward risk-taking look like, though? Author and legendary risk-taker Hunter S. Thompson once wrote, "Life should not be a journey to the grave with the intention of arriving safely in a pretty and well-preserved body, but rather to skid in broadside in a cloud of smoke, thoroughly used up, totally worn out, and loudly proclaiming 'Wow! What a Ride!'"[4]

He gets it half right. The journey of life shouldn't be all about making the safe choices. What kind of journey would that be, after all? (Obvs: a boring one.) He's wrong about the flip side, though. There's more to life than the ride. At the end of our lives, don't we want to be able to say something *more* than "What a ride"? Shouldn't we at least be striving to make it a good ride?

We live our best possible lives when we experience value in them. Risk-taking introduces novelty into our lives, which can stimulate the interesting, and that makes it a valuable strategy. But that's the piece Thompson neglects. As we embrace risk-taking, we need to remember why we're doing it. It's not—or really shouldn't be—about the risks themselves. When we forget what we are after, when risk-taking takes the shape of risk for the sake of risk, this warps its effects on our lives.

As a fan, it pains me to say this: This is the effect we see within Hunter S. Thompson's "Wow! What a Ride!" line. His attitude here reflects a relish for experiences, whatever their flavor. There's a lot of people who share this attitude, even adopt it on purpose. They go after and embrace experiences without reflecting on what they will get from those experiences. They go after experiences without concern for their meaning or purpose, even without concern for the pleasure they will derive from them. They have a distinctive attitude toward their experiences. It's an attitude very close to one that leads us to a psychologically rich life.

If we are going for a predominantly psychologically rich life, ripe with the interesting at every bite, we do give up a life structured by meaning and break free from the stability and security that bring happiness. We ditch pursuit mode. We stop evaluating the experiences that come our way and just go for them. We embrace experiences even when they come with unpleasant emotions. But unlike experience collectors, who embrace experiences without always being aware of what they derive from them, those living a psychologically rich life keep an eye on the extent to which their experiences deliver the interesting.

When I was a very young adult, I traveled around India for a summer. I was doing volunteer work, hitting monasteries for meditation retreats, trying to pull off the legendary surprise visit to the Dalai Lama's house*—doing a lot of things in the spirit of finding fulfillment—but I also spent a lot of time just traveling. There's something about the people and the country that calls to me, and immersing myself in the

---

* I will share. The Dalai Lama lives in the hills of Dharamsala in Northern India. At least when I was traveling, it was possible to arrange a visit with him, but you had to write a letter months in advance and then somehow receive a letter, while you were traveling, confirming your visit. (Yes, this was before email.) This was complicated. But you'd hear stories of people who just showed up, uninvited, rang the doorbell, and then sat down to have an intimate conversation with the Dalai Lama. You'd never meet someone who actually did this, but...legendary, irresistible. I was all set to do a pop-in during my visit to Dharamsala (or at least I told myself, and talked a lot with others about how to do it). And, alas, His Holiness was out of town. Very anticlimactic.

crowded streets and buses, walking through the dusty, busy markets, allowed me some of the most interesting experiences I've had.*

You can imagine the kinds of fellow travelers I crossed paths with. Many, like me, were there for a limited time with some sort of purpose in mind, giving their travels some structure. Others were not like me. At all. They'd been traveling for years, living on the edge. You could pinpoint them by the ease with which they moved through the bustling markets, by the clothes that by this point hung like rags off their slim frames, by their comfort walking around in sandals with very dirty feet, and by the dead looks in their eyes. It was their eyes that stuck out the most to me, that identified them as travelers in it for the long haul.

At first, I thought their eyes looked dead because they were on or had done so many drugs. But after a few failed encounters to engage with them, I realized it wasn't the drugs. Their eyes were dead because their minds were fried. They'd been on the road so long, had seen and had so many interesting experiences, that their minds just couldn't check in anymore. It's like me at the end of a long writing day: There's nothing there. Don't bother trying to have a conversation with me because I've got nothing to share. I'm fried.

That's the one limit of the interesting: As a species of cognitive engagement, it's dependent on our mind's capacity to engage, and that's a limited capacity. It's an amazing and profound capacity. While our minds are equipped with ways to preserve and protect that capacity,† our minds are simply not infinite, capable of churning out the interesting without limit. When our minds are too tired, the ripples slow to a grind. We may find ourselves lost in one thought that we're never really able to fixate on, that never goes anywhere. Or we may find ourselves

---

* Last fall, I returned to India after thirty years, with travel soulmate Kate. It did not disappoint.

† We talked about this in chapter 3. Our mind likes to make things easier on us, so it builds scripts of our habitual actions that get triggered automatically. That's why so many things are akin to "riding a bike": Once we start such a thing, our brain triggers a script, and it all comes back to us.

with no thoughts at all. When this happens, we don't literally shut down, stop moving, stop doing. We'll still move and do; we just won't be thinking. We won't notice. We most certainly won't feel the tickle of curiosity rising, and we most certainly won't feel creative. We'll just move and do.

SIGNS THAT YOUR MIND IS BURNING OUT

I'm most definitely not an expert in recognizing the signs of burnout and stopping before it happens. I'm much more familiar with the effects of burn-out. (So is my family!) This is something I struggle with, and it's likely we've all struggled with burnout at one point or another. But as I always tell my children, every time I fail on yet another plan ("I will cook dinner every night this week!" Ha), it's all about getting back after it. Even if we learn through trial and error, it's all about getting back up again and making the effort.

What are some of the signs of burnout? And what do they feel like to you?

Warning signs!	How they feel to me	How they feel to you
Loss of focus	"What was I just thinking about?"	
Lack of recall	"Why am I here?" "2 + 5 = ?????????????"	
Adrenaline kicking in for the rescue	"Here we go. Nothing else matters. Just keep going."	
Detachment	"Are my pets and children literally starving? Maybe." "Did I just walk right through a bustling, colorful, dusty Delhi market and not notice anything? I guess I did."	

These long-haul travelers had burned out long ago yet kept going. They had experiences and they collected experiences, over and over.

But they no longer experienced value in them. They couldn't. Their lives, which at one point no doubt felt like a seemingly endless chain of interesting experiences, became dull, void of value. At this point their lives consisted in one experience after the next, none of which they were fully present for, none of which stimulated anything close to the ripples of the interesting. Perhaps you have experienced this for yourself after too many hours in a museum, or on the fourth day of presentations at a weeklong conference—too much new information all at once and, suddenly, you just can't take in any more. The value of the novelty has worn off. It's not doing you any favors. And it's time for a pause.

ENHANCED EXPERIENCES

Sometimes we talk about going after experiences for the sake of experience, and it is true this attitude will help us experience psychological richness. But if we always just go after experiences, at some point we'll burn out. If we don't realize it and keep going and going, we end up like the long-haul traveler. Fried, and capable only of going through the motions of life.

The problem arises when we go after experiences for the sake of experience, forgetting what makes experiences valuable. If we don't have our eyes on the interesting and if we aren't tapped into the nature of the interesting, we set ourselves up to burn out, with few resources to turn it around. At this point, it becomes all too easy to use drugs and alcohol to enhance those experiences.

Many of the long-haul travelers I met that summer in India were doing a lot of drugs. The drugs added a dimension of value to their experiences that they craved and could no longer deliver themselves. Walking through the markets stoned added just a little something to that experience, and maybe a much-needed little something, for they'd long lost the ability to find the markets interesting using their own minds.

Recreational drugs enhance your experiences. They deliver value to your experiences. They can make things more pleasurable. And, yes, they can make things more interesting. This is why people like them. They promise a shortcut, an easy route to more valuable experiences. That's the allure, especially for those still clinging to the idea that the Good Life is supposed to be an easy one. That you have made it to chapter 9 of this book suggests you think otherwise. And I think most of us do.

There's a great thought experiment we talk a lot about in philosophy. You may have heard it before. It goes like this: Suppose there is an "experience machine" capable of delivering whatever experience you want.[5] You just punch in the experiences you're after, plug in, and get them. And that's how you live, plugged into a machine, experiencing all that you've ever imagined, and nothing that you don't want to experience. Do you plug in?

Most people would not. Time and time again, classroom after classroom, only one or two students end up saying they'd plug in. It's not just my students, it's everywhere. Very few people would choose to live in an experience machine. We can strive to find some deep explanation of why, but it also seems very straightforward: We'd rather have and be in control of our own experiences, in the moment, even if that opens us up to the possibility of having bad experiences. The easy route offered by the experience machine seems cheap and artificial, impossible to truly capture the rewards of living.

Remember the dystopian feel of Huxley's *Brave New World*, where people pop pills for pleasure? Even removing the threat of addiction, the picture is grim: a world of superficiality, where nothing seems to matter, for you can always just pop a pill and take off to another dimension, where all you feel is pleasure. This image doesn't leave us jumping out of our seats, thinking pills are the solution. We know better than that. It's a mistake to rely on drugs to develop value within your life.

It's not that you can't enjoy, indulge, or benefit from taking drugs. And it'd be ungenuine of me to deny the allure psychedelics have to deliver interesting experiences. For sure, my first time taking mushrooms was one of the most memorable experiences I've had. (It was the trees! The tiny buds!) But I hesitate to say it was a truly interesting experience, for the same reason I hesitate to say the experience machine delivers what it's truly like to live. The fast and easy route just isn't the same. We shouldn't mistake it as a substitute for interesting experiences, and we shouldn't rely on it to make our experiences interesting.

Thankfully, we can avoid having to resort to drugs to add value to our lives. By learning when to stop going after experiences, by acknowledging that our brains are limited and will burn out, and by giving ourselves time to restore, we'll position ourselves to derive value from our experiences.

This is where it comes back to the major benefit of knowing the art of the interesting. Recognizing the value experiences offer helps us to recognize when our experiences are no longer valuable. If we know we are after the interesting, we're going to stop simply collecting experiences well before the long-haul traveler does, if he ever stops. We're going to go home, to rest and to restore in our comfort zones. And then we can get back on the road.

YOU DON'T HAVE TO FLY SOMEWHERE TO EXPERIENCE NOVELTY

One of the best things about novelty is how accessible it is, and so how easy it is to find the interesting. There are also all kinds of ways to change up the little things around us, even when we are stuck in the same location, among the same people. Use chopsticks instead of a fork. Change up your handwriting and make note-taking more interesting. Take the back roads to work. Engage with the convenience store clerk you see every day. Start hitting a new coffee shop, or start hitting your favorite coffee shop at a different time of day. Pull something to wear from the depths of your closet. Get bangs. The little bits of novelty count.

Changing up the little things introduces novelty and stimulates the interesting without requiring us to do anything dramatic. We don't have to shake up our lives and transform them to make them better.

We can make them better by changing up the little things, by seizing opportunities to explore, be it vicariously or in person, and by noticing the changes around us. That's the power of novelty.

KEEPING IT INTERESTING

Novelty provides the fast track to the interesting and is easily accessible, but we've got to approach it carefully. The pursuit of novelty can morph into sensation-seeking, experience collecting, and risk for the sake of risk. By approaching novelty with an eye toward cognitive engagement, by embracing engagement strategies, and by looking for signs we're burning out, we'll keep ourselves on the fast track to the interesting.

Chapter 10:

Turning Obstacles into Adventures

GREEK MYTHOLOGY TELLS THE LEGEND OF SISYPHUS, A MAN who pissed off the gods so much, he was sentenced to an eternity spent doing one thing, and one thing only: pushing a massive boulder up to the top of a steep hill, where it'd fall back down and need to be pushed up again.

The myth of Sisyphus has come to represent many different things over the years.* Existential philosophers take the story to illustrate the complete meaninglessness of life, viewing Sisyphus's life as parallel to each of ours: We all try to keep pursuing, accomplishing something, contributing...but the reality is such that we'll never succeed. There's no way to get ahead. Our lives are all like Sisyphus's, presenting tasks that never amount to anything yet at the same time we can't help but take seriously. One obstacle after another, we strive to find something more in life than exists.

Maybe our lives are all like Sisyphus's. Maybe they aren't. One thing is for sure: Obstacles abound. Whatever form and shape they take, we each will have boulders to push up a mountain. And the attitude we take toward them has a decisive impact on our lives.

---

* Interestingly, none of them seem to be anywhere close to the original point of the story, which is all about punishing someone who repeatedly cheats death.

Be they material, emotional, of our own creation or of someone else's, removable or fixed, the question of how to live in the face of obstacles occupies some of our earliest recorded reflections on life. Each of the world's most central religions—from Hinduism to Buddhism, Islam to Christianity—contains guidance for dealing with obstacles among its most central tenets. The Hindu god Ganesha, easily recognizable by the elephant head perched atop his human body, is revered within the Vedas as the remover of all obstacles. The Buddha taught that obstacles lie within our own desires and self-doubt, hindrances of our own making that exacerbate suffering. His very first teachings pointed to the way out, first and foremost by recognizing that suffering was an inevitable condition of life that could not be changed but could be made bearable by aligning our emotions with reality. And both Islam and Christianity frame obstacles as essential to the human experience, the paths to work through as we attain spiritual development.

These early ways of approaching obstacles deeply impact how we typically attend to the challenges of life. And they really bottom out in two paths: First, we can change our perspective, especially our desires, and thereby remove the obstacle. Second, we can push through them, for doing so provides us with the opportunity for growth. These traditions provide insight into the human condition, and into the fundamental struggle of how to live in an imperfect world, in which there will always be hindrances and obstacles cropping up, interfering with our lives. Their insights are important, and no doubt serve as an important recourse for many of us as we deal with the challenges of life.

In the face of obstacles, though, there are many paths we can take. While the most common ones point to finding a perspective that removes the obstacles or gives meaning to them, there's another way. It was the only way for Sisyphus. He couldn't remove the obstacle from his life, and there was no way for him to find meaning in it. Following either of these paths would have only increased his misery and the absurd sense of his existence. Instead, Sisyphus's best option—his only option, really—was to embrace his life for what it was. To find challenge and adventure in pushing that same boulder up the same, steep hill. To find ways to engage within the journey, to create games in his head, to find ways to make his obstacle-laden life more interesting.

Our lives are not completely like Sisyphus's, devoid of meaning and possibilities for happiness. But many aspects of our lives are, and inevitably so. The good news is that, in a life where obstacles are inevitable, we can still live Good Lives. We do this by embracing the obstacles for the challenge and mixed emotions they bring and by allowing them to enrich our lives. When we do this, we turn obstacles into adventures.

EMBRACING OBSTACLES

When I was in college, I came to love the all-night study session. I'd inevitably find myself alone, walking in circles around my apartment, talking to myself. It was (and is) the best way to learn and to practice. "If you can speak it, you can write it," I often tell my students. Even better, when you try to explain something, even to yourself, you'll pick up on the weak links—the gaps in what you know—so that you can figure them out in the moment. For me, there was nothing better than walking into an exam after one of these sessions—my head was just waiting to explode with knowledge, and I'd write and write.

I tell this story to my students all the time, trying to rev them up for exam period. While the majority response is that very distinctive *you are crazy* look, I often find at least a couple of students opening their eyes with intrigue. And that's what I'm going for: to deliver a glimpse into how they might approach this particular obstacle that pays off big-time.

My approach didn't erase the challenge. Nor did it erase the emotions that inevitably come with trying to learn—anxiety, exhaustion, stress. What it did instead was and is remarkable: It heightened the challenge and the emotions that came with it. And that made it an adventure.

Life is the utmost adventure. The journey begins when we pop into this world, without a choice. It continues throughout our childhoods, where we experience, grow, feel, and think. We become adults. We develop agency and start to harness more control over how we experience life. We aspire to attain and achieve things. We become adept at planning. We try to master pursuit mode. Sometimes, if we're lucky enough, we succeed in our aspirations. We feel we've got a grip on this life thing.

Yet the more we grow, the more we aspire, and the more we succeed, the less life feels like an adventure. It becomes more important to conquer and excel, to develop mastery over life. We become quick to evaluate our circumstances. We start to see those turns life throws at us as setbacks, presenting obstacles for us to overcome. Far too often, life ends up becoming something to get through. It becomes more like an obstacle course than an adventure.

There's nothing wrong with obstacle courses. Except, of course, that adventures offer a lot more fun than obstacle courses.

If I'm stuck in this life, I'd rather it be an adventure than an obstacle course. Thankfully, the choice is mine. The choice is all of ours. In the game of life, where the end is the same for each of us, whether life becomes an obstacle course or an adventure depends entirely on our perspective. We can't choose a life without obstacles, without challenge. But we can choose to make our lives adventures—and we should because doing so adds psychological richness to our lives and makes them more interesting.

We've seen exactly how to do this. We've seen that how we look at the world changes our experience of it. We've seen that what we bring to our experiences determines what we will experience. We've learned that we can make our experiences more interesting, simply by approaching them with the right mindset. And we've seen that by becoming more comfortable with challenge, by embracing novelty when it happens, and by taking risks to introduce novelty into our lives, we can live in a way that invites the interesting into our lives. These tools deliver each of us the power to enhance our life and to live a better life without having to make any drastic changes to it. They direct us toward making the most of our day-to-day and living in a way that opens us up to the world around us, situating us to make the most of our experiences.

One important lesson we've learned along the way is that the Good Life isn't at all a matter of coasting through life—a ride we get on where things just click into place and take us to easy street. The Good Life involves a diverse range of experiences, many of which test our minds and generate complex emotions. Complexity enriches our lives. Rather than shrinking away from it, we ought to embrace it—and the tools we've learned here show us how.

And there's more: When we embrace the role psychological richness plays within the Good Life, and recognize that the Good Life involves more than happiness and meaning, we bring our best possible lives into closer alignment with the realities of life. The realities of life include much more than butterflies and beaches, aims and achievements. If we're stuck in the old dichotomy, there's a lot of life that just gets left out, dismissed as obstacles to the Good Life or, at best, as the price we must pay to get a Good Life. Embracing psychological richness as an important component of the Good Life shows us how almost all areas of our lives can be valuable, and the tools we've explored here position us to make them so.

Psychological richness provides us with a new framework to approach the road bumps that hit us all from time to time. When they do, it's easy to feel stuck. To look around and see obstacle after obstacle, stacking up, preventing us from living our best possible life. We've all been there. But we don't have to get stuck there. We can instead learn to see the obstacles as adventures.

I remember a family vacation years ago—I must have been in college at the time. My family was sprawled all over the country by this point. We all gathered in San Francisco and set off on a drive to Lake Tahoe, where we would ski and spend Christmas together. A few hours in, squalls hit, and the mountain pass closed. We had no other option (I guess, but I most certainly was leaving that up to my dad at the time) but to find a room in the very small town sitting at the base of the mountain, which was Truckee, California. We stayed there for two nights before the pass opened and we drove it, like caterpillars, with chains on the tires of our rental cars.

I don't remember that Christmas at all. I don't remember the skiing, either, except for the day it rained, and we still stayed out until the lifts closed. But I remember Truckee. I remember the motel room, I remember the roadside restaurant, I remember the odd, then new, feeling of being stuck in limbo, with nothing to do and nowhere to go, the feeling of just being.

My family members' experiences of that trip, I know, were different. And I'm sure they were different in all sorts of ways, but let's just say that was the last time we took a family ski vacation. For whatever the reason—and it is indeed mysterious to me, even now—I simply gave in to the experience. Even though those storms were quite literally an obstacle to the glorious ski vacation waiting for me, I was able to keep an open mind about the whole experience, so I could see it as an adventure and harness something valuable out of it.

I hope we've all had times like these, where for whatever the reason, we go along with the adventures life brings us. It's kind of like taking a *why not?* attitude toward it. It's easiest to do this when things are clearly not within our ability to change and when they don't seem that bad. It's much harder to find the adventure in things when maybe, if we try hard enough...and just keep trying, we can change them. And it's much harder to find adventures in things that feel bad or that we see as bad. These are the times when we find ourselves on an obstacle course, railing against the challenges of life and the uncertainty they bring...to no avail.

This struggle is now made classic by the completely absorbing TV show *Schitt's Creek*. It's about a wealthy, urban family, so used to living in luxury the materialism screams from their (clear and tight) pores, who find themselves broke and living in a motel in the middle of nowhere, in a small town they'd bought as a joke, years before.

The show is notoriously difficult to get into. The first few episodes, which set up and track the downfall of the filthy-rich family, depict characters so materialistic, petty, and completely obnoxious that it is hard to imagine there is anything redeeming about them or even worth watching. But if you are open to the experience, and stick out those first few episodes, watching these characters transform becomes a completely engrossing experience. While they each engage in their own battles and individual struggles in accepting their new conditions—in coming to see their new conditions as presenting adventures rather than obstacles—they each transform in the most magical of all ways. Without the materialistic veil shaping and coloring their perspectives, their personality quirks bloom, and each character becomes completely endearing.*

This is what happens when we choose to fully engage with our lives and to embrace the adventure to be found within them. Life starts to feel more like play than work. We've just got to choose to see it that way and to embrace the challenges life throws at us, rather than begrudging them, to no avail, and letting them bring us down. The more rapidly we see obstacles as adventures, the better lives we'll live.

BUT WHAT ABOUT WHEN THINGS ARE ACTUALLY JUST REALLY BAD?

Alas, I get that, for most of us, this is way easier said than done. It flies against routine thought patterns, built up through our life. Snakes = Bad. Cold water = Bad. Anything forced = Bad. The unknown = Bad.

That's where practice helps. This is where it pays to pause and really think about what it means to be truly open to experiences, and how we can develop that openness. One thing we can do right away is start paying attention to those little nuances I just slipped in about things being "bad," and the difference between things that seem bad and things that really are bad, that are tragic. Really bad, hard stuff

---

* It's not that their transformations are magical, but much more so that their transformations are magical for the viewer to experience themselves: You find yourself moving from feeling disdain and horror when first meeting the family, to then finding them so endearing that you root for them. That's the power of our minds, by the way; we can engage with something to the extent that vicariously witnessing the transformation of others becomes itself a source of psychological richness. Experiencing the value of the interesting is always at our fingertips.

exists, and we'll grapple with that in a few pages. A lot of the stuff we think is bad, though, really isn't bad. We just see it that way. Often, when we see things as bad, what we really mean is that they get in the way. They impede our progress, or they prevent us from getting something we want. They get in between us and our happiness or our purpose—the only templates that, until now, we've had for living the Good Life.

We've all got those immediate tendencies to categorize, to associate some things as always bad, and to see them as obstacles. Rain is a big one for a lot of us, as is especially hot or cold weather—events beyond our control, which we react to by immediately seeing them as bad. But are they, really?

Obstacles arise when we see things through the lens of our desires, our wants. You want to go running after work, but it just started raining. You think, *Ugh. Rain, again. This sucks.* All of a sudden, rain becomes bad. Why? Because it interferes with what you want to do. It's "bad" because you can't go outside, or now you have to run on a treadmill. But it's just as easy to counter each of these thoughts: That's what they make raincoats for! Or, if you really hate running on the treadmill, why do it? Maybe you could sleep in instead.

Let me tell you, though, about the adventures to be had running in the rain! The freedom it delivers. Being so drenched that there is simply no point in even trying to avoid the puddles. Sure, you're not likely to get that personal record on a rainy run. Who cares? Just let that go and embrace the moment. When we let go and loosen the grip of our desires and wants, we open our minds. We find adventures rather than obstacles.

I know at least one of you is thinking: *But, really, Lorraine? I need that PR today. My desires aren't just fickle little things. They represent things I've invested myself in, that I care about. Why would I ever let that go?*

There's a difference between having desires and caring about the things you want, and seeing everything that happens as either contributing to or detracting from your desire satisfaction. By taking our desires to serve as the only metric of something's value, we miss out on a lot of value. We miss out on adventures, and we most certainly miss out on a lot of the interesting.

PANDEMIC ADVENTURES

Are you ready to start seeing some of those pandemic experiences as adventures? It can be easier to see obstacles as adventures in retrospect when we are not bogged down by the grueling details. If we struggle to see our obstacles as adventures in the moment, it'll help to consider how some of these experiences will look further down the line. Doing so now may help you to shift in the moment.

I remember very clearly my first grocery store trip of the pandemic. It was the first time I'd gone out in public after the lockdown. No one had real masks at that point, and our faces were covered with scarves, bandanas, neck-warmers. I might have been wearing gloves. The details are hard to remember but the adventure is not. Walking through the store that day was surreal. How do I negotiate the other people? How far back should I stand? Across the way, I thought I saw someone I knew...my dear close friend Puanani. "Pua? Is that you?" I asked in a desperate, crazy tone. Everyone's guards were up. It took her a minute. Then it clicked in. We did our first fake hugs, so awkwardly, having no idea how regular they would soon become. It had been five whole days since I'd seen her, yet it felt like a lifetime. "Is this what our lives have come to?!" I guess it was.

A chance encounter, under forced and pressing conditions. Yet the conditions were so off, so weird, even in that moment, I felt the adventure. Seeing Pua all covered up, across the way, just sweetened the deal. It made my week.

Do you remember the first time you hit the grocery store under pandemic conditions? Or the first time you had to negotiate the masks, the absence of hugs and handshakes? Wasn't it at least a little bit like an adventure?

If you didn't feel it then, and, especially, if you don't see it now, it's worth thinking about what was holding you back. What interfered with your ability to see all these new obstacles as adventures to jump into?

It's also actually just a weird perspective to take on life. A tempting one, I know, but a weird one. Does the world exist to satisfy our desires? Of course not. Then why should we look at everything life has to offer in terms of our desires? From the big picture, it seems rather remarkable we ever get what we want. We know we can't always get what we want. Why do we try so hard? Is it because of a well-known line from a song written in the 1960s? It might be. Let it go.

Life does not always deliver what we want. But it does deliver opportunities, which present adventures. If we stop trying so hard to get what we want, and shed the lenses of desire for pleasure and fulfillment, we find opportunity and adventure.

OPENNESS TO EXPERIENCE

We've talked already about how important keeping an open mind is to the art of the interesting. And we've talked a lot about the mode we can get into, of evaluating everything for what it will bring us or what we can do with it. This inhibits us on a lot of grounds, but especially because it prevents us from being open to experiences. So, as we shed the lenses of desires, we should strive to develop openness to experience.

What exactly is openness to experience? Conceived one way, it is a matter of being willing to engage in a wide variety of experiences. Saying yes without hesitation. That's kind of what we're talking about (and it's not a bad way to start), but openness to experience runs much deeper. It's not simply about being willing to do things but is much more about the way we approach and process our activities. It's a feature of our inner experience, an active process of our minds. While sometimes we talk about an open mind in terms of a passive mind—one that takes things in without evaluation—openness to experience comprises a set of cognitive, affective, and motivational patterns activated through experience, patterns that shape that experience.

We're never passive receptors of experience. Things don't just happen, they happen to us—creatures laden with thoughts, emotions, dispositions, all built up uniquely within us through our past experiences.

I like to think of experience as a synthesis between what we are doing and what we bring to that experience. This is why each person's experience is always unique. And this is why we have the power to shape our experiences. Our minds shape our experiences one way or another. We may as well use them to shape our experiences in ways that are more likely to deliver the Good Life, right? Developing openness to experience helps, particularly when it comes to how we address and confront the obstacles life throws at us.

Psychologists frame openness to experience as a personality trait, taking it to present itself along a spectrum. Those at the highest end? Psychologists Robert R. McCrae and Paul T. Costa Jr. point to artists and writers:

Dreamers with keen imaginations, seeing possibilities that others miss. They are sensitive and passionate, with a wide and subtle range of emotional reactions. They are adventurous, bored by familiar sights, and stifled by routine. They have an insatiable curiosity, as if they retained into adulthood the child's wonder at the world. And they are unorthodox, free-thinking, and prone to flout convention.[1]

What they're describing should sound *very* familiar to those of us familiar with the interesting. And look at how much here points simply to the outlook these individuals bring to their experiences. That's what we've been focusing on all along. We live more interesting lives not by doing certain things but by reframing our perspective, by shaping our inner experience to make what we are doing that much more novel, complex, engaging, and emotionally varied.

Through developing openness to experience, we transform obstacles into adventures. But if we're used to seeing obstacles, developing openness to experience may take some practice.

Early research on personality traits led many psychologists to believe that personality traits were fixed, stable, and largely inherited—things you've either got or not. And while it's true that personality traits describe enduring dispositions that we bring to our experiences, research over the years shows that personality traits can change, and given their impact on our well-being, that it can benefit us when they do so.[2] There's no surefire recipe to change our personality overnight, but there's also no reason not to try.

THE SIX FACETS OF OPENNESS

It'll help to get a little more concrete on what openness to experience encapsulates. Typically, psychologists construe openness to experience as an umbrella covering six facets. Think through them and see where you tend to fall on the spectrum.

Dimension	Description	Does this sound like you? Yes/No/ A little
Adventurousness	"Adventurousness" describes the attitudes we take toward our actions. Highly adventurous people display a willingness to take chances and risks, and to engage in new activities.	
Intellect	Typically, this describes one's proneness toward abstract and philosophical thinking. Yet the high correlation between divergent thinking and openness to experience suggests that most important to the intellectual dimension may very well be a tendency to question the ideas that one encounters. Divergent thought resists black-and-white answers, looks for new connections, and explores alternative approaches.	
Imagination	This tracks the ease with which one lets their imagination play. While those low in openness to experience stick to the concrete aspects of their experiences, those high in openness let their imaginations run. They daydream and think about what could be.	

Artistic Experience	Aesthetics is a deep and profound subject. But its subject matter is basic: How do we react to beauty? One cool way in which openness to experience shows itself is through "aesthetic chills"—spontaneous reactions to beauty, or any kind of profound experience.[3]	
Emotionality	Those open to experience can experience mixed emotions, rather than let the positive (or negative) feelings dominate. Those less open may get fixated on the positive or the negative, feeling and focusing on only one emotion.	
Values	Openness to experience is correlated with liberal orientations toward social and political issues.	

I'm guessing we can all safely identify where we are on this spectrum of openness. The degree to which we are open to experience influences almost every choice we make, from where to eat lunch, to whom to have lunch with, to what to eat for lunch. But that we start from our own place on the spectrum doesn't mean we can't move along it. It just takes work. It may take conscientious effort to develop more openness to experience. It's worth it.

We develop openness to experience through being exposed to different forms of experience. You can probably see the connections between your current level of openness and the culture in which you were raised. Many of us weren't exposed to a lot of new experiences growing up. Many of us weren't encouraged to think outside the box. Many of us were told we weren't creative. All this shapes who we are today. But it's just information. Information we can use to think about where we might strive to develop more openness to experience, and how we might do so.

And here's the coolest part: We can develop openness to experience by seeking out new experiences, ideas, and ways of thinking.[4] Your parents didn't force you to try new things at dinnertime? No problem—you can do it for yourself now. Take the time to think about the specific areas where you lack openness to experience. Then, start trying out new experiences in that area. Even if you have to fake it, you'll become more open to experiences simply by having new ones. And at some point, your perspective will shift. You won't be faking it anymore.

DEVELOPING OPENNESS 101: VICARIOUS ADVENTURES

Psychological richness is all about having experiences that penetrate one's mind, that stimulate new thoughts, and that evoke a wide range of emotions. This is how it generates the interesting, which describes how these experiences feel. Both psychological richness and the interesting describe the internal effects of whatever we're doing or thinking about. They are found in the inner lives of our minds.

While we could develop more adventurousness by throwing ourselves out of a plane, I'm thrilled to report that we can also experience adventurousness vicariously, by reading about people who do. While we could expose ourselves to new cultures by traveling across the world, we can experience them vicariously, by watching a documentary. While we could go to great lengths to find a place to eat tripe, we could just watch Anthony Bourdain do it for us. While we could develop more liberal attitudes by seeking out those living without homes, or talking to those who've had their reproductive rights trampled upon, we could sit at home and read about them.

These vicarious experiences help us take baby steps toward developing more openness to experience. They offer a cheap, low-stakes way of broadening our horizons. And even better: They let us have an interesting experience along the way. All sorts of vicarious experiences generate psychological richness, and the interesting doesn't discriminate. Whether we're reading about Hinduism or traveling to India, we'll have interesting experiences.

Trying out vicarious experiences is an easy way to experience the interesting while also developing more openness to experience. If you aren't jumping out of your seat yet, eager to try on new experiences, stay put. Open a book. Find something on TV. Vicarious adventures are easy to find. And while you're experiencing them, try to learn from the experience. Feel the goose bumps of the artistic chills. Feel the mixed emotions of another's heartbreak and journey to recovery. Take in the descriptions of foreign places and cultures. Try to imagine you are there yourself. Seek out books and shows that make you think or that present differing values or lines of thought. Notice how they shift your perspective. By letting vicarious stories feed you, you'll experience the interesting and prep yourself to bring more openness to your experiences.

BRINGING OPENNESS TO THE CHALLENGES OF LIFE

One huge and important way bringing openness to your experiences will change your life is that it gives you a new frame to deal with the challenges you face. The realities of life are such that we don't always get what we want, and changes are often forced on us. Your partner gets a new job across the country, forcing you to quit your job and uproot your family. You get laid off from a job you loved. You graduate from college and now must do something. You can no longer afford your dream house and have to find a new home. In these moments, you feel forced to change. And while it can be really hard not to see these moments as obstacles, the value to be had by bringing openness to these moments is worth it.

We can't control every aspect of our lives, so often our best strategy is to approach them with openness. The good and the bad. The parts we desired and the ones we didn't. Some psychologists even frame openness to experience in terms of a "challenge perspective."[5] Their idea is straightforward: We can see challenges as threats and obstacles. We do this and we'll trigger negative emotions, such as fear, frustration, anger, and despair. Or we can see challenges as adventures and adopt an open, optimistic attitude toward them. When we do this, we'll trigger the positive emotions, such as hope, pride, inspiration, and equanimity. These emotions propel us toward embracing our lives, challenges and all, rather than avoiding or sabotaging them. They'll make it more likely we'll have adventures that enhance our lives.

USING THE FRAMEWORK OF THE
INTERESTING TO DEAL WITH TRAGEDY

While they might seem bad, many of the challenges of life aren't obstacles to the Good Life. They aren't all the things that hold us back, and many can be opportunities to explore and to engage. Recognizing them as such helps us live better lives. Letting go of the idea that the Good Life is an easy one, and learning to appreciate the opportunities that challenges present for interesting experiences, helps us reorient our perspective and reactions to the things that seem bad.

But of course, life doesn't only throw challenges at us. Sometimes life throws tragedies—the kinds of things that present more as earthquakes than bumps in the road. Not the cold that had you canceling your kid's birthday party, but the cancer diagnosis that has you questioning how many more of them you'll get to celebrate. Not losing your job, but losing a child. These tragedies shatter one's world. When they happen, it's difficult to know how to move forward, much less to think about living a Good Life. But psychological richness promises a unique way of looking at the really bad, hard stuff in our lives.

Without the interesting, when tragedy hits, all we've got to work with is the old dichotomy that says a Good Life is either a happy one or a meaningful one, which puts us only between a rock and a hard place. The pain of our lives comes with deeply rooted negative emotions but, from the perspective of happiness, these negative emotions simply have no place. We're told not to focus on them and to embrace the positivity in our lives, always, or we're given some paltry, ridiculous story about silver linings. We're told not to dwell in the bad, hard stuff or, even worse, we're forced to say that it's good that it happened.

That's just a painful approach. And an insulting one. It's asking someone to sweep that bad, hard thing under the rug and go on with a smile. It invalidates traumatic experience, and the negative emotions people justifiably feel. Even worse, the whole approach suggests there is something wrong with those of us who can't see that silver lining, or who can't silence the negative feelings. It makes us feel as if the Good Life is no longer an option for us...and that we don't deserve one, anyway.

If, in the face of tragedy, we aren't being told to find silver linings and to be positive at all costs, forced into (or out of) the happiness camp, chances are we are being told to find meaning in it. This approach seems a little less offensive than toxic positivity, but only slightly less so.

We often hear stories of someone making it through tragic circumstances by finding meaning in their lives. Viktor Frankl's is one of the most compelling.[6] *Awesome*, even. He spent three years living in Nazi concentration camps. He survived while the rest of his family did not. What saved him, he wrote, was the spiritual freedom he found within his mind. This freedom gave him the space to find meaning in life, which he described in terms of finding the right answer to the challenges life presents, and to finding a way to address the challenges of life through actions and conduct. What this means for any one person is an individual thing, but Frankl believed that everyone needs to find meaning in life to function and get through it.

Let's just be very clear: Anyone who survived the Holocaust has a remarkable perspective on life. Anyone who felt anything other than terror, grief, and hopelessness in those circumstances is remarkable. That anyone survived and was able to share and tell their story is remarkable. It speaks to the downright remarkable capacity of human beings. There's just no other word for it. Remarkable.

It's also true that some conditions may be so devoid of any meaning that our only recourse through them may be to find meaning. But it's not true that finding meaning is always the best, nor only, response to tragedy, nor is it the only way to live a Good Life in the face of challenge.

Remember Aaron Elster?* He, too, found something within his mind

---

* You didn't skip the introduction, did you?

to make life worth living. Stuck, as a young child, hiding in an attic, he turned his mind into a playground. He daydreamed. He wrote novels in his head. He was the hero all the time. Heck, he invented the art of the interesting all by himself. Frankl's insight about spiritual freedom—about the ability to hold space in your mind—doesn't always have to take the shape of meaning.

For many of us dealing with the more common yet nonetheless severe and tragic obstacles of life, the recommendation to turn those challenges into sources of meaning—along with the thought that that's the only way to move forward—is offensive and insulting, for a few reasons.

First, the advice to find meaning in tragedy suggests that we should start to see tragic occurrences as good things that happened for a reason. Yet bad, hard stuff doesn't always happen for a reason. It just doesn't. It certainly doesn't happen for a good reason. Do not tell a survivor of sexual assault that she was raped for a reason. Do not lead her to think she'd be better off if she thought that way. Sexual assault is bad, period. Just as there's no silver lining, there's no underlying meaning. What meaning could there possibly be? There is none. Do not tell someone who has lost their entire family to floods that it happened for a reason. Do not lead them to think they'd be better off if they thought that way.

Tragedy is bad. By trying to frame it in a context that makes it look good, we deny its reality, and the effects of that denial can be devastating. It's one thing if someone like Frankl finds meaning within the bad, hard stuff. But to suggest that one's only recourse is to find meaning in it in order to live a Good Life makes the bad, hard stuff intolerable.

The suggestion is not just offensive, it's also too much to ask. Does anyone really need to find the meaning in being abused as a child? In having their loved ones swept away by floods? In surviving a school shooting? Finding meaning in tragedy can be very hard, especially for those without religious faith to draw on. To suggest victims ought to places them under a double burden. They must live with what happened to them. And they are supposed to find meaning within it? This is simply too much to ask.

Tragic stuff happens, and it is bad. It brings negative emotions that simply can't—and shouldn't—be ignored. Our ordinary approaches toward helping those who've suffered tragedies do not help, and can even make their situation worse. We ought to jettison them, along with the old dichotomy.

Thinking about the nature of psychological richness can help. Psychological richness describes the range of experiences that evoke new thoughts and new emotions, and that often change one's perspective. That people view psychological richness as part of the Good Life, that there is value to the robust cognitive engagement such experiences stimulate, affirms that any experience can enrich our lives, even the bad, hard stuff. It affirms that negative emotions can be and are part of a Good Life. It teaches us that the Good Life is not an easy one and that there is nothing wrong with us if we find ourselves struggling to find happiness, or if we can't find the meaning in something that has happened to us.

Now, I want to be clear: Evoking the interesting is not going to make all of that stuff good—that's not the point. It will still be painful. Heartbreaking. But if we can approach the bad, hard stuff with Mindfulness 2.0, curiosity, and creativity; with open-mindedness; with awareness of when we've pushed our nervous systems too far—the same skills we bring to cultivate the interesting under better circumstances—we can learn to recognize how much it's shaped our perspective, and to sit with negative emotions. Best of all, we can remember that even though horrible, painful things have happened, we aren't prevented from living a Good Life. There is reason for hope.

Life is not perfect. There's not a reason for everything. Obstacles crop up and tragic stuff happens. This makes it hard to live a Good Life. By remembering that a Good Life isn't an easy one, we'll be better equipped to deal with tragedy. By cultivating the mindset of the interesting, we'll have a way to deal with it that fits with its reality. Reframing our perspective on challenge makes sense. Doing so won't erase the bad, hard stuff or turn it into an adventure. But you just may gain the tools you need to deal with it.

KEEPING IT INTERESTING

What's the difference between an adventure and an obstacle course? Obstacle courses present challenges that must be met to get to the finish line, to the good stuff. Adventures contain challenges, the surmounting of which is itself good. Seeing life as an adventure involves embracing its challenges and finding value within them. Too often we equate challenge with something bad. By reframing our perspective, by resisting our urge to see everything that interferes with our wants as bad and instead developing more openness to experience, we turn obstacles into adventures and invite the interesting to arise. We also set ourselves up with a framework that'll actually help us cope with the bad, hard stuff.

Chapter 11:

Friends Make Everything Better

M Y HUSBAND, JODY, IS A SUPER-HUMBLE GUY. HE SOMEHOW has no need for public attention, much less public praise. He can dismiss praise of any kind in literally a blink of an eye. This is all to say that he's going to be downright mortified by the existence of this particular story. But it's all true, and a writer has got to be honest, right?

Jody has taught me more about how to appreciate the interesting in life than anyone else. I know I would have been drawn to the research on psychological richness on my own, but without him, I wouldn't have had much to draw on. It certainly would have made this whole project more difficult. That's one of the most remarkable features of relationships. Whether romantic or not, friends help us grow. The best ones help us grow in ways that can't be taught or learned. I'm doing my best here to describe the mindset of the interesting and the steps we can take to cultivate it. But one of the very best ways to master the art of the interesting is to be around someone who models it. When you're around a master of the interesting, your life simply becomes more interesting. The interesting spreads like that, remember?

As I began to talk with Oishi about psychological richness, and started thinking about this important question of why the psychologically rich life is a good one, bit by bit I started thinking through different times I'd been having with Jody. We'd been dating for a couple of years at that point. It was already crystal clear how much our time together had enriched my life, in ways I'd never really imagined were possible.

It happened through the little things. The drives around town, where he'd point and notice things I'd driven past a billion times before. The weekend trips we'd take, with only a vague plan and not a single reservation. The clarity he had toward things that bored him and the ease with which he simply refused to engage in the boring things—things I'd often feel pressure to pretend I was interested in, like conversations about food. The stories he'd tell, reflecting his endless curiosity for thinking about what and why someone ended up being here, or even why a stranger was driving down the road at that moment.

Bit by bit, I felt my passions more. I let them fuel me. I stopped worrying about what others would think. I stopped pretending to be interested in things I wasn't. I let go of the planning. I looked past the pleasure. I started to see and embrace the interesting.

Our life was hectic in many ways. We soon moved in together, blending the kids, dogs, and cats. At one point, we had three boys, three dogs, three cats, and a variable number of chickens running around the yard. Kids were coming in and going out of the door, which was always open. I'd never know how many would show up for dinner, or who would be sleeping on the couch in the morning. It was the kind of situation you'd look at and think lacked stability. But the opposite was the case. Our stability grew from within. Together, we created one interesting life. And we knew it. I grew from freaking out about not knowing how many people to cook for to thinking broadly and creatively, on the spot.* I learned how much better it was to live with a little uncertainty than to live by the book. When the chaos was simply undeniable, we'd say to each other: "At least it's not boring."

And we were right. Meeting Jody shook up my life, dislodged the

---

* I call this "Iron Chef" night, which makes it way more interesting, obvs.

plans and expectations I'd been clinging to, and introduced me to a complexity of emotions. My old life paled in comparison. I'd never go back.

See, this is the thing about relationships: The best kinds don't give you the space to flourish; the best kinds spark seeds within you that just take off. They've got the best power of all.

Remember Sam and Joel from chapter 1? Sitting around, stuck in the old dichotomy of the Good Life, never realizing the interest their friendship brought? Bit by bit, it started to sink in. They still didn't have the words for it, but together their lives became more psychologically rich, and the dichotomy's hold on them loosened. Fast-forward a year or so, and Sam spends way less time sitting around alone, drinking wine in her underwear. Instead, with Joel by her side, encouraging and supporting her, she's putting herself out there—challenging herself by showing up at a church mixer, or by getting up onstage and putting her beautiful voice to work. Joel, in turn, has cut way back on his seemingly endless pursuit of meaning: With Sam by his side, he stops going to church, he stops scheduling all his time, he starts to spend more time with friends, and he opens himself up to love.

It was their friendship that drove these changes, changes that brought each of them away from living the scripted lives they thought they were supposed to be living, and closer to their true selves. Friends give us permission to be ourselves, and it is so often in the context of friendships that we grow into ourselves, that we discover our passions, and that we start living the lives our passions direct us toward, rather than the lives we might be told to live.

MORE THAN JUST HAPPINESS

Have you heard that relationships are the secret to happiness? Ha. Yes. Me too, about a thousand billion times. It's all true. There's no question of that. It's important, too. Beyond the fact that this is an exceptional instance where study after study affirms the same thing, thereby producing a shit-ton of research that can help us improve our lives, there's something really affirming about knowing that relationships are the secret to happiness.

It gives us a good measure of what makes for a bad relationship, that's for sure. If we're in a relationship that consistently makes us feel bad about ourselves, with someone who deflates our burgeoning feelings of pleasure, or with someone who brings no benefit to our lives whatsoever, we should end it. We should remember that friendships and romantic relationships are voluntary relationships. We choose to be in them. We choose to be in them because they enhance our lives. And if it becomes clear that a particular relationship does not enhance our lives, we should end it. And then we should find people who do enhance our lives. We all need friends.

I know sometimes people think they don't need friends. Over the past few years, I've heard this on two occasions from loved ones, both of whom lived long distances away. Both times I held my tongue. And both times, I watched my loved ones go through months of a very mellow kind of existence, with very little pleasure, and certainly nothing close to exuberance that I witnessed. Both times, I watched my loved ones start to shift, and emerge back. When I say "emerge back," I mean they emerged back to their selves. To people who were comfortable enjoying happiness and engaging in the pleasurable stuff that makes it happen. Friends spark and fuel you.

It's easy to forget this. It's easy to see and approach friendships as optional, and to deprioritize them in your life, especially if you're caught up in pursuit mode. I know I did this for a long time. Thank goodness my divorce had the helpful "shaking it up" effect, and a recently divorced friend, Laura, had given me the exact advice I needed. Laura's one of the happiest people I know. She brings a smile and enthusiasm to anything and everything. And her smile didn't fade away, even while going through a difficult divorce. "How do you do it?" I asked one night. "Friends," she replied.

Sometimes the answers are easy and obvious, and this was no exception. Friends provide an outlet. The familiarity that develops between

friends brings the safety and stability we need to let go, to allow ourselves to feel pleasure, to be happy, even if there's a bunch of crap waiting for us the next day.

With Laura's excellent advice at the top of my mind, I knew what
to do the second my marriage started to dissolve. I reached out to my
friends. I committed, then and there, to prioritizing my friendships,
most of which had been long neglected at that point. That first year
of being single was one of the hardest of my life. It was also chock-full
of some of my happiest times. We'd spend hours drinking wine on my
front porch, turning our struggles into funny stories marked by endless
laughter. I rediscovered that feeling of laughing so hard your stomach
hurts. We'd go on weekend road trips, with and without the kids. Our
dance parties were downright legendary, somehow always involving a
headstand, and more than once involving car roofs.

Those happy times were exactly what I needed. I don't know that I
had the energy to strive for more. Spending time with friends was easy
and effortless, delivering quick shots of pleasure and many moments of
happiness.

There's no question that the secret to happiness is relationships. But
in the wake of all this talk of the importance of relationships to happiness, I worry we'll miss out on the many powers of relationships and
start treating our friends as gumball machines again, seeing them as
valuable only as long as they deliver happiness. Yet friendships support
us in a variety of ways, such as helping us to make our lives more psychologically rich.

RELATIONSHIPS CHANGE OUR PERSPECTIVE

Relationships bring together people with different experiences, different responsiveness, and different interests. Anytime we form a new relationship, it's going to be an interesting experience. Even if we look the
same on paper, we are different people. By embracing the differences,
we set up the interesting. And sometimes, we'll find ourselves moved
and changed by those differences. Through forming relationships, we

create little windows into each other's very perspectives. If we are open, we'll let the other's perspective influence our own.

This is exactly what it felt like when Jody and I started dating. I'd never encountered anyone who lived with such passion and whose life prioritized passion. Jody had figured out very early on that he'd live his best possible life by following his passions and shrugging away society's expectations. His dad showed him the way. "You've got to be happy in what you're doing. If not, what is the point?"

Jody repeats this frequently and often. I let the loose usage of "happy" slip, and always take it in, always appreciative and still a little taken aback. It's so obviously true, the depths of which, though, I'd never really appreciated. I love my job and appreciate that I get paid to do something I love. Yet I don't always love the day-to-day, and most certainly can get sucked into weeks and weeks of not loving it. Hearing this attitude, so foreign to the family I was raised in, helps me put into perspective my priorities. Even if I can't change my work day-to-day in that moment, I make sure I check out of work when I go home. I make sure to find a couple of hours, at least, to enjoy the present. To help those seeds that drive me to keep their flame and prevent them from getting stomped down. The easiest way to do this 99 percent of the time? Just spending time with the people who spark and fuel me.

How do we find the people who spark and fuel us? That's not exactly the right question to ask. People spark and fuel us when we let them— not everyone, of course, but almost everyone deserves the chance to try. When we bring the mindset of the interesting to our relationships, we invite others to spark and fuel us. Consider what happens when we bring these skills to the table.

First, we follow our instincts. We don't prejudge, we don't evaluate, we don't let the opinions of others influence how we think or behave. We follow our gut and use our responsiveness to direct our interactions. If it points us to following up on a chance encounter with someone who looks worlds different from us, we do it. We let our instincts take us out of our comfort zones and into the zone of the interesting, but we always keep an eye on the warning signs of danger. If an interaction with someone else starts to trigger those warning signs, we listen to them.

Second, we use Mindfulness 2.0. We notice things about the person. We look at the other with our eyes and minds. We pause on the details. We think about the details. We notice what drives them. We pick up on the passions fueling them.

Third, we're curious. We wonder why someone acts the way they do. We wonder what would happen if we did the same. We wonder what will become of this interaction. We wonder how we can include the other in our lives, and what that would look like.

Fourth, we're creative. We're not just interacting to learn and wonder, we're in a relationship to experience—to experience each other, and to allow our paths to converge. We can use our creativity to leap past the typical boundaries, to create a new space for this person, to find ways to share the interesting, to find ways to create the interesting together. We use our creativity to be more active in shaping our relationships so that they become a source of the interesting, so that together we discover new things about ourselves and the world.

Bringing the art of the interesting to our relationships unlocks the power that relationships have to enrich our lives, so that we all lead more interesting lives.

RELATIONSHIPS HELP US FEEL

Just the other night I said to Jody: "Hey, we should start doing three-minute planks together every night. It'll be less boring that way." It's true. Doing something with a friend, a loved one, really anyone you are compatible with, makes everything better. It's obvious.

One often-overlooked way friends make everything better, though, is by helping us feel. Do you know those horrible, awful stories of young children raised in a closet only to emerge after years, unable to function, their minds simply stalled out? They illustrate, in a painfully sad way, just how much of our psychological development occurs through our interactions.

This was one of David Hume's greatest insights into human nature: Our minds are such that we rely on others to feel or realize our own emotions. "A perfect solitude is, perhaps, the greatest punishment we can suffer," he wrote.* Why? It's not because friends make our lives easier, or provide opportunities for us to get ahead, or anything like that. It is because "every pleasure languishes when enjoyed apart from company, and every pain becomes more cruel and intolerable."[1]

Have you ever tried to do a happy dance on your own? Did it come close to the good feelings the *Seinfeld* gang generates when they're doing it together? I doubt it. There's something about sharing your emotions with others that lets them blossom. Hume sometimes describes this effect in terms of having others affirm and share your emotions. It's a rudimentary point. How often do we look to others for clues as to how we react? How often do we stifle our emotions when we sense that others don't share them? And how good does it feel when others do share our emotions? How much more robust do our emotions feel? Whatever emotion it is, we'll feel it more strongly when we share it with others.

Among the many TV shows I love,† there's no better presentation of friendship than *Derry Girls*. Set in Northern Ireland in the 1990s, the show follows a group of teenagers navigating the challenges of growing up in the heightened political climate dominating Ireland at the time. The group is not all girls but a crew of four girls plus one guy, who is so tight and close with the girls he doesn't bat an eye at being consistently referred to as a girl. They develop an amazing bond through the years that's really like no other. They never let petty differences interfere. If one is annoyed with the other over something stupid, and the other turns out to need them, the annoyance immediately drops. They

---

* Read carefully here: It's not that there are no benefits to solitude, for of course there are. It's that a perfect solitude, in which we never experience other human beings, is awful.
† It's hard to do philosophy all the time.

always come together to support one another. They support each other so magnificently well because, at root, they share all the same feelings, to the same degree. It is almost magical.

In one of the final episodes, there's a funeral procession for a girl's father, who unexpectedly passed away. Despite some surface-level conflict bubbling for the group, they come together immediately. They share. They are one.

If you jumped right into this scene of sadness and turmoil, of dark colors and desperation, you'd have no idea which member of the group's father had died. The emotions each expresses are of real, genuine, heartbreaking tragedy. It is as if each of them suffered the same loss. And rather than sucking up their personal grief and trying to comfort and support the girl whose father had died, they walk the procession with her, sharing completely and fully in her grief.

It is impossible to watch this scene and not wish you had friends like this. Friends who are so in tune with your emotions, with what is important to you, that there is no distinguishing your grief from theirs. The support derived from sharing in one another's emotions is incomparable. And one lesson to take away is this (it was also Hume's): Relationships enhance our lives, but the best kinds of relationships are ones in which parties connect with each other's mental states.

When we connect with others in this way, and share their emotions, our mental lives become more psychologically rich. Psychological richness involves the experience of a wide variety of emotions, and through our relationships we simply feel more emotions. Moreover, when we share our emotional experiences, and feel the mixed emotions of life with another, we strengthen those very emotions.

It's easier to feel sad with a friend—which doesn't mean that we feel less sad when we are with the friend, but that experiencing difficult emotions together often allows us to experience them more fully. When we're alone, feeling difficult emotions, it can be hard to let them settle. We may feel the glimmer of tension, or the shock of fear, or even the bursts of pleasure, but we don't always give in to them and let them envelop us fully. Relationships offer a space to feel. And our minds are such that when we feel together, we feel more deeply than we might when we're alone.

Feeling a wide range of emotions generates the ripples of the interesting, especially the ones that shift your perspective and beget more of the interesting. If there are emotions you struggle to feel on your own, you might reach out to a friend next time and see the magic that happens when you share your emotions and feel together. No matter what the emotions, it's just better that way. Kind of like those three-minute planks.

HOW EASILY DO YOU CONNECT?

The ways in which we connect to others are deeply influenced by the attachment styles we develop from a young age. Some of us share feelings and empathize with ease, while for others it's more difficult—which sucks, because sharing feelings is one of the easiest ways to develop relationships that help us thrive. If you've been missing out because it's hard for you to connect, it's not too late to start trying. You can start by striving to be more honest, with yourself and others. When we hide our feelings, we sabotage our chances of forming a real connection. Our friendships end up resting on a superficial level, focusing only on sharing the good stuff, or maybe not on sharing at all. When we share our feelings, we open ourselves up to forming deep connections, laden with the emotional exchange and empathy that enrich our emotional lives.

It can be scary to be honest about your feelings. But having no connections is scarier. And there's just no better way to tell whether someone will make a good friend than to see how they react to your honesty. The good ones will react with empathy, curiosity, concern. The bad ones will barely react. There's nothing to lose here, except the bad "friends." Just do it. Next time someone asks how you are, or next time you meet a friend for drinks, share. Share your feelings, good or bad, and don't just rehash your day-to-day. That's how you connect. That's how you reap the emotional benefits of relationships.

RELATIONSHIPS KEEP US OUT OF THE DANGER ZONE

I've been talking a lot about the deep impacts our relationships have upon our very experiences, about how they stimulate individual growth, shape our perspectives, help us feel. These are all ways in which relationships provide the context for the interesting to spring and will be especially important to those of us who need the nurturing. There's a different role that relationships play in helping us lead more interesting lives, though, and it may seem counterintuitive at first. Relationships serve as anchors that keep us from going over the edge as we strive to lead more interesting lives.

Stable, anchoring relationships may be among the most difficult to maintain, but they're irreplaceable. The anchoring power of having a family is well-known. Families give us something to come home to, preventing us from burning out and from getting caught up in sensation-seeking, or the mere collecting of experiences. They remind us that there is more than just us and our needs in the world, and they encourage us to think of others before ourselves. That thought, and the connection that stimulates it, can keep us grounded as we pursue the interesting.

The effect is not at all limited to family but can include the deep connections you have with anyone, be they a partner, a friend, or a sibling. It's the deep emotional connections that do the important work, not the kind of connections they are.

In 2022, results from the longest scientific study of happiness were released. Researchers tracked participants over an eighty-year period.[2] The results were not surprising—relationships are essential—but the fine print was revealing, and worth highlighting. What it showed was not solely that relationships are essential, but that the most important relationships to our well-being are the deep connections we have with people.

This puts a different spin on the ways in which we typically think relationships make us happier. It shows that it is way more important to our well-being to have people we know we can count on, to whom we are deeply connected, than to have the book clubs and trivia teams. All relationships are important, yet this study shows that the key is to ensure you've got people in your life with whom you can share the best and the worst of yourself without hesitation. In other words, it's not just about having people who make you happy, and around whom you share only your happiness—the emotional experience is far more varied and profound than that.

In the context of trying to live a psychologically rich life, the value of deep relationships goes beyond its anchoring effect, but its anchoring effects are important to take note of. Deep connections keep us anchored by giving us something to return home to and by giving us perspective. They can help us learn more about ourselves. They can help us recognize when experiences start to lose their interest. They can help us recognize when we need a restorative break. They can remind us that other things count and that other values count, too, even if they resonate less for us than they do for others. And, of course, thank goodness, they can remind us that it is never a good idea to get bangs.

ON ANCHORS

I most certainly get my love of adventure from my family. For years my dad took these insane canoe trips with his buddies into very remote territories. I remember one trip where the group failed to make their pickup point and were stranded for days without being able to contact anyone. Understandably, the wives were freaking out. Predictably, the husbands were doing just fine, with plenty of whiskey to pass the time.

My sister learned to sail the big boats in her twenties, and for a good run she'd captain family trips for us. My brothers would always oversee the anchor. We learned a lot about anchors during those trips. It turns out that good anchors don't feel at all like anchors. We think anchors will weigh us down, hold on to us too tightly, and prevent us from going where we want to go. But good anchors feel quite the opposite. A good anchor keeps you stable enough so you don't have to constantly pay attention to the boat, worrying about it drifting away. You can go for a swim, dinghy to shore for a hike or to gather supplies. A good anchor doesn't feel like it's holding you back. It feels like it sets you free.

The big exception, of course, is during the storms. I remember one year, facing a huge storm, we anchored in a "hurricane hole," a place known for its protection. We anchored and settled in for a wild night; the boat was always in motion, random objects got tossed around, and the wind was just howling. During a storm, a good anchor feels like an anchor. And thank goodness it does. During a storm, the winds overtake any power of the sail. Without the anchor, we would have literally been blown away.

Good anchors don't feel like anchors when things are calm, but they do feel like anchors when things are stormy. During rough times, you lean on the anchor, relishing in its power, allowing it to keep you safe. This is what we need to keep in mind when we think about the anchoring effect of our relationships. Relationships anchor us, but if they are healthy relationships, they function like good anchors. When things are going well for us, healthy relationships allow us to thrive, to find our independence. They don't weigh us down or hold us back. But when the shit hits the fan, and the storm threatens, healthy relationships keep us steady. They keep us safe.

We all need anchors, even the most independent-minded of us. We shouldn't be threatened by the anchoring effect of relationships. We should just make sure they are good anchors.

A fierce sense of independence might lead you to think you don't *need* deep relationships, that they only serve to hold you back—especially from living an interesting life. But that's simply a misguided form of independence. Genuine independence requires a solid sense of self, and we build and maintain that sense of self through our deep connections. This is the underlying source of their anchoring power, and it is not a constraining one. It's a freeing one. Finding people we are really compatible with, who bring out our best *and* are there for our worst, has a liberating effect. They strengthen our sense of self and so make possible genuine independence.

RELATIONSHIPS MAKE THE INTERESTING SPREAD

While a great thing about the interesting is that we can cultivate it and create it on our own, we all need a little help once in a while. Even the best of us get stuck in moments where being creative just seems too hard. In these moments, we fall back on routines, settling for familiarity, even though we're seeking more. Here's where it pays to know which of our friends to call, to help us find the interesting.

We know how much the interesting spreads between friends. And if anyone needs black-and-white evidence of this, just compare the novel Jack Kerouac wrote before meeting Neal Cassady—*The Town and the City*—to the one he wrote after, *On the Road*. Both are largely autobiographical, discussing roughly the same set of characters, yet the difference in style overwhelms. *The Town and the City* is written in a conventional style. It was long and boring, and it did not sell well. The stories Jack tells within it didn't spread. Conversely, *On the Road* is written in the spontaneous prose style Kerouac would go on to be famous for—a stream of consciousness delightfully ridden with random thoughts, observations, personality shining through and through. The most blatant explanation for this shift? Kerouac's burgeoning friendship with Neal Cassady, stimulated through the old-school, long-distance practice of writing letters. Neal's letters famously illustrated the stream of consciousness Kerouac would go on to incorporate into his own writings. Neal's perspective, Neal's zest for living, simply shine through these letters. Neal inspired Kerouac to write, and to live, in ways that were just that much more interesting. Interesting friends are the best. They can make everything—and everyone—more interesting.* In one of the most interesting episodes of *Ted Lasso*, Coach Beard has just broken up with his girlfriend, Jane, and drags two of his players out to the pub to help him drown his sorrows. The outing turns into a wild, madcap night of one adventure after the next. The wee

---

* The moral philosopher in me observes: As being interesting ourselves inspires the interesting to arise in those around us, we can see ourselves as having a moral obligation to be more interesting!

hours of the morning find Coach, who is at this point dressed in someone else's sequined bell-bottom pants, in a church. He'd spent the entire night in a booze-filled state driven by a downright zeal to turn every obstacle—from closing time, to dress codes, to tunnels—into an adventure, but here he is, somehow in a church, hit by a single revelation. He finds himself begging—to God. He wants Jane back. He knows she isn't going to solve every problem in his life, but he also knows what is most important: With her, he cries, "the world just feels more interesting."

It's clear that the night has been a chase to experience the interesting, and it's revelatory: All the crazy adventures of a booze-soaked night can't hold a candle to the way in which just one person can make your life that much more interesting. There is nothing better than that.

The more interesting we are, the more we invite the interesting into the lives of those around us. In bringing the interesting to our own lives—whether we have more interesting parties, start more interesting conversations, or dress more interestingly—we bring it to our relationships.

Be the interesting friend. If you need to draw on an interesting friend to do it, go right ahead. That's how it starts. Our lives become more interesting when we're around interesting people. And by becoming more interesting ourselves, we make our friends' lives more interesting. It's a double whammy, a much-needed explosion of the interesting.

HAVE MORE INTERESTING PARTIES

One great thing interesting friends do is throw interesting parties. And, really, we've all sat through some boring parties in our lives. There's nothing worse. You make the effort to go out, and find yourself sitting around, having the most boring conversation of the day, thinking, *Why did I think this would be fun?* * We should all be striving to throw more interesting parties.

---

* If you are like me, this question is immediately followed by *One more glass of wine might help.*

This is something I think my generation, and, sorry, especially the women, falls short on. There are exceptions, of course, but on the whole it feels like we've forgotten about the value of doing more than just socializing over drinks and food. Gone are the days of bridge nights, where couples would come together to play cards. Or charades, where people are forced to use their imaginations and engage. Or knitting circles, where people can socialize while creating. We've got book clubs, yes, but those just aren't the same, especially when they devolve into just another night of wine and food. I will give the guys this one: They've done a better job at making socializing more interesting—think poker, trivia nights, darts, watching football together, that sort of thing.

As we seek to incorporate more of the interesting into our lives, we might think about making our social lives a little more interesting. Everyone stands to benefit. Here are some ideas for more interesting parties—stolen (with permission, of course!) from some of my most interesting friends.

It takes all of two seconds to talk with Marshall and realize she is one superinteresting person. Her mind just operates on a different wavelength, and she tells the best stories.[*] Any party at Marshall's house involves both a theme and costumes. Even if you are lame, like me, and consistently show up without a costume, she's always got a stockpile of something for you to wear. That's an important trick to get everyone together, on the same, much more interesting, wavelength.

My favorite of Marshall's parties are the scavenger hunts. She'd run all over town beforehand planting clues and party supplies. Then the group would split into teams and head out (costumed, of course) in what was often a ferocious fight to be the first to reach the end. One time the end was a bar; another time the end was an impromptu fireworks show on the riverbank. We're talking full-grown, middle-aged men and women running

---

[*] Marshall Highet writes, too: a completely unique blend of science fiction / historical drama / teenage adventure. Check out her latest series of young adult novels, coauthored with Bird Jones: *Hold Fast* and *Blue-Eyed Slave*.

all over town, dressed *Game of Thrones*-style in heavy fur coats, or in *Star Trek*-themed uniforms with goofy lights, having the time of their lives. Unforgettable and so very interesting.

Lisa is one of the most creative organizers I know. She's got the perfect combination of social goodwill, a young and free spirit, and the talent and drive to pull off unique events that enrich our small community. Her fortieth birthday party was downright legendary. It was officially a casino theme, but I don't think I made it to the casino tables at all that night, though, because I—along with lots of others—was caught up in a game that structured the night. It was a game of villains and heroes. At the beginning of the night, each person drew a "villain" or "hero" card and kept their card secret. The goal of the villains was "death by selfie": to take the heroes down by shooting a selfie with them. The game made the night. It was hysterical watching the lengths to which some would go to trick people into taking selfies with them, and the lengths to which some would go to avoid being tricked. (I got taken out early. It didn't stop the fun.) Having a mission, particularly a sneaky one, makes any party just that much more interesting.

Stacy and Mary don't throw a ton of parties, but they throw ones that count, and they go all out. They throw parties for the purpose of bringing people together. We're a small community, and that sometimes means we know people's faces but not their names, or their names but not their faces. Stacy and Mary try to fill in these gaps for us all, by bringing together circles of friends from all different corners.

Their parties work to bring people together because we are there to play a game. Playing games with people functions as the best icebreaker ever. Even if you've just met the person across the table, and have barely gotten through the niceties, playing a game with them creates a bond that bypasses the need for the boring niceties. It brings people together rapidly and much more so than they might have had they met over the charcuterie board.

One great tradition they've started are old-school bingo nights. Well, not old-school, because their bingo games get very hard. They have us aiming for shapes on the bingo card, not just straight lines. They read the numbers fast. It gets hard and forces engagement. Tables unite to help one another out, and the competition between tables can get fierce. And then the party ends. That's probably an important secret to pulling off a successful game night: Don't let it go on too long. You go on too long, you risk people getting bored and checking out from the game, threatening a ripple effect. Get the timing right, then people will leave fully engaged, with never a dull moment to drag the party down.

RELATIONSHIPS HELP US EXPERIENCE VALUE

An old friend once taught me that no one person could be everything for another, that every friend, partner, sibling, and so on delivers something unique to our lives. It's easy to take this point at the superficial level: one friend to run with, one group of friends to meet for cocktails, that kind of thing. But it helps to go a little deeper. What each relationship delivers depends on how they help you experience the stuff that counts in your life: fulfillment, pleasure, and the interesting.

When I first started thinking about psychological richness and why it was a distinct form of the Good Life, different from meaning and happiness, it helped to think where my friends lined up, about which of these three forms of the Good Life clearly resonated with them. And it was surprisingly easy.

Puanani is always up for a trip to Mexico, shares my deep love for massages, would need no more than one week's notice to hop on a flight to Hawaii, and predictably balked at the thought of joining me on a trek to Machu Picchu. The happy life suits her; pleasure resonates for her most strongly. I turn to her for lots of things, but especially in moments where I need help settling down, getting out of my head, and getting those good feelings flowing.

And then there is my husband, Jody, who is always up for an

adventure, who observes and notices everything, who taught me how to find the interesting. There's no question he strongly resonates with the interesting, and spending any time with him—even if it is just talking on a drive to the airport—sparks the interesting in me and strengthens my connection to it. He has less patience for the life of pleasure: lazy beach days, nice dinners, feel-good movies…not his thing. It's harder for me to find pleasure in these things when around him. Thank goodness I have Pua.

Other friends are more like Lesley, always up for the interesting but craving fulfillment as well. I remember her, predictably, jumping on board the Machu Picchu trip. And I remember her, predictably, praying as we built stone cairns at the snowcapped peak. Watching her seek fulfillment, sharing in her passion, helped me in that moment to see past the adventure. I didn't start praying, but instead took the moment to sit and stack in awe.

WHAT ARE YOUR FRIENDS LIKE?

You can try now to think of which of your friends are the best fit to a particular dimension of the Good Life. That'll help you understand how they enrich your life and why you are compatible. And this in turn can help you know who to reach for when you need help finding what you need, be it fulfillment in a time of need, pleasure in a time of stress, or the interesting in a time of boredom. Going through this process will also help you tune in even more to your own sense of resonance. What would your life rest at mediocrity without? What is essential to your Good Life?

Me? I'd say there's no question the interesting resonates most strongly; without the interesting in my life I'm shrinking, living in mediocrity. That's why Jody and I are so compatible: Together, we bring value to each other's lives. Our experiences of the interesting resonate, even reverberate and become better when we are together. Pleasure and fulfillment resonate for me as well, but I find for these values it's always in different degrees and in different times.

By appreciating what our friends bring to our lives, we make the pursuit of our best possible lives that much easier. Our best possible lives contain more than just the interesting, and through our friendships we can find the balance we need when we need it.

KEEPING IT INTERESTING

If you're all in on the interesting yet are tempted to think you can go it alone, don't. Don't underestimate the effect deep connections have on our lives. Relationships, especially the deep ones, are key ingredients to living Good Lives. Whatever shape your Good Life takes, it is going to be a better one when you've nourished the deep connections in your life. By sharing your emotions, by helping you to find and follow your passions, by inspiring the interesting, and anchoring you when you need it, relationships help you lead a more interesting life.

Conclusion

Leo Tolstoy thought a lot about death. He used it as a springboard for thinking about life. The approach is a little dark for me: Do we have to confront our mortality to understand what counts in life? I don't think so. But Tolstoy did. And sometimes he nailed it. In his memoir *A Confession*, he describes an Eastern fable.[1] It goes like this.

A traveler is being chased by a wild beast. He's in despair—there's no way out. He jumps into a well to hide from the beast. But at the very bottom of the well is a dragon, its tongue dripping, waiting to devour him. The traveler is stuck...if he climbs out, the beast will get him. If he goes farther into the well, the dragon will get him. But he sees a branch, growing magically (as they do) from a crack in the wall. He grabs it.

Hanging from the branch, the traveler's safe...for now. For not only is he hanging from a branch, there are two mice (one white, one black) gnawing away at the branch. What's a lost and scared traveler, hunted by beasts and dragons, to do? The traveler "knows that he will inevitably perish, but while still hanging, he looks around, sees some drops of honey on the leaves of the twig, reaches them with his tongue and licks them."

Yes. The traveler goes after the sweet, simple pleasure and licks some honey while he awaits his gruesome death. It's exactly what he should do.

But there's only a few drops! How long is that goodness going to last? If you are the traveler, what are you going to do when the honey dries up?

You know exactly what to do. You're going to look around at the branches. You're going to wonder where those drops of honey came from and maybe start thinking about bees and flowers. You're going to watch those two mice gnaw away at the branch and wonder how sharp their teeth are. You're going to marvel at the contrast between the purity of the white mouse and the jet-black darkness of the other. You're going to wonder whether being eaten by a dragon is worse than being chased down by a wild beast. You are going to find, you are going to create, an endless source of interesting experiences to ride out that time hanging on a branch. You'll be able to infuse that time with value.

We are all mortal, yes. But we are all alive now. And we should all be striving to make the most of our lives, to live our best possible lives, even—and especially—during those times when we feel just like that traveler, stuck in a world where the odds seem so stacked against us. No reason not to enjoy the honey when it presents itself, but we should go for a lot more. Of course.

Really Good Lives have it all. They have happiness, meaning, *and* psychological richness. They are full of pleasure, fulfillment, and the interesting. They don't often have all of these at the same time— pleasure comes in drops and fulfillment is elusive. It's only the interesting that we can create that is completely up to us. And now you've got the skills you need to turn any experience into an interesting one.

You've also got the skills to balance your life so that you'll have your best shot at having it all. There's no secret formula, for your Good Life is all about you. You'll find your best possible life by tapping into your passions, learning what resonates with you and to what degree, and by recognizing what you need to enhance your life and when you need it.

Getting to know yourself is the essential to developing the art of the interesting. Take some time to do it if you haven't already or do it again now. Go back to those quizzes, see what they do for you, and see what you can learn from them. Then commit to using this knowledge. Take stock of those areas in your life that don't feel good, that lack value, and try to enhance them.

These days, my Good Life is laden with the interesting along with many fulfilling experiences and some pleasant ones. Pleasure has taken a back seat lately, which at this moment works for me. I make a point of getting out and seeing friends when I can, but it's been less often now than in times past. I'm sure those tides will shift and I'll start to crave more bouts of happiness at some point. For certain, come summer the water and the wind will be calling. Teaching and writing give me purpose and are almost always rewarding, although every time I finish a big project, I'm increasingly aware of how elusive fulfillment is. I try to appreciate my achievements, but I don't stress about it when fulfillment evades me. And those long, boring pandemic years have given me even more motivation to travel. I always find the interesting while traveling, and the more I travel, the more my life is psychologically rich.

Thankfully my day-to-day continues to deliver the interesting. As I write this, it's the start of ski season, and the return of our winter family. Every day it seems someone's coming home from the mountain with a new story to share, from failed backflips and sightings of the *entire* glade family to getting yelled at by our favorite ski patroller, Sean (a badge of honor, obvs). We all keep a count of our ski days on the chalkboard wall in our great room. It's still early, but it looks like both of my sons may beat Jody for the first time, and there's endless chatter over how many ski runs it takes to count as a "day."

Looking at that chalkboard wall this morning, the richness of our lives screams out. I gave up putting inspirational messages on it years ago and rarely erase it, preferring instead to keep it as an ongoing reflection of our lives. It's loaded with our ski count, my older son's very detailed predictions of the football season, a Happy Birthday message to **Kagen Beck Camden Noah**. I wonder whose birthday is going to hit next. There's some kind of geometric diagram involving the sun and a dog that I can't quite remember the origins of, but it makes me smile. My kids' friends have taken to signing their names, which I love. They are all clustered, in very small print, around the outlet at the bottom of the wall. I have no idea why. There's my stepson's favorite strawberry doodle, and a sweet note from my stepdaughter. Way at the top, where no one can reach, is the word "Merry" and a star. All of the scattered parts of our lives, all on one wall. The wall prompts all of us, all the time, to think, to feel, and to wonder. Each time I pause on it, something hits me in a new way. Each time I walk away, though, the perspective it delivers feels the same: Our lives are rich, and never boring. Life is Good.

A CHEAT SHEET FOR INCORPORATING INTERESTING EXPERIENCES INTO YOUR GOOD LIFE

1. Embrace curiosity, Mindfulness 2.0, and creativity. Tap into your inner child. These states are within all of us, just waiting to be nourished.
2. Stop planning everything. Give yourself some breathing room from the pursuit. Allow yourself to experience something without evaluating what you'll get from it, without caring what it will do for you.
3. Explore your boundaries and see how far you can roam while staying safe and anchored. Be alert to the signs that you are getting too close to your danger zone, but don't let them stop you from pushing the boundaries of your comfort zone. Find the zone of the interesting that works for you.
4. Embrace novelty, even if doing so involves some risks. Just remember you're after the interesting.
5. Pay attention to what you're getting out of your experiences. Remember that if you're not stimulating your mind, you've lost the path to the interesting.
6. Try to stop seeing things as bad just because they interfere with what you want. Perspective changes everything.
7. Don't shy away from challenges—challenges stimulate the interesting. And if they don't? Remember that's because either they weren't challenging enough or they were too difficult. Seek the sweet spot.

8. Remember that vicarious experiences deliver the interesting and can be just as good as the real thing. They also present a great opportunity to develop more openness to experience.

9. Time in solitude is a great opportunity to practice the art, but balance is important. Friends will make your life more interesting if you let them.

10. Find your people. Know what they do for you. Maintain those deep connections, and remember that sometimes your people know you better than you might know yourself, especially in the moment. Listen to them.

Acknowledgments

I'm deeply grateful to all of those who have supported this project through its development, including Micheal Bishop, Gwen Bradford, John Doris, Dale Dorsey, Alison Gopnik, Dan Haybron, Christian Miller, Laurie Patton, Jim Ralph, Valerie Tiberius, and Justin Weinberg. I'm particularly thankful for my agent, Mark Tauber, who proposed this idea; and to my editor, Hannah Robinson, for her steady support and insight. Together, both helped me find my voice for this new venture. The initial research informing this book began with funding from the Happiness and Well-Being Project, sponsored by the John Templeton Foundation in conjunction with St. Louis Univeristy. I am grateful for their support, as well as for ongoing institutional support from Middlebury College. To my engaging, smart research assistants, Ben Awtrey and Lilly Jones, thank you. In writing this book, I've had the opportunity to recognize and appreciate so many of the interesting people who've helped to make my life better, and I can only hope that I do the same in return. There are many more of you out there.

Quizzes
and
Worksheets

A PRIMER ON THE GOOD LIFE

This can help you make sense of the moving parts and gives some insight into how to understand the perspective contributions of psychology and philosophy.

FRAMEWORKS OF GOOD LIVES[1]

	Happy life	Meaningful life	Psychologically rich life
Scientifically established correlations	Pleasant Secure Comfortable Safe Satisfies desires	Purpose-driven activities Structured by ends Often invokes virtue Involves development and use of our intellectual capacities	Complex experiences that are often: Challenging Perspective-changing Generative of wide range of emotional states Unplanned Novel
Philosophical analysis of the *underlying value* that makes these Good Lives	Pleasure Physically based, affective form of arousal that feels good The opposite: pain	Fulfillment Satisfaction of contributing/ achieving; intellectually based and often defined in terms of one's ends and goals The opposite: pointlessness	Interesting Cognitive engagement and arousal Highlights unique role of unstructured cognitive activity The opposite: boredom

WHAT DOES YOUR BEST POSSIBLE LIFE LOOK LIKE?

There's a classic deathbed test people often invoke to think about what they really want. Sometimes it goes in terms of regrets: *What will you regret not doing?* Sometimes it is used to help us make a choice: *At the end of the day, will you remember that day of work you think is so important that you should skip your child's third-grade play, or will you remember the third-grade play?* It's a gut test. We can use it to consider what our best possible life looks like. And then this information can help us understand how our best possible life aligns with the established dimensions of the Good Life.

The following three quizzes are intended to help you get a feel for your best possible life by tapping into your passions and values. Your passions reflect who you are and what lights you up, while your values reflect what you want. Let's figure out the foundation of your Good Life!

What do you want?
Rank the top five things you want to see in your obituary.

1. "Her life was one adventure after the next."
2. "She made an impact on the world."
3. "He was the life of the party."
4. "Her work will be long remembered and discussed into the future."
5. "He devoted his life to his family."
6. "She traveled the world."
7. "Her smile was contagious, and she brought joy to those around her."
8. "She was committed to her career and rose to the top of her profession."
9. "She was a hard worker, but she was never happier than at home with her family and friends."

10. "She knew how to turn anything into an adventure."
11. "She was a voracious reader with an insatiable appetite for [name a genre]."
12. "Her favorite place to vacation was anywhere warm, with a beach."

Now let's see how your choices line up with the dimensions of the Good Life. If you are curious about how the scoring runs, it may be helpful to revisit the primer on the Good Life earlier in this chapter.

Items that reflect psychological richness are: 1, 9, 10, 12.
Items that reflect meaning are: 2, 4, 5, 6.
Items that reflect happiness are: 3, 7, 8, 11.

Where do your choices end up? Does any one dimension dominate? Are any missing? If so, take note and start to ask questions. For example, do you attribute your score more to your inner preferences or your upbringing? Do you feel good about the extent to which this dimension dominates your life? How is it working out for you? Could your life be better if there were more of one dimension than you have currently?

What are you like?

*It's not enough to think about what you **want**.*
*You've also got to think about and confront what you are **like**.*
Be honest with yourself!

1. Change scares me.
   Agree
   Disagree

2. It is hard to feel good about myself when I'm not contributing.
   Agree
   Disagree

3. I feel most alive when (choose one):
   I'm basking in the sun.
   I've met a big deadline.
   I'm scared.

4. I feel the worst when (choose one):
   I haven't accomplished anything all day.
   I've been stuck in a daylong meeting.
   Everything feels like the same old routine.

5. The best experience I've had lately was planned.
   Agree
   Disagree

6. If I could choose my dream vacation, it would involve:
   Art museums.
   The spa.
   A new country.

7. Select which of these feels worst:
   Being bored.
   Doing something pointless.
   Feeling pain.

8. My best friend is:
   Always happy.
   Feisty and somewhat unpredictable.
   Devoted to her community.

Let's see how your choices here line up with the dimensions of the Good Life. I've indicated below how your responses reflect the values of the interesting (associated with psychological richness), the pleasant (associated with happiness), and the fulfilling (associated with meaning).

1. Change scares me.
   Agreement indicates resonance with pleasure.
   Disagreement signals resonance with the interesting.

2. It is hard to feel good about myself when I'm not contributing.
   Agreement indicates resonance with fulfillment.
   Disagreement indicates higher degrees of resonance with pleasure and the interesting than with fulfillment.

3. I feel most alive when (choose one):
   I'm basking in the sun. *(pleasure)*
   I've met a big deadline. *(fulfillment)*
   I'm scared. *(interesting)*

4. I feel the worst when (choose one):
   I haven't accomplished anything all day. *(fulfillment)*
   I've been stuck in a daylong meeting. *(pleasure)*
   Everything feels like the same old routine. *(interesting)*

5. The best experience I've had lately was planned.
   Disagreement signals resonance with the interesting.

6. If I could choose my dream vacation, it would involve:
   Art museums. *(fulfillment)*
   The spa. *(pleasure)*
   A new country. *(interesting)*

7. Select which of these feels worst:
   Being bored. *(interesting)*
   Doing something pointless. *(fulfillment)*
   Feeling pain. *(pleasure)*

8. My best friend is:

Always happy. *(pleasure)*

Feisty and somewhat unpredictable. *(interesting)*

Devoted to her community. *(fulfillment)*

What *are* you like? What values resonate with you the most? And the least?

What lights you up?

*Here we are looking for the spark: those activities we do that **do** something for us. Start by thinking just about what lights you up, what sparks something in you. Your answers will help show what those things **do** for you and how they enhance your life.*

This is a good one to take notes on!

For each of the following, think about whether, how often, and when the activity (or another activity like it) sparks something in you.

Friday night activities. What gets you out of the house after a long week?

1. Happy hour
   Always   Never   Sometimes (when? _____)

2. Your antiracist book club
   Always   Never   Sometimes (when? _____)

3. Trivia night
   Always   Never   Sometimes (when? _____)

It's the weekend. What are you looking forward to?

1. Watching the new documentary that just came out
   Always   Never   Sometimes (when? _____)

2. Catching up on sleep
   Always   Never   Sometimes (when? _____)

3. Getting your friends together for "green-up" day
   Always   Never   Sometimes (when? _____)

It's 1990 and you have a three-disc CD player in your car. What's in there?

1. Dance music
   Always   Never   Sometimes (when? _____)

2. Country ballads
   Always   Never   Sometimes (when? _____)

3. Nothing—NPR all the way
   Always   Never   Sometimes (when? _____)

Summer vacations are on the horizon. What are you excited to do?

1. Sit in the sun
   Always   Never   Sometimes (when? _____)

2. Build a Habitat for Humanity house
   Always   Never   Sometimes (when? _____)

3. Anything, as long as it is new

    Always   Never   Sometimes (when? _____)

SCORING

Below, find the dimension of value each item tracks. This is what each of these activities *does* for you, that is, how they enhance your life. Then, learn from what lights you up!

What always does it for you?
What never does it for you?
What sometimes does it for you? When and why does it do it for you only sometimes?

Pleasure: 1, 5, 7, 10
Fulfillment: 2, 6, 8, 11
The interesting: 3, 4, 9, 12

PLEASURE, FULFILLMENT, AND THE INTERESTING: A WORKSHEET

It's important to this project that we can wrap our heads around how these values are distinct. But it's tricky because they each describe experiences that in some sense feel good and are all part of a Good Life. We'll live better lives when we learn to distinguish them, understand the degree to which each resonates with us, and come to learn what we need and when we need it. We don't want to go on blindly shooting in the dark for the good stuff. We can do better.

Start by looking at the differences in how these values operate. Each tracks a quality of our experience—something we feel. Each arises within a certain context and invokes different aspects of our nature. And each has its own limitations. They can all overlap, and they can conflict with one another. But it is important to understand each as distinct before considering the ways in which they overlap and conflict.

The value	Common descriptions	Draws on...	Distinctive contexts	Limitations
Pleasure	Warm feelings Sensation that fills the body Dopamime burst	Affect	Physical contact and touch Close, empathetic relationships Imaginative recalling	Short-lived
Fulfillment	Satisfaction with... Content with...	Reason	Stands in connection with objective facts about you and the world Invokes agency	Elusive Dependent
Interestingness	Engaged Motivating Stimulating	Mental arousal	Cognitive engagement: active thoughts and active emotional responses	Mental exhaustion

Now we can begin to think about what each of these values feels like when we experience them. Again, they all promote good feelings but they do this in different ways, and research shows that each value tracks a distinct kind of experience. We want to evoke and to feel the distinctive experience of each. It's going to help if we start with an easy, go-to case that, for us, captures the feeling. Then we'll try to take it further.

The value	Your go-to example	Feels like...	What else feels like this?
Pleasure			
Fulfillment			
Interestingness			

Now let's have some fun. Let's think about how these can conflict. They can also overlap, but for now let's make sure we see how these are distinct. The conflicts indicate that they are each distinct!

What is something that is interesting yet not fulfilling?
What is something that is pleasant yet not fulfilling?
What is something that is pleasant but not interesting?
What is something that is fulfilling yet not interesting?
What is something that is interesting but not pleasant?
What is something that is fulfilling but not pleasant?

Notes

Introduction

1. Lorraine L. Besser, *The Philosophy of Happiness: An Interdisciplinary Introduction* (New York: Routledge Press, 2021).

2. Lorraine L. Besser, "The Interesting and the Pleasant," *Journal of Ethics and Social Philosophy* 24, no. 1 (2023): 58–80.

3. Aaron shares his own story in Aaron Elster and Joy Erlichman Miller, *I Still See Her Haunting Eyes: The Holocaust and a Hidden Child Named Aaron*, 2nd ed. (Peoria, IL: BF Press, 2007). The quotes here come from the *60 Minutes* segment "Letting Future Generations Speak with Holocaust Survivors" (broadcast Jan. 27, 2021), which highlights Elster's story.

Chapter 1: An Ancient Dichotomy

1. *Somebody Somewhere*, season 1, episode 3, "Egg Shells," aired January 30, 2022, on HBO.

2. Shigehiro Oishi, Hyewon Choi, Nicholas Buttrick, et al., "The Psychologically Rich Life Questionnaire," *Journal of Research in Personality* 81 (2019): 257–70, https://doi.org/10.1016/j.jrp.2019.06.010; Lorraine L. Besser and Shigehiro Oishi, "The Psychologically Rich Life," *Philosophical Psychology* 33, no. 8 (2020): 1053–71.

3. For more on how contemporary theories relate to Aristotle, see my "Contemporary Eudaimonism," in *Handbook of Well-Being*, ed. Guy Fletcher (London: Routledge Press, 2016).

4. Martin E. P. Seligman, "Positive Psychology: A Personal History," *Annual Review of Clinical Psychology* 15, no. 1 (2019): 1–23.

5. R. M. Ryan and E. L. Deci, "On Happiness and Human Potentials: A Review of Research on Hedonic and Eudaimonic Well-Being," *Annual Review of Psychology* 52 (2001): 141–66.

Chapter 2: Happiness and the Limits of Pleasure

1. Richard A. Easterlin, "Does Economic Growth Improve the Human Lot? Some Empirical Evidence," in *Nations and Households in Economic Growth*, ed. Paul A. David and Melvin W. Reder (New York: Academic Press, 1974), 89–95.

2. G. E. Moore, *Principia Ethica*, ed. Thomas Baldwin, rev. ed. (1903; Cambridge: Cambridge University Press, 1993).

3. Dacher Keltner, *Awe: The New Science of Everyday Wonder and How It Can Transform Your Life* (New York: Penguin, 2023).

4. For a helpful explanation of this view, see Glenn Geher and Nicole Wedberg, *Positive Evolutionary Psychology: Darwin's Guide to Living a Richer Life* (New York: Oxford University Press, 2019).

5. Plenty of studies explore this paradoxical consequence. For examples, see: B. Bastian, P. Kuppens, K. De Roover, and E. Diener, "Is Valuing Positive Emotion Associated with Life Satisfaction?," *Emotion*, 14, no. 4 (2014): 639–45; Jonathan W. Schooler, Dan Ariely, and George Loewenstein, "The Pursuit and Assessment of Happiness Can Be Self-Defeating," in *The Psychology of Economic Decisions*, vol. 1, *Rationality and Well-Being*, ed. Isabelle Brocas and Juan D. Carrillo (Oxford: Oxford University Press, 2003), 41–70; and I. B. Mauss, M. Tamir, C. L. Anderson, and N. S. Savino, "Can Seeking Happiness Make People Happy? Paradoxical Effects of Valuing Happiness," *Emotion* 11, no. 4 (August 2011): 807–15.

6. Following Michael Stocker's influential paper, "The Schizophrenia of Modern Ethical Theories," *Journal of Philosophy* 73, no. 14 (August 1976): 453–66.

7. R. F. Baumeister, S. R. Wotman, and A. M Stillwell, "Unrequited Love: On Heartbreak, Anger, Guilt, Scriptlessness, and Humiliation," *Journal of Personality and Social Psychology* 64, no. 3 (1993): 377–94.

8. David Foster Wallace, "A Supposedly Fun Thing I'll Never Do Again," in *A Supposedly Fun Thing I'll Never Do Again: Essays and Arguments* (London: Hachette UK, 1998), 36.

9. Wallace, "A Supposedly Fun Thing I'll Never Do Again," 34.

Chapter 3: The Irony of Fulfillment

1. Philip Young, "On Dismembering Hemingway" *Atlantic*, August 1966, accessible at https://www.theatlantic.com/magazine/archive/1966/08/on-dismembering-hemingway/659921/.

2. Brett and Kate McKay, "Why Ernest Hemingway Committed Suicide," The Art of Manliness, updated June 16, 2021, https://www.artofmanliness.com/character/knowledge-of-men/why-ernest-hemingway-committed-suicide/.

3. Ryan Holiday, "How It Feels to Get Everything You've Ever Wanted," Medium, March 6, 2020, https://forge.medium.com/how-it-feels-to-get-everything-youve-ever-wanted-114a30604a09.

4. Michael F. Steger, Shigehiro Oishi, and Todd B. Kashdan, "Meaning in Life Across the Life Span: Levels and Correlates of Meaning in Life from Emerging Adulthood to Older Adulthood," *Journal of Positive Psychology* 4, no. 1 (January 1, 2009): 43–52, https://doi.org/10.1080/17439760802303127.

5. A. C. Shilton, "You Accomplished Something Great. So Now What?," *New York Times*, May 28, 2019.

6. Suzanne Gelb, "Why Accomplishment Often Leaves Us Feeling 'Empty,'"

Psychology Today, May 11, 2019, https://www.psychologytoday.com/us/blog/all-grown/201905/why-accomplishment-often-leaves-us-feeling-empty.

7. Adam Dorr, "Common Errors in Reasoning About the Future: Three Informal Fallacies," *Technological Forecasting and Social Change* 116 (March 2017): 322–30, https://doi.org/10.1016/j.techfore.2016.06.018.

8. John Stuart Mill, *Autobiography* (New York: Columbia University Press, 1924), 97.

9. Mill, *Autobiography*, 97.

10. Plato, *Plato: Republic*, ed. and trans. G. M. A. Grube and C. D. C. Reeve (Indianapolis: Hackett Publishing, 1992).

11. Larissa MacFarquhar, *Strangers Drowning: Voyages to the Brink of Moral Extremity* (London: Penguin, 2015), 4.

12. Susan Wolf, "Moral Saints," *Journal of Philosophy* 79, no. 8 (1982): 419.

13. George Orwell, "Reflections on Gandhi," in *A Collection of Essays* (New York: Harcourt Brace Jovanovich, 1946). Quoted in MacFarquhar, *Strangers Drowning*, 9.

14. Yolanda Mayo, "Machismo, Fatherhood and the Latino Family: Understanding the Concept," *Journal of Multicultural Social Work* 5, no. 1–2 (May 15, 1997): 49–61, https://doi.org/10.1300/J285v05n01_05.

Chapter 4: The Unique Promise of the Interesting

1. Grateful Dead, "The Faster We Go, the Rounder We Get" (aka "The Other One"), by Bill Kreutzmann and Bob Weir, track 1, part 3 on *Anthem of the Sun*, Warner Bros.–Seven Arts Records WS 1749, 1968.

2. Neal Cassady, *The Joan Anderson Letter: The Holy Grail of the Beat Generation*, 2nd ed. (London: Black Spring Press Group, 2021).

Chapter 5: Passions and Values

1. Anatole Broyard, "Good Books About Being Sick," *New York Times*, April 1, 1990, https://www.nytimes.com/1990/04/01/books/good-books-abut-being-sick.html.

2. Oliver Sacks, *On the Move: A Life* (New York: Alfred A. Knopf, 2015), 61.

3. Sacks, *On the Move*, 222.

4. Sacks, *On the Move*, 108.

5. Sacks, *On the Move*, 109.

6. Sacks, *On the Move*, 170.

7. Sacks, *On the Move*. His previous book, *Uncle Tungsten: Memories of a Chemical Boyhood* (New York: Alfred A. Knopf, 2001), explores his childhood.

8. Oliver Sacks, *Oaxaca Journal* (New York: Vintage, 2012), xiv–xv.

9. Oliver Sacks, *Gratitude* (New York: Alfred A. Knopf, 2015).

Chapter 6: Stepping Away from Pursuit Mode

1. Lorraine L. Besser and Shigehiro Oishi, "The Psychologically Rich Life," *Philosophical Psychology* 33, no. 8 (2020): 1053–71; Shigehiro Oishi, Hyewon Choi,

Nicholas Buttrick, et al., "The Psychologically Rich Life Questionnaire," *Journal of Research in Personality* 81 (2019): 257–70, https://doi.org/10.1016/j.jrp.2019.06.010.

2. Timothy D. Wilson and Daniel T. Gilbert, "Affective Forecasting: Knowing What to Want," *Current Directions in Psychological Science* 14, no. 3 (June 2005): 131–34; and Gilbert's popular discussion of this in *Stumbling on Happiness* (New York: Vintage, 2007).

3. Joseph Butler, *Five Sermons*, ed. Stephen L. Darwall (1726; Indianapolis: Hackett Publishing, 1983).

4. Oliver Sacks, *On the Move: A Life* (New York: Alfred A. Knopf, 2015), 113.

5. Oliver Sacks, *Oaxaca Journal* (New York: Vintage, 2012), 26, 30, 58.

6. Sacks, *Oaxaca Journal*, xiv.

7. For more discussion, see Maggie Koerth-Baker, "Why Boredom Is Anything but Boring," *Nature* 529, no. 7585 (2016): 146–48.

8. John Rawls, *A Theory of Justice* (Cambridge, MA: Harvard University Press, 1971).

9. Jennifer L. Smith, Virginia Thomas, and Margarita Azmitia, "Happy Alone? Motivational Profiles of Solitude and Well-Being Among Senior Living Residents," *International Journal of Aging and Human Development* 96, no. 3 (April 2023): 312–34, https://doi.org/10.1177/00914150221112283.

10. Virginia Thomas, "Solitude Skills and the Private Self," *Qualitative Psychology* 10, no. 1 (2023): 127, https://doi.org/10.1037/qup0000218.

Chapter 7: Developing an Interesting Mindset

1. "Art Critic Jerry Saltz on His New Book 'How to Be an Artist,'" interview by Scott Simon, *Weekend Edition*, NPR, March 28, 2020, audio and transcript, https://www.npr.org/2020/03/28/823071293/art-critic-jerry-saltz-on-his-new-book-how-to-be-an-artist.

2. For an explanation, see Jordan Litman, "Curiosity and the Pleasures of Learning: Wanting and Liking New Information," *Cognition & Emotion* 19, no. 6 (2005): 793–814.

3. A 2013 study deliberately set out to debunk the right brain–left brain myth through functional MRI (fMRI) analysis of the brain activity of more than one thousand people. Jared A. Nielsen, Brandon A. Zielinski, Michael A. Ferguson, et al., "An Evaluation of the Left-Brain vs. Right-Brain Hypothesis with Resting State Functional Connectivity Magnetic Resonance Imaging," *PLoS ONE* 8, no. 8 (August 14, 2013): e71275. Roger Beaty's research uses fMRI to explore what actually happens when subjects engage in creative work, and locates creativity within the connections made across the brain, which he describes as "whole-brain functional connectivity." See Roger E. Beaty, Yoed Nissan Kenett, Alexander P. Christensen, et al., "Robust Prediction of Individual Creative Ability from Brain Functional Connectivity," *Proceedings of the National Academy of Sciences* 115, no. 5 (January 30, 2018): 1087–92.

4. "Art Critic Jerry Saltz," interview by Scott Simon.

5. Alan Sillitoe, *The Loneliness of the Long-Distance Runner: Stories* (New York: Open Road Media, 2016), ebook.

Chapter 8: Finding Your Zone of the Interesting

1. Alison Gopnik, "A Good Life Doesn't Mean an Easy One," *Wall Street Journal*, August 28, 2020, https://www.wsj.com/articles/a-good-life-doesnt-mean -an-easy-one-11598623184.

Chapter 9: Harnessing the Power of Novelty

1. William N. McBain, "Arousal, Monotony, and Accidents in Line Driving," *Journal of Applied Psychology* 54, no. 6 (1970): 509–19, https://doi.org/10.1037 /h0030144.

2. McBain, "Arousal, Monotony, and Accidents in Line Driving," 518.

3. Jason Duvall, "Enhancing the Benefits of Outdoor Walking with Cognitive Engagement Strategies," *Journal of Environmental Psychology* 31, no. 1 (March 2011): 27–35, https://doi.org/10.1016/j.jenvp.2010.09.003.

4. Hunter S. Thompson, *The Proud Highway: Saga of a Desperate Southern Gentleman, 1955–1967* (New York: Ballantine Books, 1998).

5. Robert Nozick, *The Examined Life: Philosophical Meditations* (New York: Simon and Schuster, 1989).

Chapter 10: Turning Obstacles into Adventures

1. Robert R. McCrae and Paul T. Costa Jr., "Conceptions and Correlates of Openness to Experience," in *Handbook of Personality Psychology*, ed. Robert Hogan, John Johnson, and Stephen Briggs (San Diego: Academic Press, 1997), 825.

2. W. Bleidorn, P. L. Hill, M. D. Back, et al., "The Policy Relevance of Personality Traits," *American Psychologist* 74, no. 9 (2019): 1056–67, https://doi .org/10.1037/amp0000503.

3. McCrae and Costa, "Conceptions and Correlates of Openness to Experience."

4. Christian Jarrett, *Be Who You Want: Unlocking the Science of Personality Change* (New York: Simon and Schuster, 2021).

5. Jim Taylor, "Embrace Life as a Challenge to Pursue, Not a Threat to Avoid," *Psychology Today*, April 20, 2022, https://www.psychologytoday.com/us/blog /the-power-prime/202204/embrace-life-challenge-pursue-not-threat-avoid.

6. Viktor E. Frankl, *Man's Search for Meaning* (Boston: Beacon Press, 1992).

Chapter 11: Friends Make Everything Better

1. David Hume, *A Treatise of Human Nature*, ed. David Fate Norton and Mary J. Norton (Oxford: Clarendon Press, 2000), 2.2.5.15.

2. Robert Waldinger and Marc Schulz, *The Good Life: Lessons from the World's Longest Scientific Study of Happiness* (New York: Simon and Schuster, 2023).

Conclusion

1. Leo Tolstoy, *A Confession and Other Religious Writings*, trans. Jane Kentish (London: Penguin Classics, 1987).

Quizzes and Worksheets

1. Lorraine L. Besser and Shigehiro Oishi, "The Psychologically Rich Life," *Philosophical Psychology* 33, no. 8 (2020): 1053–71; Lorraine L. Besser, "The Interesting and the Pleasant," *Journal of Ethics and Social Philosophy* 24, no 1 (2023): 1–23.

Glossary

Cognitive: This describes the mind's operations as a whole. A generic form of "using the mind."

Desire: A psychological state of wanting something.

Eudaimonia: Aristotle's theory of human flourishing, according to which we flourish through the development of reason and virtue.

Eudaimonism: The view that well-being consists in flourishing as a human being, where this is most often understood in terms of using one's rational capacities to develop purpose or meaning.

Fulfillment: The mental state of satisfaction derived from using one's mind to accomplish or to attain an objective state of affairs.

Happiness: The state of mind that feels pleasurable.

Hedonia (hedonism): The view that happiness consists in feelings of pleasure.

Instrumental Value: Something valuable for what it brings about.

Interesting: The qualitative aspect of our experience of a robust form of cognitive engagement that stimulates new thoughts and emotions. What the experience of psychological richness feels like.

Intrinsic Value: Something valuable in itself.

Meaning: The cluster of views, evolving from eudaimonia, that understands the Good Life in terms of using our rational capacities to attain or to achieve.

Objective Value: Value that is independent of any one person.

Passion: Instinctual drives to pursue certain experiences.

Phenomenology: What it feels like to experience something.

Pleasure: A physiological response experienced as a reward.

Prudential Value: That which benefits the subject. Often called welfare or well-being. A form of subjective value.

Psychological Richness: The set of complex, novel, and challenging experiences that stimulate and engage the mind, that evoke different emotions, and that change our perspective.

Rational: The part of our mind that plans, pursues, and thinks about meaning.

Resonance: The feeling of concordance between our passions and our activities.

Index

NOTE: *Italic page references* indicate illustrations

About the Author

Lorraine Besser, PhD, is a professor of philosophy at Middlebury College who specializes in the philosophy and psychology of the Good Life and teaches popular courses for undergraduates on happiness, well-being, and ethics. An internationally recognized scholar, she was a founding investigator on the research team studing psychological richness. She is the author of two academic books (*The Philosophy of Happiness: An Interdisciplinary Introduction* and *Eudaimonic Ethics: The Philosophy and Psychology of Living Well*) and dozens of professional journal articles on moral pyschology.